Hands-On Generative Adversarial Networks with PyTorch 1.x

Implement next-generation neural networks to build powerful GAN models using Python

John Hany
Greg Walters

BIRMINGHAM - MUMBAI

Hands-On Generative Adversarial Networks with PyTorch 1.x

Commissioning Editor: Sunith Shetty
Acquisition Editor: Devika Battike
Content Development Editor: Roshan Kumar
Senior Editor: Jack Cummings
Technical Editor: Dinesh Chaudhary
Copy Editor: Safis Editing
Project Coordinator: Aishwarya Mohan
Proofreader: Safis Editing
Indexer: Tejal Daruwale Soni
Production Designer: Deepika Naik

First published: December 2019

Production reference: 1111219

Published by Packt Publishing Ltd.
Livery Place
35 Livery Street
Birmingham
B3 2PB, UK.

ISBN 978-1-78953-051-3

www.packt.com

Packt.com

Subscribe to our online digital library for full access to over 7,000 books and videos, as well as industry leading tools to help you plan your personal development and advance your career. For more information, please visit our website.

Why subscribe?

- Spend less time learning and more time coding with practical eBooks and Videos from over 4,000 industry professionals

- Improve your learning with Skill Plans built especially for you

- Get a free eBook or video every month

- Fully searchable for easy access to vital information

- Copy and paste, print, and bookmark content

Did you know that Packt offers eBook versions of every book published, with PDF and ePub files available? You can upgrade to the eBook version at www.packt.com and as a print book customer, you are entitled to a discount on the eBook copy. Get in touch with us at customercare@packtpub.com for more details.

At www.packt.com, you can also read a collection of free technical articles, sign up for a range of free newsletters, and receive exclusive discounts and offers on Packt books and eBooks.

Contributors

About the authors

John Hany received his master's degree and bachelor's degree in calculational mathematics at the University of Electronic Science and Technology of China. He majors in pattern recognition and has years of experience in machine learning and computer vision. He has taken part in several practical projects, including intelligent transport systems and facial recognition systems. His current research interests lie in reducing the computation costs of deep neural networks while improving their performance on image classification and detection tasks. He is enthusiastic about open source projects and has contributed to many of them.

Greg Walters has been involved with computers and computer programming since 1972. He is well-versed in Visual Basic, Visual Basic .NET, Python, and SQL and is an accomplished user of MySQL, SQLite, Microsoft SQL Server, Oracle, C++, Delphi, Modula-2, Pascal, C, 80x86 Assembler, COBOL, and Fortran. He is a programming trainer and has trained numerous people on many pieces of computer software, including MySQL, Open Database Connectivity, Quattro Pro, Corel Draw!, Paradox, Microsoft Word, Excel, DOS, Windows 3.11, Windows for Workgroups, Windows 95, Windows NT, Windows 2000, Windows XP, and Linux. He is semi-retired and has written over 100 articles for Full Circle Magazine. He is also a musician and loves to cook. He is open to working as a freelancer on various projects.

About the reviewers

Sarit Ritwiruneis did a BSc. in Physics and an MSc. in Computer Science at Mahidol University. Proven tracks of projects are mainly POS (Point of Sales), IoT. Sarit recently started to get back into computer science research after doing some Python programming while being a senior software engineer. Sarit currently works in a small office of a big insurance company in Thailand. Sarit dreams about intelligent and friendly websites using A.I.

Sandeep Singh Kushwaha has a master's degree from the Indian Institute of Technology, Kanpur, and he currently works with Aegon as Assistant Vice President, Analytics. As part of the Center of Excellence in Aegon, he is driving Analytics, ML/AI, Digitization, and Innovation for several countries in Europe and Asia. He is passionate about data science, ML/AI, InsurTech and MarTech, and has developed many AI solutions using deep learning algorithms to accelerate businesses. As a real-life problem solver using Machine learning, Sandeep also echoes that GAN is *the coolest idea in Machine Learning in the last twenty years,* and he believes that readers are going to learn a lot from this book to develop AI solutions using GANs.

Packt is searching for authors like you

If you're interested in becoming an author for Packt, please visit authors.packtpub.com and apply today. We have worked with thousands of developers and tech professionals, just like you, to help them share their insight with the global tech community. You can make a general application, apply for a specific hot topic that we are recruiting an author for, or submit your own idea.

Table of Contents

Preface

With continuously evolving research and development, **Generative Adversarial Networks (GANs)** are the next big thing in the field of deep learning. This book highlights the key improvements in GANs over traditional generative models and shows you how to make the best out of GANs with the help of hands-on examples.

This book will help you understand how GAN architecture works using PyTorch. You will get familiar with the most flexible deep learning toolkit and use it to transform ideas into actual working code. You will apply GAN models to areas such as computer vision, multimedia, and natural language processing using a sample-generation methodology.

Who this book is for

This book is for machine learning practitioners and deep learning researchers looking to get hands-on guidance on implementing GAN models using PyTorch 1.0. You'll become familiar with state-of-the-art GAN architectures with the help of real-world examples. Working knowledge of the Python programming language is necessary to grasp the concepts covered in this book.

What this book covers

Chapter 1, *Generative Adversarial Networks Fundamentals*, exploits the new features of PyTorch. You will also learn how to build a simple GAN with NumPy to generate sine signals.

Chapter 2, *Getting Started with PyTorch 1.3*, introduces how to install CUDA in order to take advantage of the GPU for faster training and evaluation. We will also look into the step-by-step installation process of PyTorch on Windows and Ubuntu and build PyTorch from source.

Chapter 3, *Best Practices in Model Design and Training*, looks at the overall design of the model architecture and the steps that need to be followed to choose the required convolutional operation.

Chapter 4, *Building Your First GAN with PyTorch*, introduces you to a classic and well-performing GAN model, called DCGAN, for generating 2D images. You will also be introduced to the architecture of DCGANs and learn how to train and evaluate them. Following this, you will learn how to use a DCGAN to generate hand-written digits and human faces, and take a look at adversarial learning with autoencoders. You will also be shown how to efficiently organize your source code for easy adjustments and extensions.

Chapter 5, *Generating Images Based on Label Information*, shows how to use a CGAN to generate images based on a given label and how to implement adversarial learning with autoencoders.

Chapter 6, *Image-to-Image Translation and Its Applications*, shows how to use pixel-wise label information to perform image-to-image translation with pix2pix and how to translate high-resolution images with pix2pixHD. You will also learn how to flexibly design model architectures to accomplish your goals, including generating larger images and transferring textures between different types of images.

Chapter 7, *Image Restoration with GANs*, shows you to how to perform image super-resolution with SRGAN to generate high-resolution images from low-resolution ones and how to use a data prefetcher to speed up data loading and increase your GPU's efficiency during training. You will also learn how to train a GAN model to perform image inpainting and fill in the missing parts of an image.

Chapter 8, *Training Your GANs to Break Different Models*, looks into the fundamentals of adversarial examples and how to attack and confuse a CNN model with **FGSM (Fast Gradient Sign Method)**. After this, we will look at how to use an accimage library to speed up your image loading even more and train a GAN model to generate adversarial examples and fool the image classifier.

Chapter 9, *Image Generation from Description Text*, provides basic knowledge on word embeddings and how are they used in the NLP field. You will also learn how to design a text-to-image GAN model to generate images based on one sentence of description text.

Chapter 10, *Sequence Synthesis with GANs*, covers commonly used techniques in the NLP field, such as RNN and LSTM. You will also learn some of the basic concepts of reinforcement learning and see how it differ from supervised learning (such as SGD-based CNNs). You will also learn how to use SEGAN to remove background noise and enhance the quality of speech audio.

Chapter 11, *Reconstructing 3D Models with GANs*, shows how 3D objects are represented in **computer graphics (CG)**. We will also look at the fundamental concepts of CG, including camera and projection matrices. You will then learn how to construct a 3D-GAN model with 3D convolutions and train it to generate 3D objects.

To get the most out of this book

You should have basic knowledge of Python and PyTorch.

Download the example code files

You can download the example code files for this book from your account at www.packt.com. If you purchased this book elsewhere, you can visit www.packtpub.com/support and register to have the files emailed directly to you.

You can download the code files by following these steps:

1. Log in or register at www.packt.com.
2. Select the **Support** tab.
3. Click on **Code Downloads**.
4. Enter the name of the book in the **Search** box and follow the onscreen instructions.

Once the file is downloaded, please make sure that you unzip or extract the folder using the latest version of:

- WinRAR/7-Zip for Windows
- Zipeg/iZip/UnRarX for Mac
- 7-Zip/PeaZip for Linux

The code bundle for the book is also hosted on GitHub at https://github.com/PacktPublishing/Hands-On-Generative-Adversarial-Networks-with-PyTorch-1.x. In case there's an update to the code, it will be updated on the existing GitHub repository.

We also have other code bundles from our rich catalog of books and videos available at https://github.com/PacktPublishing/. Check them out!

Download the color images

We also provide a PDF file that has color images of the screenshots/diagrams used in this book. You can download it here:
http://www.packtpub.com/sites/default/files/downloads/9781789530513_ColorImages.pdf.

Conventions used

There are a number of text conventions used throughout this book.

CodeInText: Indicates code words in text, database table names, folder names, filenames, file extensions, pathnames, dummy URLs, user input, and Twitter handles. Here is an example: "Mount the downloaded WebStorm-10*.dmg disk image file as another disk in your system."

A block of code is set as follows:

```
# Derivative with respect to w3
d_w3 = np.matmul(np.transpose(self.x2), delta)
# Derivative with respect to b3
d_b3 = delta.copy()
```

Any command-line input or output is written as follows:

```
$ python -m torch.distributed.launch --nproc_per_node=NUM_GPUS
YOUR_SCRIPT.py --YOUR_ARGUMENTS
```

Bold: Indicates a new term, an important word, or words that you see onscreen. For example, words in menus or dialog boxes appear in the text like this. Here is an example: "Select **System info** from the **Administration** panel."

Warnings or important notes appear like this.

Tips and tricks appear like this.

Get in touch

Feedback from our readers is always welcome.

General feedback: If you have questions about any aspect of this book, mention the book title in the subject of your message and email us at customercare@packtpub.com.

Errata: Although we have taken every care to ensure the accuracy of our content, mistakes do happen. If you have found a mistake in this book, we would be grateful if you would report this to us. Please visit www.packtpub.com/support/errata, selecting your book, clicking on the Errata Submission Form link, and entering the details.

Piracy: If you come across any illegal copies of our works in any form on the Internet, we would be grateful if you would provide us with the location address or website name. Please contact us at copyright@packt.com with a link to the material.

If you are interested in becoming an author: If there is a topic that you have expertise in and you are interested in either writing or contributing to a book, please visit authors.packtpub.com.

Reviews

Please leave a review. Once you have read and used this book, why not leave a review on the site that you purchased it from? Potential readers can then see and use your unbiased opinion to make purchase decisions, we at Packt can understand what you think about our products, and our authors can see your feedback on their book. Thank you!

For more information about Packt, please visit packt.com.

Section 1: Introduction to GANs and PyTorch

In this section, you will be introduced to the basic concepts of GANs, how to install PyTorch 1.0, and how you can build your own models with PyTorch.

This section contains the following chapters:

- Chapter 1, *Generative Adversarial Networks Fundamentals*
- Chapter 2, *Getting Started with PyTorch 1.3*
- Chapter 3, *Best Practices in Model Design and Training*

1
Generative Adversarial Networks Fundamentals

Generative Adversarial Networks (GANs) have brought about a revolutionary storm in the **machine learning** (ML) community. They, to some extent, have changed the way people solve practical problems in **Computer Vision (CV)** and **Natural Language Processing (NLP)**. Before we dive right into the storm, let's prepare you with the fundamental insights of GANs.

In this chapter, you will understand the idea behind adversarial learning and the basic components of a GAN model. You will also get a brief understanding on how GANs work and how it can be built with NumPy.

Before we start exploiting the new features in PyTorch, we will first learn to build a simple GAN with NumPy to generate sine signals so that you may have a profound understanding of the mechanism beneath GANs. By the end of this chapter, you may relax a little as we walk you through many showcases about how GANs are used to address practical problems in CV and NLP fields.

The following topics will be covered in this chapter:

- Fundamentals of machine learning
- Generator and discriminator networks
- What GAN we do?
- References and a useful reading list

Fundamentals of machine learning

To introduce how GANs work, let's use an analogy:

> *A long, long time ago, there were two neighboring kingdoms on an island. One was called Netland, and the other was called Ganland. Both kingdoms produced fine wine, armor, and weapons. In Netland, the king demanded that the blacksmiths who specialized in making armor worked at the east corner of the castle, while those who made swords worked at the west side so that the lords and knights could choose the best equipment the kingdom had to offer. The king of Ganland, on the other hand, put all of the blacksmiths in the same corner and demanded that the armor makers and sword makers should test their work against each other every day. If a sword broke through the armor, the sword would sell at a good price and the armor would be melted and reforged. If it didn't, the sword would be remade and men would strive to buy the armor. One day, the two kings were arguing over which kingdom made better wine until the quarrel escalated into war. Though outnumbered, the soldiers of Ganland wore the armor and swords that had been improved for years in the daily adversarial tests, and the Netland soldiers could not break their strong armor nor withstand their sharp swords. In the end, the defeated king of Netland, however reluctant he was, agreed that Ganland had better wine and blacksmiths.*

Machine learning – classification and generation

ML is the study of recognizing patterns from data without hardcoded rules given by humans. The recognizing of patterns (**Pattern Recognition** or **PR**) is the automatic discovering of the similarities and differences among raw data, which is an essential way to realize **Artificial Intelligence** (**AI**) that only exists in novels and movies. Although it is hard to tell when exactly real AI will come to birth in the future, the development of ML has given us much confidence in recent years. ML has already been vastly used in many fields, such as CV, NLP, recommendation systems, **Intelligent Transportation Systems** (**ITS**), medical diagnoses, robotics, and advertising.

A ML model is typically described as a system that takes in data and gives certain outputs based on the parameters it contains. The **learning** of the model is actually adjusting the parameters to get better outputs. As illustrated in the following diagram, we feed training data into the model and get a certain output. We then use one or several criteria to measure the output, to tell how well our model performs. In this step, a set of desired outputs (or ground truth) with respect to the training data would be very helpful. If ground truth data is used in training, this process is often called **supervised learning**. If not, it is often regarded as **unsupervised learning**.

We constantly adjust the model's parameters based on its performance (in other words, whether it gives us the results we want) so that it yields better results in the future. This process is called **model training**. The training of a model takes as long as it pleases us. Typically, we stop the training after a certain number of iterations or when the performance is good enough. When the training process has finished, we apply the trained model to predict on new data (testing data). This process is called **model testing**. Sometimes, people use different sets of data for training and testing to see how well the model performs on samples it never meets, which is called the **generalization** capability. Sometimes an additional step called **model evaluation** is involved, when the parameters of the model are so complicated that we need another set of data to see whether our model or training process has been designed well:

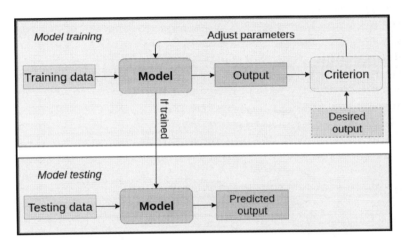

A typical machine learning system, with model training and testing

What types of problems this model can solve is essentially determined by the types of input and output data we want. For example, a classification model takes an input of any number of dimensions (audio, text, image, or video) and gives a 1-dimension output (single values indicating the predicted labels). A generative model typically takes a 1-dimension input (a latent vector) and generates high-dimension outputs (images, videos, or 3D models). It maps low-dimensional data to high-dimensional data, at the same time, trying to make the output samples look as convincing as possible. However, it is worth pointing out that we'll meet generative models that don't obey this rule in the future chapters. Until Chapter 5, *Generating Images Based on Label Information*, it's a simple rule to bear in mind.

When it comes to AI, there are two groups of believers in the community. The symbolists acknowledge the necessity of human experience and knowledge. They believe the low-level patterns constitute high-level decisions based on explicit rules given by humans. The connectionists believe that AI can be realized by an analogous network similar to human neural systems and adjusting the connections between simple neurons is the key to this system. Apparently, the exploding development of deep learning adds a score to the connectionists' side. What is your opinion?

Introducing adversarial learning

Traditionally, generative problems are solved by statistics-based methods such as a **Boltzmann machine**, **Markov chain**, or **variational encoder**. As mathematically profound as they are, the generated samples are as of yet far from perfect. A classification model maps high-dimension data to low-dimension, while a generative model often maps low-dimension data to high-dimension ones. People in both fields have been working hard to improve their models. Let's look back to the little made-up opening story. Can we get the two different models to work against each other and improve themselves at the same time? If we take the output of a generative model as the input of the classification model, we can measure the performance of the generative model (the armor) with the classification model (the sword). At the same time, we can improve the classification model (the sword) by feeding generated samples (the armor) along with real samples, since we can agree that more data is often better for the training of ML models.

The training process where the two models try to weaken each other and, as a result, improve each other is called **adversarial learning**. As demonstrated in the following diagram, the models, **A** and **B**, have totally opposite agendas (for example, classification and generation). However, during each step of the training, the output of **Model A** improves **Model B**, and the output of **Model B** improves **Model A**:

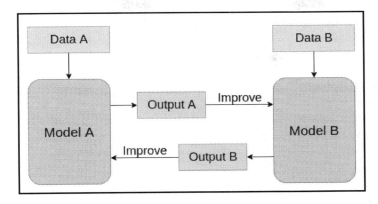

A typical adversarial learning system

GANs are designed based on this very idea, which was proposed by Goodfellow, Pouget-Abadie, Mirza, et al in 2014. Now, GANs have become the most thriving and popular method to synthesize audio, text, images, video, and 3D models in the ML community. In this book, we will walk you through the basic components and mechanisms of different types of GANs and learn how to use them to address various practical problems. In the next section, we will introduce the basic structure of GANs to show you how and why they work so well.

Generator and discriminator networks

Here, we will show you the basic components of GANs and explain how they work with/against each other to achieve our goal to generate realistic samples. A typical structure of a GAN is shown in the following diagram. It contains two different networks: a generator network and a discriminator network. The **generator** network typically takes random noises as input and generates fake samples. Our goal is to let the fake samples be as close to the real samples as possible. That's where the discriminator comes in. The **discriminator** is, in fact, a classification network, whose job is to tell whether a given sample is fake or real. The generator tries its best to trick and confuse the discriminator to make the wrong decision, while the discriminator tries its best to distinguish the fake samples from the real ones.

In this process, the differences between fake and real samples are used to improve the generator. Therefore, the generator gets better at generating realistic-looking samples while the discriminator gets better at picking them out. Since real samples are used to train the discriminator, the training process is therefore supervised. Even though the generator always gives fake samples without the knowledge of ground truth, the overall training of GAN is still **supervised**:

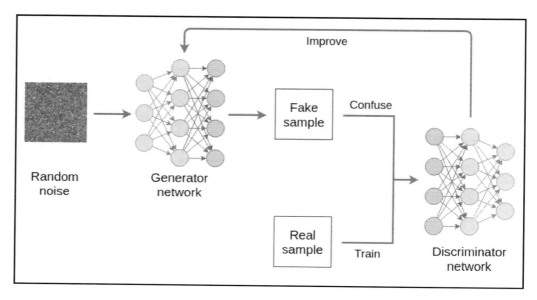

Basic process of a GAN

Mathematical background of GANs

Let's take a look at the math behind this process to get a better understanding of the mechanism. Let G and D represent the generator and discriminator networks, respectively. Let V represent the performance criterion of the system. The optimization objective is described as follows:

$$\min_{G} \max_{D} V(D, G) = \mathbb{E}_{x}[\log D(x)] + \mathbb{E}_{x^{*}}[\log(1 - D(x^{*}))]$$

In this equation, x is the real sample, $x^* = G(z)$ is the generated sample, and z is the random noise that G uses to generate fake samples. $\mathbb{E}_x[f]$ is the expectation over x, which means the average value of any function, f, over all samples.

As mentioned before, the goal of the discriminator, D, is to maximize the prediction confidence of real samples. Therefore, D needs to be trained with **gradient ascent** $\max$ (the operator in the objective). The update rule for, D, is as follows:

$$\theta_d \leftarrow \theta_d + \frac{1}{m} \nabla_{\theta_d} \sum_{i=1}^{m} (\log D(x_i) + \log(1 - D(x_i^*)))$$

In this formula, θ_d is the parameter of D (such as convolution kernels and weights in fully-connected layers), m is the size of the mini batch (or batch size for short), and i is the index of the sample in the mini-batch. Here, we assume that we are using mini-batches to feed the training data, which is fairly reasonable since it's the most commonly used and empirically effective strategy. Therefore, the gradients need to be averaged over m samples.

There are 3 different ways to feed training data into models: (1) one sample at a time, which is often referred to as **stochastic** (for example, **Stochastic Gradient Descent** or **SGD**); (2) a handful of samples at a time, which is called **mini-batch**; and (3) all samples at one time, which is, in fact, called **batch**. The stochastic way introduces too much randomness so that one bad sample could jeopardize the good work of several previous training steps. The full batch requires too much memory to calculate. Therefore, we feed data to all of the models by mini-batch in this book, even though we might slothfully refer to it as just batch.

The goal of the generator network, G, is to fool the discriminator, D, and let D believe that the generated samples are real. Therefore, the training of G is to maximize $D(G(z))$ or minimize $1 - D(G(z))$. Therefore, G needs to be trained with **gradient descent** $\min$ (the operator in the objective). The update rule for G is as follows:

$$\theta_g \leftarrow \theta_g - \frac{1}{m} \nabla_{\theta_g} \sum_{i=1}^{m} \log(1 - D(G(z_i)))$$

In this formula, θ_g is the parameters of D, m is the size of the mini-batch, and i is the index of the sample in the mini-batch.

If you are unfamiliar with the concept of GD, think of it as a little boy kicking a sticky ball on bumpy terrain. The boy wants the ball to be at the bottom of the lowest pit so that he can call it a day and go home. The ball is sticky so it doesn't roll after it hits the ground, even on a slope. Therefore, where the ball will hit is determined by which direction and how hard the boy kicks it. The amount of force the boy kicks the ball with is described by the step size (or the **learning rate**). The direction of kicking is determined by the characteristics of the terrain under his feet. An efficient choice would be the downhill direction, which is the negative gradient of the loss function with respect to the parameters. Therefore, we often use gradient descent to minimize an objective function. However, the boy is so obsessed with the ball that he only stares at the ball and refuses to look up to find the lowest pit in a wider range. Therefore, the GD method is sometimes inefficient because it takes a very long time to reach the bottom. We will introduce several tips on how to improve the efficiency of GD in Chapter 3, *Best Practices for Model Design and Training*. The **gradient ascent** is the opposite of gradient descent, which is to find the highest peak.

Using NumPy to train a sine signal generator

Maybe math is even more confusing than a big chunk of code to some. Now, let's look at some code to digest the equations we've thrown at you. Here, we will use Python to implement a very simple adversarial learning example to generate sine (sin) signals.

In the following example, we will be only using NumPy, a powerful linear algebra Python library to implement a GAN model. We will need to calculate the gradients by ourselves so that you can have an in-depth understanding of what might be happening beneath the popular deep learning toolkits such as PyTorch. Rest assured that we won't do this in future chapters because we can use the powerful computational graph provided by PyTorch to calculate the gradients for us!

Designing the network architectures

The architecture of the generator network is described in the following diagram. It takes a 1-dimension random value as input and gives a 10-dimension vector as output. It has 2 hidden layers with each containing 10 neurons. The calculation in each layer is a matrix multiplication. Therefore, the network is, in fact, a **Multilayer Perceptron (MLP)**:

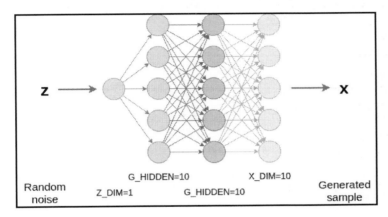

Structure of the generator network

The architecture of the discriminator network is described in the following diagram. It takes a 10-dimension vector as input and gives a 1-dimension value as output. The output is the prediction label (real or fake) of the input sample. The discriminator network is also an MLP with two hidden layers and each containing 10 neurons:

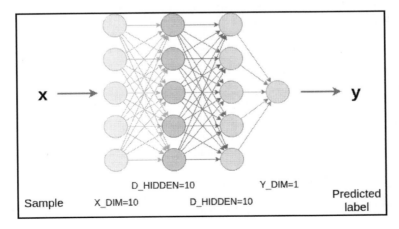

Structure of the discriminator network

Defining activation functions and the loss function

We will be only using NumPy (http://www.numpy.org) to calculate and train our GAN model (and optionally using Matplotlib (https://matplotlib.org) to visualize the signals). If you don't already have the Python environment on your machine, please refer to Chapter 2, *Getting Started with PyTorch 1.3*, to learn how to set up a working Python environment. If your Python environment is properly set up, let's move on to the actual code.

All of the following code can be placed in a simple.py file (such as simple_gan.py). Let's look at the code step by step:

1. Import the NumPy library:

   ```
   import numpy as np
   ```

2. Define a few constant variables that are needed in our model:

   ```
   Z_DIM = 1
   G_HIDDEN = 10
   X_DIM = 10
   D_HIDDEN = 10

   step_size_G = 0.01
   step_size_D = 0.01
   ITER_NUM = 50000

   GRADIENT_CLIP = 0.2
   WEIGHT_CLIP = 0.25
   ```

3. Define the real sine samples (with numpy.sin) that we want to estimate:

   ```
   def get_samples(random=True):
       if random:
           x0 = np.random.uniform(0, 1)
           freq = np.random.uniform(1.2, 1.5)
           mult = np.random.uniform(0.5, 0.8)
       else:
           x0 = 0
           freq = 0.2
           mult = 1
       signal = [mult * np.sin(x0+freq*i) for i in range(X_DIM)]
       return np.array(signal)
   ```

In the previous snippet, we use a `bool` variable, `random`, to introduce randomness into the real samples, as real-life data has. The real samples look like this (50 samples with `random=True`):

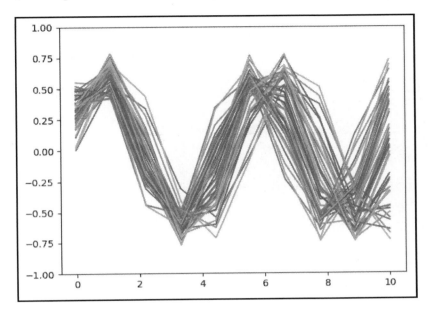

The real sine samples

4. Define the activation functions and their derivatives. If you are not familiar with the concept of activation functions, just remember that their jobs are to adjust the outputs of a layer so that its next layer can have a better understanding of these output values:

```
def ReLU(x):
    return np.maximum(x, 0.)

def dReLU(x):
    return ReLU(x)

def LeakyReLU(x, k=0.2):
    return np.where(x >= 0, x, x * k)

def dLeakyReLU(x, k=0.2):
    return np.where(x >= 0, 1., k)

def Tanh(x):
    return np.tanh(x)
```

```
def dTanh(x):
    return 1. - Tanh(x)**2

def Sigmoid(x):
    return 1. / (1. + np.exp(-x))

def dSigmoid(x):
    return Sigmoid(x) * (1. - Sigmoid(x))
```

5. Define a `helper` function to initialize the layer parameters:

```
def weight_initializer(in_channels, out_channels):
    scale = np.sqrt(2. / (in_channels + out_channels))
    return np.random.uniform(-scale, scale, (in_channels,
out_channels))
```

6. Define the `loss` function (both forward and backward):

```
class LossFunc(object):
    def __init__(self):
        self.logit = None
        self.label = None

    def forward(self, logit, label):
        if logit[0, 0] < 1e-7:
            logit[0, 0] = 1e-7
        if 1. - logit[0, 0] < 1e-7:
            logit[0, 0] = 1. - 1e-7
        self.logit = logit
        self.label = label
        return - (label * np.log(logit) + (1-label) * np.log(1-
logit))

    def backward(self):
        return (1-self.label) / (1-self.logit) - self.label /
self.logit
```

This is called **binary cross-entropy**, which is typically used in binary classification problems (in which a sample either belongs to class A or class B). Sometimes, one of the networks is trained too well so that the `sigmoid` output of the discriminator might be either too close to 0 or 1. Both of the scenarios lead to numerical errors of the `log` function. Therefore, we need to restrain the maximum and minimum values of the output value.

Working on forward pass and backpropagation

Now, let's create our generator and discriminator networks. We put the code in the same `simple_gan.py` file as well:

1. Define the parameters of the generator network:

```
class Generator(object):
    def __init__(self):
        self.z = None
        self.w1 = weight_initializer(Z_DIM, G_HIDDEN)
        self.b1 = weight_initializer(1, G_HIDDEN)
        self.x1 = None
        self.w2 = weight_initializer(G_HIDDEN, G_HIDDEN)
        self.b2 = weight_initializer(1, G_HIDDEN)
        self.x2 = None
        self.w3 = weight_initializer(G_HIDDEN, X_DIM)
        self.b3 = weight_initializer(1, X_DIM)
        self.x3 = None
        self.x = None
```

We keep track of the inputs and outputs of all the layers because we need them to calculate the derivatives to update the parameters later.

2. Define the forward calculation (to generate samples based on random noise):

```
def forward(self, inputs):
    self.z = inputs.reshape(1, Z_DIM)
    self.x1 = np.matmul(self.z, self.w1) + self.b1
    self.x1 = ReLU(self.x1)
    self.x2 = np.matmul(self.x1, self.w2) + self.b2
    self.x2 = ReLU(self.x2)
    self.x3 = np.matmul(self.x2, self.w3) + self.b3
    self.x = Tanh(self.x3)
    return self.x
```

It's basically the same calculation process repeated 3 times. Each layer calculates its output according to this formula:

$$x_{l+1} = f(x_l \cdot w_{l+1} + b_{l+1})$$

In this equation, x represents the output value of a layer, f represents the activation function, and subscript l represents the index of the layer. Here, we use ReLU in the hidden layers and Tanh in the output layer.

Now it's time to define the backward calculation for the generator network (to calculate the derivatives and update the parameters). This part of the code is a bit long. It's really repeating the same process 3 times:

1. Calculate the derivatives of loss with respect to the output of this layer (for example, the derivative with respect to `output` or `x2`).
2. Calculate the derivatives of loss with respect to the parameters (for example, the derivative with respect to `w3` or `b3`).
3. Update the parameters with the derivatives.
4. Passing the gradients to the preceding layer. The derivatives are calculated as follows:

$$\delta = \frac{\partial L}{\partial x_{l+1}}$$

$$\nabla_{w_{l+1}} L = \frac{\partial L}{\partial w_{l+1}} = \frac{\partial L}{\partial y_{l+1}} \cdot \frac{\partial y_{l+1}}{\partial w_{l+1}} = x_l^T \cdot \delta$$

$$w_{l+1} \leftarrow w_{l+1} - \mu \nabla_{w_{l+1}} L$$

In this process, the derivative of the loss with respect to the output, which is denoted by `delta` in the code, is the key to propagate the gradients from layer *l+1* to layer *l*. Therefore, this process is called **backpropagation**. The propagation from layer *l+1* to layer *l* is described as follows:

$$\delta \leftarrow \frac{\partial L}{\partial x_l} = \frac{\partial L}{\partial x_{l+1}} \cdot \frac{\partial x_{l+1}}{\partial x_l} = \delta \cdot w_{l+1}^T$$

3. Calculate the derivatives with respect to the output:

```
def backward(self, outputs):
    # Derivative with respect to output
    delta = outputs
    delta *= dTanh(self.x)
```

Calculate the derivatives with respect to the parameters in the third layer:

```
# Derivative with respect to w3
d_w3 = np.matmul(np.transpose(self.x2), delta)
# Derivative with respect to b3
d_b3 = delta.copy()
```

Pass the gradients to the second layer:

```
# Derivative with respect to x2
delta = np.matmul(delta, np.transpose(self.w3))
```

And update the parameters of the third layer:

```
# Update w3
if (np.linalg.norm(d_w3) > GRADIENT_CLIP):
    d_w3 = GRADIENT_CLIP / np.linalg.norm(d_w3) * d_w3
self.w3 -= step_size_G * d_w3
self.w3 = np.maximum(-WEIGHT_CLIP, np.minimum(WEIGHT_CLIP,
 self.w3))

# Update b3
self.b3 -= step_size_G * d_b3
self.b3 = np.maximum(-WEIGHT_CLIP, np.minimum(WEIGHT_CLIP,
 self.b3))
delta *= dReLU(self.x2)
```

4. Update the parameters in the second layer and pass the gradients to the first layer:

```
# Derivative with respect to w2
d_w2 = np.matmul(np.transpose(self.x1), delta)
# Derivative with respect to b2
d_b2 = delta.copy()

# Derivative with respect to x1
delta = np.matmul(delta, np.transpose(self.w2))

# Update w2
if (np.linalg.norm(d_w2) > GRADIENT_CLIP):
    d_w2 = GRADIENT_CLIP / np.linalg.norm(d_w2) * d_w2
self.w2 -= step_size_G * d_w2
self.w2 = np.maximum(-WEIGHT_CLIP, np.minimum(WEIGHT_CLIP,
    self.w2))

# Update b2
self.b2 -= step_size_G * d_b2
self.b2 = np.maximum(-WEIGHT_CLIP, np.minimum(WEIGHT_CLIP,
```

```
        self.b2))
    delta *= dReLU(self.x1)
```

5. Update the parameters in the first layer:

```
# Derivative with respect to w1
d_w1 = np.matmul(np.transpose(self.z), delta)
# Derivative with respect to b1
d_b1 = delta.copy()

# No need to calculate derivative with respect to z
# Update w1
if (np.linalg.norm(d_w1) > GRADIENT_CLIP):
    d_w1 = GRADIENT_CLIP / np.linalg.norm(d_w1) * d_w1
self.w1 -= step_size_G * d_w1
self.w1 = np.maximum(-WEIGHT_CLIP, np.minimum(WEIGHT_CLIP,
  self.w1))

# Update b1
self.b1 -= step_size_G * d_b1
self.b1 = np.maximum(-WEIGHT_CLIP, np.minimum(WEIGHT_CLIP,
  self.b1))
```

You will notice that the following code looks similar to the preceding code. It is only mentioned here to point out that these lines help to keep the data from becoming unstable. You don't have to add these three lines:

```
if (np.linalg.norm(d_w3) > GRADIENT_CLIP):
    d_w3 = GRADIENT_CLIP / np.linalg.norm(d_w3) * d_w3
self.w3 = np.maximum(-WEIGHT_CLIP, np.minimum(WEIGHT_CLIP, self.w3))
```

This code is included because the training of GANs can be very unstable and we need to clip the gradients and the parameters to ensure a stable training process.

 We will elaborate on the topics of activation functions, loss functions, weight initialization, gradient clipping, weight clipping, and more in Chapter 3, *Best Practices for Model Design and Training*. These are extremely useful for stabilizing and improving the training of GANs.

Now, let's define the discriminator network:

```
class Discriminator(object):
    def __init__(self):
        self.x = None
        self.w1 = weight_initializer(X_DIM, D_HIDDEN)
        self.b1 = weight_initializer(1, D_HIDDEN)
        self.y1 = None
```

```
self.w2 = weight_initializer(D_HIDDEN, D_HIDDEN)
self.b2 = weight_initializer(1, D_HIDDEN)
self.y2 = None
self.w3 = weight_initializer(D_HIDDEN, 1)
self.b3 = weight_initializer(1, 1)
self.y3 = None
self.y = None
```

And now define its forward calculation (to predict the label based on the input sample):

```
def forward(self, inputs):
    self.x = inputs.reshape(1, X_DIM)
    self.y1 = np.matmul(self.x, self.w1) + self.b1
    self.y1 = LeakyReLU(self.y1)
    self.y2 = np.matmul(self.y1, self.w2) + self.b2
    self.y2 = LeakyReLU(self.y2)
    self.y3 = np.matmul(self.y2, self.w3) + self.b3
    self.y = Sigmoid(self.y3)
    return self.y
```

Here, we use LeakyReLU as the activation function for hidden layers and sigmoid for the output layer. Now, let's define the backward calculation for the discriminator network (to calculate the derivatives and update the parameters):

```
def backward(self, outputs, apply_grads=True):
    # Derivative with respect to output
    delta = outputs
    delta *= dSigmoid(self.y)
    # Derivative with respect to w3
    d_w3 = np.matmul(np.transpose(self.y2), delta)
    # Derivative with respect to b3
    d_b3 = delta.copy()
    # Derivative with respect to y2
    delta = np.matmul(delta, np.transpose(self.w3))
    if apply_grads:
        # Update w3
        if np.linalg.norm(d_w3) > GRADIENT_CLIP:
            d_w3 = GRADIENT_CLIP / np.linalg.norm(d_w3) * d_w3
        self.w3 += step_size_D * d_w3
        self.w3 = np.maximum(-WEIGHT_CLIP, np.minimum(WEIGHT_CLIP,
          self.w3))
        # Update b3
        self.b3 += step_size_D * d_b3
        self.b3 = np.maximum(-WEIGHT_CLIP, np.minimum(WEIGHT_CLIP,
          self.b3))
    delta *= dLeakyReLU(self.y2)
    # Derivative with respect to w2
    d_w2 = np.matmul(np.transpose(self.y1), delta)
```

```
# Derivative with respect to b2
d_b2 = delta.copy()
# Derivative with respect to y1
delta = np.matmul(delta, np.transpose(self.w2))
if apply_grads:
    # Update w2
    if np.linalg.norm(d_w2) > GRADIENT_CLIP:
        d_w2 = GRADIENT_CLIP / np.linalg.norm(d_w2) * d_w2
    self.w2 += step_size_D * d_w2
    self.w2 = np.maximum(-WEIGHT_CLIP, np.minimum(WEIGHT_CLIP,
        self.w2))
    # Update b2
    self.b2 += step_size_D * d_b2
    self.b2 = np.maximum(-WEIGHT_CLIP, np.minimum(WEIGHT_CLIP,
        self.b2))
delta *= dLeakyReLU(self.y1)
# Derivative with respect to w1
d_w1 = np.matmul(np.transpose(self.x), delta)
# Derivative with respect to b1
d_b1 = delta.copy()
# Derivative with respect to x
delta = np.matmul(delta, np.transpose(self.w1))
# Update w1
if apply_grads:
    if np.linalg.norm(d_w1) > GRADIENT_CLIP:
        d_w1 = GRADIENT_CLIP / np.linalg.norm(d_w1) * d_w1
    self.w1 += step_size_D * d_w1
    self.w1 = np.maximum(-WEIGHT_CLIP, np.minimum(WEIGHT_CLIP,
        self.w1))
    # Update b1
    self.b1 += step_size_D * d_b1
    self.b1 = np.maximum(-WEIGHT_CLIP, np.minimum(WEIGHT_CLIP,
        self.b1))
return delta
```

Please note that the main difference in the backward calculation of the discriminator is that it's trained with gradient ascent. Therefore, to update its parameters, we need to add the gradients. So, in the preceding code, you will see lines like this that take care of it for us:

```
self.w3 += step_size_D * d_w3
```

Training our GAN model

Now that all the necessary components are defined, we can begin the training of our GAN model:

```
G = Generator()
D = Discriminator()
criterion = LossFunc()

real_label = 1
fake_label = 0

for itr in range(ITER_NUM):
    # Update D with real data
    x_real = get_samples(True)
    y_real = D.forward(x_real)
    loss_D_r = criterion.forward(y_real, real_label)
    d_loss_D = criterion.backward()
    D.backward(d_loss_D)

    # Update D with fake data
    z_noise = np.random.randn(Z_DIM)
    x_fake = G.forward(z_noise)
    y_fake = D.forward(x_fake)
    loss_D_f = criterion.forward(y_fake, fake_label)
    d_loss_D = criterion.backward()
    D.backward(d_loss_D)

    # Update G with fake data
    y_fake_r = D.forward(x_fake)
    loss_G = criterion.forward(y_fake_r, real_label)
    d_loss_G = D.backward(loss_G, apply_grads=False)
    G.backward(d_loss_G)
    loss_D = loss_D_r + loss_D_f
    if itr % 100 == 0:
        print('{} {} {}'.format(loss_D_r.item((0, 0)), loss_D_f.item((0,
0)), loss_G.item((0, 0))))
```

As you can see from the preceding code, the training of the GAN model mainly has 3 steps:

1. Train the discriminator with real data (and recognize it as real).
2. Train the discriminator with fake data (and recognize it as fake).
3. Train the generator with fake data (and recognize it as real).

The first two steps teach the discriminator how to tell the difference between real and fake data. The third step teaches the generator how to fool the discriminator by generating fake data that is similar to real data. This is the core idea of adversarial learning and the reason why GANs can generate relatively realistic audio, text, images, and videos.

Here, we use SGD to train the model for 50,000 iterations. If you are interested, feel free to implement a mini-batch GD to see whether it produces better results in a shorter time. You are also welcome to change the network architectures (for example, the number of layers, the number of neurons in each layer, and the data dimension, X_DIM) to see how results change with the hyperparameters.

Finally, let's use Matplotlib to visualize the generated samples:

```
import matplotlib.pyplot as plt
x_axis = np.linspace(0, 10, 10)
for i in range(50):
    z_noise = np.random.randn(Z_DIM)
    x_fake = G.forward(z_noise)
    plt.plot(x_axis, x_fake.reshape(X_DIM))
plt.ylim((-1, 1))
plt.show()
```

It may take a few seconds to finish the training, depending on how powerful your CPU is. When the training is finished, the samples generated by the generator network may look like this (50 samples):

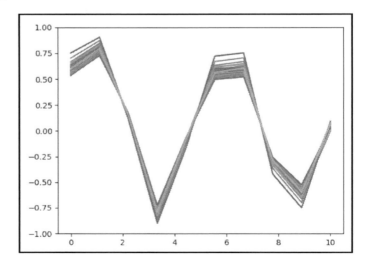

The generated sine samples

Pretty convincing, right? It's amazing to see how it captures the peaks and valleys of the original sine waves. Imagine what GANs are capable of with much more complex structures!

What GAN we do?

GANs can do a lot more than generating sine signals. We can apply GANs to address many different practical problems by altering the input and output dimensions of the generator and combining them with other methods. For example, we can generate text and audio (1-dimension), images (2-dimension), video, and 3D models (3-dimension) based on random input. If we keep the same dimension of input and output, we can perform denoising and translation on these types of data. We can feed real data into the generator and let it output data with larger dimensions, for example, image super-resolution. We can also feed one type of data and let it give another type of data, for example, generate audio based on text, generate images based on text, and so on.

Even though it has only been 4 years since GANs first came out (at the time of writing), people have kept working on improving GANs and new GAN models are coming out almost weekly. If you take a look at `https://github.com/hindupuravinash/the-gan-zoo`, you can see that there have been at least 500 different GAN models. It's nearly impossible for us to learn and evaluate each one of them. You'll be amazed to see that it is actually common to find several models sharing the same name! Therefore, in this book, we won't even try to introduce you to most of the GAN models out there. We will, however, help you to get familiar with the most typical GAN models in different applications and learn how to use them to address practical problems.

We will also introduce you to some useful tricks and techniques to improve the performance of GANs. We hope that, by the time you finish this book, you have a wide yet in-depth understanding of the mechanisms of various GAN models so that you will feel confident to design your own GANs to creatively solve the problems you may encounter in the future.

Let's take a look at what GANs are capable of and what their advantages are compared to traditional approaches in these fields: image processing, NLP, and 3D modeling.

Image processing

In the field of image processing, GANs are applied to many applications, including image synthesis, image translation, and image restoration. These topics are the most common in the study and application of GANs and make up most of the content in this book. Images are one of the easiest to show and spread media form on the internet; therefore, any latest breakthrough in the image-wise application of GANs would receive overwhelming attention in the deep learning community.

Image synthesis

Image synthesis is, in short, the creation of new images. Early in 2015, **DCGANs (Deep Convolutional Generative Adversarial Networks)** came out. It was one of the first well-performing and stable approaches to address the hard-to-train issues presented in earlier GAN models. It generates 64 x 64 images based on a random vector with a length of 100. Some images generated by DCGANs are shown in the following screenshot. You may notice that some of the images are far from being realistic because of the blocky appearance of the pixels. In the paper by Radford, Metz, and Chintala (2015), they present many interesting and inspiring visual experiments and reveal even more potential of GANs. We will talk about the architecture and training procedure of DCGANs later in `Chapter 4`, *Building Your First GAN with PyTorch*:

Images generated by a DCGAN (left: human faces; right: bedroom)

Now, GANs perform extraordinarily in image synthesis. Take BigGAN, for example. It was proposed in a paper submitted to ICLR 2019 (7th *International Conference on Learning Representations*) by Brock, Donahue, and Simonyan. It received a lot of attention on social media even during the open review process. It's capable of generating images as large as 512 x 512 with high quality.

In future chapters, we will also take a look at GAN models that look further into attributes of images, rather than just class conditions. We will talk about Conditional GANs, which allow you to generate images interactively, and Age-cGAN, which generates human faces of any age of your desire. We will also look into how to use GANs to generate adversarial examples that even the best classifiers cannot correctly recognize in Chapter 8, *Training Your GANs to Break Different Models*.

Image translation

If we describe image synthesis as a process where we expect the outputs to be 2-dimension images when feeding 1-dimension vector into the models (again, note that there are exceptions since you can generate images based on other types of data if you want), image translation (more precisely, image-to-image translation) would be the process where we feed 2-dimension images into models that also give 2-dimension data as outputs. A lot of interesting things can be done with image translation. For example, pix2pix (Isola, Zhu, Zhou, et al, 2016) transforms label maps into images, including turning edge sketches into colorized images, generating street view photos based on semantic segmentation information, transferring image styles, and so on. We will get to an upgraded version of pix2pix, pix2pixHD, in Chapter 6, *Image-to-Image Translation and Its Applications*, along with other image-to-image translation methods such as CycleGAN and DiscoGAN.

Image-to-image translation can be used in other computer vision applications and address more traditional problems, such as image restoration, image in-painting, and super-resolution. Image restoration is one of the most important research areas in computer vision. Mathematicians and computer scientists have been trying to figure out how to remove the annoying noises off photos or reveal more information out of blur images for decades. Traditionally, these problems are solved by iterative numerical calculations, which often require profound mathematical backgrounds to master. Now, with GANs at hand, these problems can be solved by image-to-image translation. For example, SRGAN (Ledig, Theis, Huszar, et al, 2016) can upscale images to 4X of size with high quality, which we will talk about in detail in Chapter 7, *Image Restoration with GANs*. Yes, Chen, Lim, et al (2016) proposed using a DCGAN-like model to address human face inpainting problems. More recently, Yu, Lin, Yang, et al (2018) designed a GAN model that fills in an arbitrary shape of blank holes in images and the generated pixels are quite convincing as well.

Text-to-image translation is also a good application of GANs, in which new images are generated based on the description text. Reed, Akata, Yan, et al (2016) came up with a procedure that extracts distinguish features from detailed description text and uses the information to generate flower or bird images that match perfectly to the description. Months later, Zhang, Xu, Li, et al (2016) proposed StackGAN to generate 256 x 256 images with high fidelity based on description text. We will talk about text-to-image translation in Chapter 9, *Image Generation from Description Text*.

Video synthesis and translation

A video is a sequence of images. Therefore, most of the image translation methods can be directly applied to video. However, a crucial performance criterion of video synthesis or translation is the calculation speed. For example, if we want to develop a camera application with different image styles for mobile devices, our users would certainly hope that they can see the processed results in real-time. Take video surveillance systems as another example. It is completely feasible to use GANs to denoise and enhance the video signals (provided that your clients trust your models without reservation). A fast model that processes each frame in milliseconds to keep up with the frame rate would certainly be worth considering.

We'd like to point out an interesting gesture transfer project called **Everybody Dance Now**. It extracts the movements of the dancer from a source video, then maps the same movements to the person in the target video by image-to-image translation. This way, anyone can use this model to make dancing videos of their own!

NLP

NLP is the study of how to use computers to process and analyze natural human languages. Other than generating images, GANs can also be used to generate sequential and time-dependent data, such as text and audio. SeqGAN, proposed by Yu, Zhang, Wang, et al (2016), is designed to generate sequential signals, like poems and music. Shortly after, Mogren (2016) proposed C-RNN-GAN, which is designed to generate classical music under acoustic restraints. In 2017, Dong, Hsiao, Yang, et al designed MuseGAN to generate polyphonic music of multiple instruments, including bass, drums, guitar, piano, and strings. Feel free to visit the following web[10] site to enjoy the generated music!

Speech enhancement is one of the main research areas in audio signal processing. Traditionally, people use spectral subtraction, Wiener filtering, subspace approaches, and more to remove the noises in audio or speech signals. However, the performances of these methods have only been satisfactory under certain circumstances. Pascual, Bonafonte, and Serrà (2017) designed SEGAN to address this problem and achieved impressive results[11]. We will talk about the applications of GANs in the field of NLP in Chapter 10, *Sequence Synthesis with GANs*.

3D modeling

Now that we know GANs can generate 2D data based on 1D inputs, it's only natural to consider leveling this up to generate 3D data based on 1D or 2D signals with GANs. 3D-GAN (Wu, Zhang, Xue, et al, 2016) is designed exactly for this purpose. It learns the mapping between the latent vector and 3D models to generate 3D objects based on a 1D vector. It is also completely feasible to use GANs to predict 3D models based on 2D silhouettes. Gadelha, Maji, and Wang (2016) designed PrGAN to generate 3D objects based on binary silhouette images from any viewpoint. We will discuss how to generate 3D objects with GANs in detail in Chapter 11, *Reconstructing 3D Models with GANs*.

Summary

We've covered a tremendous amount of information just in this first chapter. You've seen how GANs came about and have a basic grasp of the roles of generators and discriminators. You've even seen a few examples of some of the things that GANs can do. We've even created a GAN program using just NumPy. Not to mention we now know why Ganland has better blacksmiths and wine.

Next, we'll dive into the wondrous world of PyTorch, what it is, and how to install it.

The following is a list of references and other helpful links.

References and useful reading list

1. Goodfellow I, Pouget-Abadie J, Mirza M, et al. (2014). Generative adversarial nets. NIPS, 2672-2680.

2. Wang, J. (2017, Dec 23). *Symbolism vs. Connectionism: A Closing Gap in Artificial Intelligence*, retrieved from https://wangjieshu.com/2017/12/23/symbol-vs-connectionism-a-closing-gap-in-artificial-intelligence.

3. Radford A, Metz L, Chintala S. (2015). *Unsupervised Representation Learning with Deep Convolutional Generative Adversarial Networks*. arXiv preprint arXiv:1511.06434.

4. "Dev Nag". (2017, Feb 11). **Generative Adversarial Networks (GANs)** in 50 lines of code (PyTorch), retrieved from https://medium.com/@devnag/generative-adversarial-networks-gans-in-50-lines-of-code-pytorch-e81b79659e3f.

5. Brock A, Donahue J, Simonyan K. (2018). *Large Scale GAN Training for High Fidelity Natural Image Synthesis*. arXiv preprint arXiv:1809.11096.

6. Isola P, Zhu J Y, Zhou T, Efros A. (2016). *Image-to-Image Translation with Conditional Adversarial Networks*. arXiv preprint arXiv:1611.07004.

7. Ledig C, Theis L, Huszar F, et al (2016). *Photo-Realistic Single Image Super-Resolution Using a Generative Adversarial Network*. arXiv preprint arXiv:1609.04802.

8. Yeh R A, Chen C, Lim T Y, et al (2016). *Semantic Image Inpainting with Deep Generative Models*. arXiv preprint arXiv:1607.07539.

9. Yu J, Lin Z, Yang J, et al (2018). *Free-Form Image Inpainting with Gated Convolution*. arXiv preprint arXiv:1806.03589.

10. Reed S, Akata Z, Yan X, et al (2016). *Generative Adversarial Text to Image Synthesis*. arXiv preprint arXiv:1605.05396.

11. Zhang H, Xu T, Li H, et al (2016). *StackGAN: Text to Photo-realistic Image Synthesis with Stacked Generative Adversarial Networks*. arXiv preprint arXiv:1612.03242.

12. Yu L, Zhang W, Wang J, et al (2016). *SeqGAN: Sequence Generative Adversarial Nets with Policy Gradient*. arXiv preprint arXiv:1609.05473.

13. Mogren O. (2016). *C-RNN-GAN: Continuous recurrent neural networks with adversarial training*. arXiv preprint arXiv:1611.09904.

14. Dong H W, Hsiao W Y, Yang L C, et al (2017). *MuseGAN: Multi-track Sequential Generative Adversarial Networks for Symbolic Music Generation and Accompaniment*. arXiv preprint arXiv:1709.06298.

15. Pascual S, Bonafonte A, Serrà J. (2017). *SEGAN: Speech Enhancement Generative Adversarial Network*. arXiv preprint arXiv:1703.09452.

16. Wu J, Zhang C, Xue T, et al (2016). *Learning a Probabilistic Latent Space of Object Shapes via 3D Generative-Adversarial Modeling*. arXiv preprint arXiv:1610.07584.

17. Gadelha M, Maji S, Wang R. (2016). *3D Shape Induction from 2D Views of Multiple Objects*. arXiv preprint arXiv:1612.05872.

Getting Started with PyTorch 1.3

2

PyTorch 1.3 has finally arrived! Are you ready to exploit its new features and functionalities to make your research and production easier?

In this chapter, we will walk you through the breaking changes introduced in PyTorch, including switching from eager mode to graph mode. We will look at how to migrate older code to 1.x and walk you through the PyTorch ecosystem along with Cloud support.

Also, we will introduce how to install CUDA so that you can take advantage of GPU acceleration for faster training and evaluation with your PyTorch code. We will show you the step-by-step installation process of PyTorch on Windows 10 and Ubuntu 18.04 (with pure Python or an Anaconda environment) and how to build PyTorch from source.

Finally, as bonus content, we will present how to configure Microsoft VS Code for PyTorch development and some of the best extensions to make your work more enjoyable.

The following topics will be covered in this chapter:

- What's new in PyTorch 1.3?
- CUDA - GPU acceleration for fast training and evaluation
- Installing Pytorch on Windows and Linux
- References and useful reading list

What's new in PyTorch 1.3?

PyTorch (`https://pytorch.org`) is an open source machine learning platform for Python. It is specifically designed for deep learning applications, such as **Convolutional Neural Networks (CNNs)**, **Recurrent Neural Networks (RNNs)**, and **Generative Adversarial Networks (GANs)**, and it includes extensive layer definitions for these applications. It has built-in tensor operations that are designed to be used in the same way as NumPy arrays, and they are also optimized to run on GPUs for fast computation. It provides an automatic computational graph scheme so that you won't need to calculate derivatives by hand.

After around 3 years of development and improvements, PyTorch has finally reached its newest milestone, version 1.3! What comes with it is a big package of new features and new functionalities. Don't worry about whether you'll have to re-learn the tool; even when it's a totally new version, PyTorch has always been good at keeping its core functionality consistent. In fact, its core modules haven't changed much since its alpha release (version 0.1.1): `torch.nn`, `torch.autograd`, and `torch.optim`, unlike some other platforms. (Yes! We're talking about you, TensorFlow!) Now let's take a look at some of the new features in PyTorch.

Easy switching from eager mode to graph mode

When PyTorch first caught people's attention around 2 years ago, one of its biggest advantages over other deep learning tools was its dynamic graph support. It might be the main reason people ditch their old tools and embrace PyTorch. As you might have noticed, recently, more authors of the latest deep learning papers are using PyTorch to implement their experiments.

However, it doesn't mean that PyTorch is not fit for production environments. In version 1.0, PyTorch provides a **hybrid frontend** that easily transfers your code from eager mode (dynamic graph) to graph mode (static graph). You can write your code in as flexible a way as before. When you are satisfied with your code, just by changing a few lines of code in your model, it will be ready to be optimized for efficiency in graph mode. This process is accomplished by the torch.jit compiler. **JIT (Just-In-Time)** compiler is designed to serialize and optimize PyTorch code into **TorchScript**, which can run without a Python interpreter.

This means that, now, you can easily export your model to an environment where Python is not available or efficiency is extremely important, and call your model with C++ code. Two modalities are provided to convert traditional PyTorch code to TorchScript: tracing and scripting. **Tracing** is perfect for directly transforming your fixed model scheme with fixed inputs to graph mode.

However, if there is any data-dependent control flow in your model (for example, RNN), **scripting** is designed for this type of scenario, where all possible control flow routes are converted into TorchScript. Bear in mind that, for now (at the time of writing this book), scripting still has its limitations.

Dynamic graph means that the computational graph is established each time you run your model and can be changed between different runs. It's like everyone driving their own cars around the streets, when anyone can go anywhere each time they leave their home. It's flexible for research purposes. However, the additional resource overheads that building the graphs before each run requires cannot be overlooked. Therefore, it might be a little inefficient for production purposes. **Static graph** means that the computational graph has to be established before the first run and it cannot be changed once established. It's like everyone going to work on the bus. It's efficient, but if the passengers want to travel to different destinations, they have to talk to the bus driver, who will then talk to the public transportation authorities. Then, the bus route can be changed the next day.

Here's an example of how to change your models to graph mode.

Assume that we already have `model` on a given `device`:

```
model = Net().to(device)
```

We only need to add these lines to `trace` the `model`:

```
trace_input = torch.rand(BATCH_SIZE, IMG_CHANNEL, IMG_HEIGHT,
IMG_WIDTH).to(device)
traced_model = torch.jit.trace(model, trace_input)
```

Then, we can `save` the traced model to file:

```
traced_model.save("model_jit.pth")
```

Note that you should avoid using `torch.save(traced_model.state_dict(),` `"model_jit.pth")` to save the traced model, because, at the time of writing this book, the checkpoint file created in this way cannot be properly processed by the C++ API.

aced model can be used in the same way as a normal `torch.nn.Module` in
l can also be used by other C++ code, which we will cover later. The full code for
, _e, where we train and export a CNN for classification on MNIST can be found
in the `jit/mnist_jit.py` file located in the code repository for this chapter. You can refer
to the official tutorial for more information about the hybrid frontend: `https://pytorch.`
`org/tutorials/beginner/deploy_seq2seq_hybrid_frontend_tutorial.html`.

The C++ frontend

Even though the backend of PyTorch is mostly implemented by C++, its frontend API has
always been focused on Python. It's partly because Python has already been very popular
among data scientists and it has tons of open source packages that help you focus on
solving the problems, rather than re-creating the wheel. Also, it's extremely easy to read
and write. However, Python is not known for computation and memory resource
efficiency. Big companies often develop their own tools in C++ for better performance. But
smaller companies or individual developers find it difficult to divert their main focus to
developing their own C++ tools. Luckily, PyTorch has now shipped the C++ API with
version 1.0. Now, anyone can build efficient projects with it.

 Note that, right now, the C++ API of PyTorch is still under development
and may undergo some changes in the future. In fact, the changes
between v1.0.1 and v1.0.0 are so huge that the official documents and
tutorials for v1.0.0 would not fit v1.0.1.

Here's an example of how to use the C++ API provided by PyTorch.

Let's load the traced model we exported previously:

```
torch::Device device = torch::kCUDA;
std::shared_ptr<torch::jit::script::Module> module =
torch::jit::load("model_jit.pth");
module->to(device);
```

Then, let's feed a dummy input image to the model:

```
std::vector<torch::jit::IValue> inputs;
inputs.push_back(torch::ones({BATCH_SIZE, IMG_CHANNEL, IMG_HEIGHT,
IMG_WIDTH}).to(device));
at::Tensor output = module->forward(inputs).toTensor();
```

The full code for the C++ example can be found under the `jit` directory located in the code repository for this chapter, including a `CMakeLists.txt` file for compiling the `.cpp` file. You can refer to the official documentation for more information about C++ APIs: `https://pytorch.org/cppdocs`.

The redesigned distributed library

Debugging multithreading programs on a CPU is painful. Designing efficient GPU programs on distributed systems can be even more so. Fortunately, PyTorch keeps delivering ease-of-use distributed solutions for this very purpose. In version 1.0, the `torch.distributed` module is performance-driven and runs asynchronously for all backends, including Gloo, NCCL, and MPI. The new distributed library is designed to deliver near-optimal performance on both single-node and multi-node systems. It's also specially optimized for less advanced network communication scenarios by reducing bandwidth exchanges and thus improves the performance of these systems.

The NCCL backend is used for distributed GPU training, and the Gloo backend is used for distributed CPU training. The new distributed package also provides a helper utility, `torch.distributed.launch`, which is designed to launch multiple processes on both single-node and multi-node systems. An example of how to use it for distributed training is as follows:

- Single-node `distributed` training:

  ```
  $ python -m torch.distributed.launch --nproc_per_node=NUM_GPUS
  YOUR_SCRIPT.py --YOUR_ARGUMENTS
  ```

- Multi-node `distributed` training:

  ```
  # Node 1
  $ python -m torch.distributed.launch --nproc_per_node=NUM_GPUS --
  nnodes=2 --node_rank=0 --master_addr=MASTER_IP --
  master_port=MASTER_PORT YOUR_SCRIPT.py --YOUR_ARGUMENTS
  # Node 2
  $ python -m torch.distributed.launch --nproc_per_node=NUM_GPUS --
  nnodes=2 --node_rank=1 --master_addr=MASTER_IP --
  master_port=MASTER_PORT YOUR_SCRIPT.py --YOUR_ARGUMENTS
  ```

In the preceding, `MASTER_IP` is a string containing the IP address of the master node, for example, `192.168.1.1`.

> check out the official tutorial on distributed training with PyTorch 1.3: `https://`
`org/docs/master/distributed.html, https://pytorch.org/tutorials/`
`.iate/dist_tuto.html, https://pytorch.org/tutorials/beginner/former_`
`s/parallelism_tutorial.html` **and** `https://pytorch.org/tutorials/beginner/`
`aws_distributed_training_tutorial.html.`

Better research reproducibility

You may have heard complaints about how hard it is to reproduce the experimental results in deep learning papers. Apparently, we need to trust the reviewers, even though they have to review thousands of papers for each top conference every year. However, does it mean we cannot trust our abilities to follow the exact steps written on paper? Now PyTorch has announced torch.hub to help with the research reproducible problem. Authors can now publish their trained models with Torch Hub and users can directly download and use them in their code.

Here's an example of how to publish and use pre-trained models with Torch Hub.

To publish your model, you need to create a `hubconf.py` file in a GitHub repository and define the entrypoint (for example, named `cnn`) like this:

```
dependencies = ['torch']

def cnn(pretrained=True, *args, **kwargs):
    model = Net()
    checkpoint = 'models/cnn.pth'
    if pretrained:
        model.load_state_dict(torch.load(checkpoint))
    return model
```

In the preceding code, `dependencies` is a list of the dependencies required to run your model, and `Net()` is the class that defines your model. Note that the published models have to live under certain a branch/tag, for example, the **master** branch. You can also upload your `pretrained` model files to other sites and download them in this way:

```
if pretrained:
    import torch.utils.model_zoo as model_zoo
    model.load_state_dict(model_zoo.load_url(checkpoint))
```

Say we have published our model to `https://github.com/johnhany/torchhub`. To use a published model, you only need to call `torch.hub`:

```
import torch.hub as hub
model = hub.load("johnhany/torchhub:master", "cnn", force_reload=True,
pretrained=True).to(device)
```

The full code for the Torch Hub example can be found under the `torchhub` directory located in the code repository for this chapter.

Miscellaneous

Other than what we've mentioned previously, there are other things we can benefit from in the new version of PyTorch. By the end of this section, we will also talk about how to migrate your old PyTorch code to version 1.x.

The PyTorch ecosystem

There are many wonderful tools and projects built on the PyTorch platform. They explore the full potential of PyTorch in many domains. For example, **AllenNLP** (`https://allennlp.org`) is an open source natural language processing library. Check out their demo site and see what state-of-the-art NLP algorithms are capable of: `https://demo.allennlp.org`. **Fastai** (`https://docs.fast.ai`) provides a simplified procedure of model training with PyTorch, and also offers practical deep learning courses at `https://course.fast.ai`. **Translate** (`https://github.com/pytorch/translate`) is a PyTorch library that's dedicated to natural language translation.

Check out this site to find out more about the PyTorch ecosystem: `https://pytorch.org/ecosystem`.

Cloud support

PyTorch is fully supported by popular cloud platforms such as Amazon AWS, Google Cloud Platform, and Microsoft Azure. If you don't currently own a CUDA-enabled GPU (which we will discuss in the next section), feel free to rent a GPU server provided by the platforms previously mentioned. Here's an official tutorial on distributed training with PyTorch on Amazon AWS: `https://pytorch.org/tutorials/beginner/aws_distributed_training_tutorial.html`.

Migrating your previous code to 1.x

Despite all the breaking changes in PyTorch 1.x, most of the APIs or coding conventions have not changed too much. Therefore, if you are already comfortable with PyTorch 0.4, your code *should* mostly work as is. API changes from v0.4 to v1.3 are listed in Breaking Changes at `https://github.com/pytorch/pytorch/releases`.

The most common issue you might run into when migrating older code to PyTorch 1.x would stem from indexing a 0-dimension tensor. You need to use `loss.item()` when, for example, printing the loss value, instead of `loss[0]`. The full code for this example is contained in the `ind-0-dim.py` file under the `pytorch_test` directory located in the code repository for this chapter.

If your code is targeted at older versions than 0.4, you should perhaps check out the migration guide for PyTorch 0.4; first: `https://pytorch.org/blog/pytorch-0_4_0-migration-guide`. There is no official migration guide for versions later than 0.4, however, you'll certainly find plenty of information on the internet with a simple web search.

CUDA – GPU acceleration for fast training and evaluation

The NVIDIA CUDA Toolkit (`https://developer.nvidia.com/cuda-toolkit`) is a fully optimized parallel computing platform for general-purpose computing on graphics processing units (GPGPU). It allows us to perform scientific computing on NVIDIA graphic cards, including linear algebra, image and video processing, deep learning, and graph analytics. It is used by a lot of commercial and open source software to enable GPU-accelerated computation across different domains. If we look back at the development of deep learning, we should realize that the latest breakthroughs in GANs would have been almost impossible without the help of CUDA and powerful GPUs. Therefore, we highly recommend you try out the experiments in this book on a CUDA-compatible GPU; otherwise, the training time of neural networks could be painfully long on CPUs.

In this section, we will walk you through the installation of CUDA on Windows 10 and Ubuntu 18.04. Before we start installing CUDA, you should make sure that your video card supports CUDA and you have installed the latest driver for your video card. To check whether your GPU is compatible with CUDA (or the exact CUDA version you want to install), you should first make sure you have an NVIDIA video card on your machine.

On Windows, you can use third-party tools such as GPU-Z (`https://www.techpoweru|
com/gpuz`) or GPU Caps Viewer (`http://www.ozone3d.net/gpu_caps_viewer`) to examine
the specifications of your video card. You can always check this web page to see if your
video card is on the list: `https://www.geforce.com/hardware/technology/cuda/
supported-gpus`. The most straightforward and practical way, however, to check whether
the latest CUDA perfectly runs on your system, is to finish the installation and evaluation
steps in the following subsections without any issues.

At the time of writing this book, the latest version of CUDA is 10.1.

Installing NVIDIA driver

On Windows 10, visit `https://www.nvidia.com/Download/index.aspx` to download the
driver by choosing the product and operating system based on your video card and system.
Installation on Windows should be very straightforward since it has a **graphical user
interface (GUI)**. You can keep the default settings during installation.

On Ubuntu 18.04, you can always download CUDA from the *How to install CUDA 10.1 on
Ubuntu 18.04* (`https://gist.github.com/eddex/707f9cbadfaec9d419a5dfbcc2042611`).
However, we recommend you install the NVIDIA driver in the following way so that your
graphics driver can be updated in the same way as other software. First, open up a
Terminal and add the proper repository to your package management source list by typing
in the following:

```
$ sudo add-apt-repository ppa:graphics-drivers/ppa
$ sudo apt-get update
```

Now, you can check your video card model and the recommended driver version
by implementing the following:

```
$ ubuntu-drivers devices
```

The output may look like this:

```
== /sys/devices/pci0000:00/0000:00:01.0/0000:01:00.0 ==
modalias : pci:v000010DEd00001B06sv00001458sd00003752bc03sc00i00
vendor : NVIDIA Corporation
model : GP102 [GeForce GTX 1080 Ti]
driver : nvidia-driver-390 - third-party free
driver : nvidia-driver-396 - third-party free
driver : nvidia-driver-415 - third-party free recommended
driver : nvidia-driver-410 - third-party free
driver : xserver-xorg-video-nouveau - distro free builtin
```

Then, install the recommended driver with the following:

```
$ sudo ubuntu-drivers autoinstall
```

If you already have CUDA installed and plan on installing a different version of CUDA, we recommend you uninstall both the NVIDIA driver and CUDA toolkit, reboot your system, and install the latest driver before re-installing CUDA.

When the installation is finished, reboot your system.

Installing CUDA

Here's the full list of CUDA toolkits: `https://developer.nvidia.com/cuda-toolkit-archive`. Click **CUDA Toolkit 10.1** to navigate to the download page for CUDA 10.1.

On **Windows 10**, select **Windows | x86_64 | 10 | exe(local)**, and download the base installer. The installer file is about 2.1 GB. Again, we won't go into details regarding the installation process since it's GUI-based. Just keep the default settings during installation.

Make sure you also install the official CUDA samples during installation. They are essential for us to evaluate the successful installation of CUDA later on and very useful for learning CUDA programming (if you are interested). Also, if you plan on installing Microsoft Visual Studio on Windows as well, make sure you install it before CUDA, because CUDA will then automatically detect Visual Studio and install the corresponding integration tool.

On Ubuntu 18.04, select **Linux | x86_64 | Ubuntu | 18.04 | runfile(local)**, and download the Base Installer. The installer file is about 2.0 GB. When the download is finished, which could take a little while (say it's downloaded under the `~/Downloads` directory), open up a Terminal and type in the following:

```
$ cd ~/Downloads
$ sudo chmod +x cuda_10.1.243_418.86.00_linux.run
$ sudo sh cuda_10.1.243_418.86.00_linux.run
```

During the installation, accept all default settings, except that we don't need to install the NVIDIA driver when prompted, since we have already installed a newer version previously.

By the end of the installation of CUDA, there might be several warning messages, such as Missing recommended library: `libGLU.so`. Simply run `apt-get install libglu1-mesa libxi-dev libxmu-dev libglu1-mesa-dev` to install those optional libraries.

Finally, add CUDA directories to your `~/.bashrc` file so that other software can find your CUDA library:

```
$ export PATH=$PATH:/usr/local/cuda/bin
$ export
LD_LIBRARY_PATH=$LD_LIBRARY_PATH:/usr/local/cuda/lib:/usr/local/cuda/lib64:
/usr/local/cuda/extras/CUPTI/lib64
```

Alternatively, you can open the file with `gedit ~/.bashrc` and manually add these two lines at the end of the file:

```
PATH=$PATH:/usr/local/cuda/bin
LD_LIBRARY_PATH=$LD_LIBRARY_PATH:/usr/local/cuda/lib:/usr/local/cuda/lib64:
/usr/local/cuda/extras/CUPTI/lib64
```

Run `sudo ldconfig` to refresh the changes we make to the `.bashrc` file. Make sure you close and re-open the Terminal before running any other bash command.

For other platforms, please visit `https://docs.nvidia.com/cuda/archive/10.0` and follow the instructions there to install CUDA 10.0.

Installing cuDNN

In order to enable the fast computation capability provided by CUDA for neural networks, we need to install cuDNN. The **NVIDIA CUDA Deep Neural Network library (cuDNN)** is a GPU-accelerated library for deep neural networks. It's basically a low-level driver that runs on GPUs that provides multiple fully optimized forward and backward computation for common neural network operations. It has been used by many deep learning platforms, including PyTorch, so that the platform developers don't have to worry about implementing the basic neural network components and can focus on delivering better APIs for us to use.

First, we need to download cuDNN from this site: `https://developer.nvidia.com/rdp/cudnn-download`. Previous versions are available at `https://developer.nvidia.com/rdp/cudnn-archive`. Look for the cuDNN release that fits your CUDA version and your OS. Normally, any version of cuDNN that's bigger than **7.0** would be acceptable for PyTorch. You can always grab the latest version, of course. Here, we will download **cuDNN v7.5.0 for CUDA 10.1** from the first of the preceding links. Please note that you will need to register an NVIDIA Developer account with a valid email address to become a member of the NVIDIA Developer Program; then all the cuDNN release files are free to download.

On Windows 10, click Download cuDNN v7.5.0 (Feb 21, 2019); for CUDA 10.0, click **cuDNN Library for Windows 10**. This will download a `cudnn-10.0-windows10-x64-v7.5.0.56.zip` file that is about 224 MB. Unzip the downloaded file and copy the unzipped files to CUDA directory as follows:

- `[UNZIPPED_DIR]\cuda\bin\cudnn64_7.dll -> C:\Program Files\NVIDIA GPU Computing Toolkit\CUDA\v10.0\bin\cudnn64_7.dll`
- `[UNZIPPED_DIR]\cuda\include\cudnn.h -> C:\Program Files\NVIDIA GPU Computing Toolkit\CUDA\v10.0\include\cudnn.h`
- `[UNZIPPED_DIR]\cuda\lib\x64\cudnn.lib -> C:\Program Files\NVIDIA GPU Computing Toolkit\CUDA\v10.0\lib\x64\cudnn.lib`

On Ubuntu 18.04, click **Download cuDNN v7.5.0 (Feb 21, 2019)**; for CUDA 10.0, click **cuDNN Library for Linux**. A `cudnn-10.0-linux-x64-v7.5.0.56.tgz` file will be downloaded. The file size is about 433 MB. When the download is finished, let's open up a Terminal and run the following scripts (we assume that your file has been downloaded to the `~/Downloads` directory):

Unzip the downloaded file:

```
$ cd ~/Downloads
$ tar -xzvf cudnn-10.0-linux-x64-v7.5.0.56.tgz
```

Copy the files to the system directory and grant the read permissions for all users (you may need to `cd` to the extracted folder first):

```
$ sudo cp cuda/include/cudnn.h /usr/local/cuda/include
$ sudo cp cuda/lib64/libcudnn* /usr/local/cuda/lib64
$ sudo chmod a+r /usr/local/cuda/include/cudnn.h /usr/local/cuda/lib64/libcudnn*
```

On other platforms, please follow the instructions at `https://docs.nvidia.com/deeplearning/sdk/cudnn-install/index.html` to install cuDNN.

Evaluating your CUDA installation

Let's see if CUDA works properly on your machine. Here, we assume that you have also installed the official CUDA samples.

 Here, Microsoft Visual Studio is needed to build and test the CUDA sample on Windows. We are using Visual Studio Community 2017 in this example.

On Windows 10, navigate to the CUDA samples directory (for example, `C:\ProgramData\NVIDIA Corporation\CUDA Samples\v10.0`). Open the `1_Utilities\deviceQuery\deviceQuery_vs2017.sln` solution file with Visual Studio 2017.

In Visual Studio, switch the **Solution Configurations** to **Release**. Then, click **Build | Build deviceQuery** to build the sample code. When the build is finished, navigate to `C:\ProgramData\NVIDIA Corporation\CUDA Samples\v10.0\bin\win64\Release` and open PowerShell under this directory. Type in the following command:

```
> .\deviceQuery.exe
```

The output should look something like this:

```
CUDA Device Query (Runtime API) version (CUDART static linking)

Detected 1 CUDA Capable device(s)

Device 0: "GeForce GTX 1080 Ti"
   CUDA Driver Version / Runtime Version 10.0 / 10.0
   CUDA Capability Major/Minor version number: 6.1
   Total amount of global memory: 11175 MBytes (11718230016 bytes)
...
Result = PASS
```

This indicates that CUDA 10.0 has been successfully installed.

On Ubuntu 18.04, navigate to the CUDA samples directory (for example, `~/NVIDIA_CUDA-10.0_Samples`). Open the Terminal and type in:

```
$ cd 1_Utilities/deviceQuery
$ make
```

This should compile the `deviceQuery` program without any issue. Then, navigate to the build directory and run the program:

```
$ cd ../../bin/x86_64/linux/release
$ ./deviceQuery
```

The output should look similar to that from Windows 10.

Now we can move on to installing PyTorch 1.0!

Installing PyTorch on Windows and Linux

To install and use PyTorch, we need to properly set up the Python development environment first. So, in this section, we will first talk about how to set up the Python environment, then how to install PyTorch either with official release binaries or by building from source. At the end of this section, we will introduce you to a lightweight, yet extremely powerful code editor tool, Microsoft VS Code, and show you how to configure it for PyTorch programming.

Setting up the Python environment

In the following sections, we will walk you through how to set up the Python environment and how to install or build PyTorch on Windows 10 and Ubuntu 18.04. We assume that, of course, you have successfully installed CUDA on your system (for example, CUDA 10.1).

Installing Python

On Windows 10, visit https://www.python.org/downloads/windows to download the Windows x86-64 executable installer. You may install any version you want. We'll install the latest version (at the time of writing), 3.7.5, as an example. Actually, 3.8.0 is the very latest version, but it's better to stay on the 3.7.x track. The downloaded `python-3.7.5-amd64.exe` file is about 25 MB. Keep the default settings during installation, except that we could change the installation path to an easier-to-find location, that is, `C:\Python37`.

Make sure you check the box for **Add Python 3.7 to PATH** during installation, otherwise, you'll have to add the environment variables manually: `C:\Python37\` and `C:\Python37\Scripts\`. The detailed process of adding environment variables on Windows 10 is described later in this chapter.

On Ubuntu 18.04, Python 2.7.15 and 3.7.1 have already been shipped with the system. So, you don't have to do anything for now.

On Ubuntu, if you plan on using the default version of Python provided by the system, think twice before you modify it (including upgrading, downgrading, or uninstalling) because it will affect many other things in your system. And always make sure you are using the right version of Python (that is, Python 2 vs 3). Sometimes, installing and using packages across Python 2 and Python 3 can be a little bit messy.

Installing Anaconda Python

On Windows 10, download the installer from `https://www.anaconda.com/distribution/#windows`. We'll download and install Python 3.7 version as an example. This will download an `Anaconda3-2018.12-Windows-x86_64.exe` file that is about 614 MB in size. Open this file to install Anaconda and keep the default settings unchanged. Note that we don't have to check the box for **Register Anaconda as the system Python 3.7** because we will create a new Python environment and add the corresponding environment variables manually later on.

At the end of the installation, you will be asked whether you want to install the Microsoft VS Code. We recommend you install one for Python development.

On Ubuntu 18.04, download the installer from `https://www.anaconda.com/distribution/#linux`. Here, we download and install Python version 3.7, for example. An `Anaconda3-2018.12-Linux-x86_64.sh` file will be downloaded. The file size is around 684 MB. Run this file to install it (assume that it's located at `~/Downloads`):

```
$ cd ~/Downloads
$ chmod +x Anaconda3-2018.12-Linux-x86_64.sh
$ ./Anaconda3-2018.12-Linux-x86_64.sh
```

During the installation, accept all default settings. By the end of the installation, you will be prompted as to whether to install Microsoft VS Code on your system. You can accept it if you haven't installed it yet.

Prerequisites before we move on

There are some important, or even necessary, Python tools and libraries we need to install before moving on to the next section, including:

- **Pip** *(required):* It is required to manage your Python packages. On Ubuntu, run `sudo apt-get install python-pip` for Python 2 or `sudo apt-get install python3-pip` for Python 3. On Windows, it's usually installed along with Python.
- **NumPy** *(required):* A scientific computing library for tensor representation, manipulation, and calculation, along with linear algebra, the Fourier transform, and random number capabilities. It is required to install PyTorch.
- **SciPy** *(optional):* A collection of numerical algorithms including signal processing, optimization, and statistics. We will use it mainly for its statistics capability, for example, initializing parameters based on a certain random distribution.
- **OpenCV** *(optional):* A cross-platform open source computer vision library for efficient and real-time image processing and pattern recognition. We will use it to preprocess or visualize the data, parameters, and feature maps in neural networks.
- **Matplotlib** *(optional):* A publication-quality plotting library. We will use it to illustrate loss curves or other plots.

On Windows 10, you can visit `https://www.lfd.uci.edu/~gohlke/pythonlibs` to download the `.whl` files for these libraries and install them with `pip install [FILENAME]` (for Python 2) or `pip3 install [FILENAME]` (for Python 3).

On Ubuntu 18.04, you can install these packages with the following:

```
#For Python 2
$ pip install numpy scipy opencv-python matplotlib
#For Python 3
$ pip3 install numpy scipy opencv-python matplotlib
```

The installation may fail due to user permission issues. If you are an administrator user on Windows, make sure you open Command Prompt as administrator. If you have root access on Ubuntu, simply add `sudo` before the installation command. If you don't have the administrator or root access at all, install the packages with `pip3 install --user`.

Installing PyTorch

You can either install PyTorch using the official release binaries or by building it from source. You can install PyTorch directly on your system, or use a package manager (such as Anaconda) to avoid potential conflicts with other tools. At the time of writing this book, the latest version of PyTorch is v1.3.1. Since we want to take advantage of the cutting-edge functionalities provided by PyTorch, we will install and use PyTorch 1.3 in all the remaining chapters of this book. You can, of course, choose any other version you wish, or install an even newer version than the one we use in this book. Simply change the version number to your own version when you follow the following instructions.

We highly recommend that you install PyTorch with Anaconda if you are using Ubuntu because it won't affect the default Python environment that's shipped with the system. If you are on Windows, you can basically delete the Python installation and re-install any other version you want, if anything goes seriously wrong.

Installing official binaries

Not too long ago, installing PyTorch was a major endeavor. However, the good folks at PyTorch.org have made it very easy for you to install PyTorch on your system. Go to `https://pytorch.org/get-started/locally/` to get started. There, you will find a very simple point and click method to get the proper installation information.

You should start with the build that you want to install, and then select the operating system. Next, you should determine the way you want to install PyTorch, if it's via Conda, pip, and so on. Next, select the version of Python you are going to target, and, finally, pick which version of CUDA you are using or whether you are going to go without a GPU:

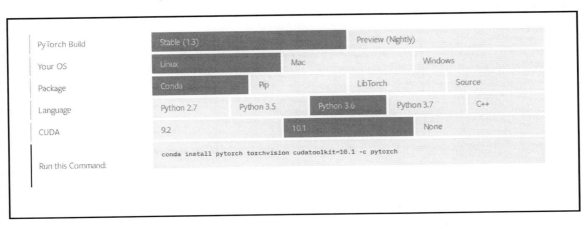

The last step is to select and copy the command from the box at the bottom of the grid. Paste this into your terminal or Command Prompt and run it. In a minute or two, you'll be all set.

You may also want to consider making the created Python environment the default Python for your system. To do that, all you need to do is add these environment variables: `C:\Users\John\Anaconda3\envs\torch` and `C:\Users\John\Anaconda3\envs\torch\Scripts`.

> How to add **environment variables** on Windows 10: (1) Right-click on the *Start* button and click *System*. (2) Click *System information* on the right in the *Settings* window, which will open up the *System Control Panel* (You may not need this step if you are on a rather old version of Windows 10). (3) Click *Advanced system settings* on the left, which will open the *System Properties* window. (4) Click *the Environment Variables* button, which will open the *Environment Variables* window. (5) Double-click the line for *Path* variable in *User variables*. Now you can add or edit the paths pointing to Anaconda or Python directories. Each time you edit environment variables, make sure that you close the *Environment Variables* window and run this script in PowerShell: `$env:Path = [System.Environment]::GetEnvironmentVariable("Path","Machine") + ";" + [System.Environment]::GetEnvironmentVariable("Path","User").`

That's it! PyTorch has now been installed on your machine and you can follow the instructions in the *Evaluating your PyTorch* installation section to see if it works properly.

Building Pytorch from source

Here, we will only talk about building PyTorch from source using Anaconda Python on Ubuntu 18.04, because the build process has a very high chance of failing on Windows. First, let's create a new Python environment called `torch-nt` for building and installing the nightly version with `conda create -n torch-nt python=3.7` and activate it with `conda activate torch-nt`.

Next, install the dependencies needed for building PyTorch:

```
(torch-nt)$ conda install numpy pyyaml mkl mkl-include setuptools cmake
cffi typing
(torch-nt)$ conda install magma-cuda100 -c pytorch
```

Then, download the source code of PyTorch with Git:

```
(torch-nt)$ git clone --recursive https://github.com/pytorch/pytorch
(torch-nt)$ cd pytorch
(torch-nt)$ export CMAKE_PREFIX_PATH="/home/john/anaconda3/envs/torch-nt"
(torch-nt)$ python setup.py install
```

Here, `CMAKE_PREFIX_PATH` points to the root directory of your Python environment. All your environments created by Anaconda are located under the `~/anaconda3/envs` folder.

Wait a moment for it to finish. When it's done, run `python` in the Terminal, type in `import torch`, and press **Enter**. If no error pops up, it means that PyTorch has been successfully built and installed.

> Do you remember, do not run `import torch` under the same directory you build PyTorch from, because Python will try to pick up the Torch library from the source files, instead of the installed package.

Evaluating your PyTorch installation

From now on, we will use the Anaconda Python environment called **torch** we previously created as the default Python environment in this book. We will also omit the (torch) indicator in front of the scripts. Also, by default, all of the code in this book is written for Python 3 (specifically, Python 3.7). If you are looking for Python 2 implementations, you might want to look at 3to2 (`https://pypi.org/project/3to2`).

Let's write a short snippet for matrix multiplication using PyTorch. Create a Python source code file named `pytorch_test.py` and copy the following lines into this file:

```
import torch

print("PyTorch version: {}".format(torch.__version__))
print("CUDA version: {}".format(torch.version.cuda))

device = torch.device("cuda" if torch.cuda.is_available() else "cpu")
print(device)

a = torch.randn(1, 10).to(device)
b = torch.randn(10, 1).to(device)
c = a @ b
print(c.item())
```

Open the Terminal and run this snippet:

```
$ conda activate torch
$ python pytorch_test.py
```

The output may look like this:

```
PyTorch version: 1.3.1
CUDA version: 10.1.243
cuda
-2.18083119392395
```

The last line is totally random, so don't worry if you get a different result. The code is also available under the `pytorch_test` directory located in the code repository for this chapter.

You can always use the jit or torchhub examples in previous sections to evaluate the installation of PyTorch. Also, feel free to check out the official examples at `https://github.com/pytorch/examples`.

> Remember the simple GAN we implemented with NumPy in `Chapter 1, Generative Adversarial Networks Fundamentals`? Now that you have your PyTorch up and ready, you can think about how you would implement it with PyTorch.

Bonus: setting up VS Code for Python coding

VS Code is a lightweight, open source code editor developed by Microsoft. It has built-in syntax highlighting, autocompleting, debugging, Git management, and it has more than 10,000 extensions developed by the community. It supports Windows, macOS, and Linux, and it is the most popular development tool among software developers, according to a StackOverflow survey: `https://insights.stackoverflow.com/survey/2018/#technology-most-popular-development-environments`. If you mainly work on your own machine for learning GANs with this book, we highly recommend you use VS Code for PyTorch development.

> If you often work remotely, which means that you have to write Python code locally and run that code on a remote server, you may consider using PyCharm Professional Edition (`https://www.jetbrains.com/pycharm`) for this purpose. It has a more mature remote development functionality than free VS Code extensions have to offer.

Configuring VS Code for Python development

Essentially, you only need the Python extension (`ms-python.python`) for Python programming in VS Code.

On Windows 10, click **File** | **Preferences** | **Settings**, click the {} button (Open Settings (JSON)) on the upper right, and type in the following:

```
"python.pythonPath": "C:\\Users\\John\\Anaconda3\\envs\\torch"
```

On Ubuntu 18.04, click **File** |**Preferences** | **Settings**, click the {} button (Open Settings (JSON)) on the upper right, and type in the following:

```
"python.pythonPath": "~/anaconda3/envs/torch/bin/python3"
```

Now, VS Code will automatically recognize it as an Anaconda Python environment and you are ready to write Python code with it!

Recommended VS Code extensions

Here are some VS Code extensions that I personally find useful in Python development. I'm sure they will make your work a lot easier as well. Many thanks to their creators!

- **Bracket Pair Colorizer** (`coenraads.bracket-pair-colorizer`): This matches each pair of brackets with different colors, which allows you to easily recognize them.
- **Code Runner** (`formulahendry.code-runner`): This allows you to run Python (and many other languages') code with a click of the button. However, we don't recommend you use it to run the training snippets of neural networks because the logging messages can be rather long and some messages might go missing in VS Code.
- **GitLens - Git supercharged** (`eamodio.gitlens`): This is a powerful tool if you rely on Git to manage your source code. For example, it shows Git history on each line you're currently looking at in the editor, shows all the local and remote changes in a tree structure, and so on.
- **indent-switcher** (`ephoton.indent-switcher`): Everyone's programming habits are different. Some like two spaces as indentation, and some like four spaces. You can switch between two-space and four-space indentation with this extension.
- **Partial Diff** (`ryu1kn.partial-diff`): This allows you to compare two code snippets across different files.
- **Path Intellisense** (`christian-kohler.path-intellisense`): This extension autocompletes filenames in your code.

- **Search - Open All Results** (`fabiospampinato.vscode-search-open-all-results`): This supports searching keywords across multiple source files.
- **Settings Sync** (`shan.code-settings-sync`): This saves the installed extensions and user settings to a Gist file and recovers from that file. It can be very useful if you work on multiple machines and systems.

References and useful reading list

1. Udacity India. (2018, Mar 8). *Why Python is the most popular language used for Machine Learning*. Retrieved from `https://medium.com/@UdacityINDIA/why-use-python-for-machine-learning-e4b0b4457a77`.

2. S Bhutani. (2018, Oct 7). *PyTorch 1.0 - A brief summary of the PTDC '18: PyTorch 1.0 Preview and Promise*. Retrieved from `https://hackernoon.com/pytorch-1-0-468332ba5163`.

3. C Perone. (2018, Oct 2). *PyTorch 1.0 tracing JIT and LibTorch C++ API to integrate PyTorch into NodeJS*. Retrieved from `http://blog.christianperone.com/2018/10/pytorch-1-0-tracing-jit-and-libtorch-c-api-to-integrate-pytorch-into-nodejs`.

4. T Wolf. (2018, Oct 15). *Training Neural Nets on Larger Batches: Practical Tips for 1-GPU, Multi-GPU and Distributed setups*. Retrieved from `https://medium.com/huggingface/training-larger-batches-practical-tips-on-1-gpu-multi-gpu-distributed-setups-ec88c3e51255`.

Summary

Wow! That was a lot of work and information. Take a minute, grab a cup of coffee or tea, and come back. I'll wait.

Let's look at all the things we've done.

We have made sure that we are up to date with our Python installation, installed CUDA (assuming we have an NVIDIA GPU graphics card) and installed PyTorch. If you are anything like me, you are *chomping at the bit* to get going and do some programming.

However, we need to get some more basics defined before we can really be productive, which is our goal. In the next chapter, we will go through some of the basics.

3
Best Practices for Model Design and Training

In this chapter, we'll take what we've learned so far and provide some basic information on it to help you move forward. We will look into the overall design of the model architecture and the steps we need to follow when choosing which convolution operation is needed. We will also learn how to adjust and tweak the loss function and learning rate.

In this chapter, we will cover the following topics:

- Model design cheat sheet
- Model training cheat sheet
- Efficient coding in Python
- Advice for deep learning beginners

Model design cheat sheet

In this section, we will provide you with an overview of the various choices you can make when it comes to designing the architecture of GAN models, and even deep learning models in general. It is always okay to directly borrow the model architectures you see in papers. It is also imperative to know how to adjust a model and create a brand new model from scratch, according to the practical problems at hand. Other factors, such as GPU memory capacity and expected training time, should also be considered when we design our models. We will talk about the following:

- Overall model architecture design
- Choosing a convolution operation method
- Choosing a downsampling operation method

Overall model architecture design

There are mainly two different design processes for deep learning models. They are fit for different scenarios and you should get comfortable with both processes:

- Design the whole network directly, especially for shallow networks. You can add/remove any layer in your network with ease. With this approach, you can easily notice any bottlenecks in your network (for example, which layer needs more/fewer neurons), which is extremely important when you are designing models that will run on mobile devices.
- Design a small block/cell (containing several layers or operations) and repeat the blocks several times to form the whole network. This process is very popular in very deep networks, especially in **network architecture search** (**NAS**). It is a bit harder to spot the weak spot in your model because all you can do is adjust the block, train the whole network for hours, and see if your adjustments lead to higher performance.

In some of the chapters in this book, U-Net-shaped (for example, pix2pixm, which we will cover in Chapter 5, *Image-to-Image Translation and Its Applications*) and ResNet-shaped (for example, SRGAN, which we will cover in Chapter 7, *Image Restoration with GANs*) networks will be used. Both architectures are designed via a block-based approach and use skip connections to connect non-adjacent layers. There are two different forms of data flow in neural networks:

- **Plain network**: Any layer within the network only has at most one input and one output direction.
- **Branching network**: At least one of the layers is connected to more than two other layers, such as ResNet and DenseNet.

You may have noticed that, in this book, plain networks are often used in discriminators and branching architectures are often used in generators. This is because generator networks are, in general, more difficult to train than discriminators and the branches (for example, skip connections) pass low-level details to deeper layers in the forward pass and help gradients flow better in the backward pass.

When we deal with branches in a network, how several branches are merged (so that the tensors can be passed to another block/cell in the uniform size) also has a great impact on the network's performance. Here are the recommended approaches:

- Concatenate all the tensors into a list and create another convolution layer to map this list to a smaller tensor. This way, information from all the input branches is reserved and the relationship between them is learned by the convolution layer. However, be careful with this approach when it comes to very deep networks since it costs more memory and more parameters means it's more vulnerable to overfitting.
- Directly sum the overall input tensors. This is easy to implement but may not perform well when there are too many input branches.
- Assign trainable weight factors to the branches before summing them up. Here, the merged tensor would be the weighted sum of the input tensors. It allows the network to figure out which inputs it should reply to and gives you a chance to remove unnecessary branches if their trained weight factors are too close to 0.

In general, if you are dealing with complex data, try using the classic models we have learned about in this book. If the classic models don't serve you well, try building a basic block (such as a residual block) and building a deep network with it. Deeper networks come with more surprises and, of course, take a longer time to train.

Choosing a convolution operation method

There are various types of convolution operations we can choose from, and different configurations in the same convolution layer lead to different results. Here, we will summarize the commonly used convolution operations and talk about their strengths and weaknesses:

1. **Vanilla convolution**: This is the most common convolution operation in CNNs. A convolution takes fewer parameters than a fully connected layer (nn.Linear) with the same input/output size and can be calculated pretty fast with im2col (see Chapter 7, *Image Restoration with GANs*, for more details). You can use the following snippet to create a ReLu-Conv-BN group (of course, feel free to change the order of the three functions):

```
class ReLUConvBN(nn.Module):
    def __init__(self, C_in, C_out, kernel_size, stride, padding,
affine=True):
        super(ReLUConvBN, self).__init__()
        self.op = nn.Sequential(
            nn.ReLU(inplace=False),
```

```
            nn.Conv2d(C_in, C_out, kernel_size, stride=stride,
    padding=padding, bias=False),
            nn.BatchNorm2d(C_out, affine=affine)
        )

    def forward(self, x):
        return self.op(x)
```

2. **Grouped convolution**: Here, the connections between the input/output neurons are separated into groups. You can create a grouped convolution by calling nn.Conv2d when assigning the groups argument to an integer larger than 1. It is often followed by another convolution layer with a kernel size of 1 so that the information from different groups can be mixed together. The GroupConv-1x1Conv combination always contains fewer parameters than a vanilla convolution as long as the kernel size is larger than 1.

3. **Depthwise separable convolution**: This is a grouped convolution where the group size equals the input channels, followed by a 1 x 1 convolution. It always contains fewer parameters than a vanilla convolution as long as the kernel size is larger than 1. Depthwise separable convolution is extremely popular among tiny networks for mobile devices and NAS (where people try to reach the highest performance under limited hardware resources). It is often used to see whether two depthwise separable convolutions appear together and result in better performance. You can use the following snippet to create a two-layer depthwise separable convolution operation:

```
class SepConv(nn.Module):
    def __init__(self, C_in, C_out, kernel_size, stride, padding,
    affine=True):
        super(SepConv, self).__init__()
        self.op = nn.Sequential(
            nn.ReLU(inplace=False),
            nn.Conv2d(C_in, C_in, kernel_size=kernel_size,
    stride=stride, padding=padding, groups=C_in, bias=False),
            nn.Conv2d(C_in, C_in, kernel_size=1, padding=0,
    bias=False),
            nn.BatchNorm2d(C_in, affine=affine),
            nn.ReLU(inplace=False),
            nn.Conv2d(C_in, C_in, kernel_size=kernel_size,
    stride=1, padding=padding, groups=C_in, bias=False),
            nn.Conv2d(C_in, C_out, kernel_size=1, padding=0,
    bias=False),
            nn.BatchNorm2d(C_out, affine=affine)
        )
    def forward(self, x):
        return self.op(x)
```

4. **Dilation convolution**: This has a larger reception field compared to vanilla convolution. For example, a 3×3 vanilla convolution has a 3×3 sliding window, but a 3×3 dilation convolution has a 5×5 sliding window, in which input pixels are samples – one for every two adjacent steps. However, it is not recommended to use dilation convolution with other types of convolutions (for example, depthwise separable convolution) in the same network. This is because dilation convolutions normally need much smaller learning steps to train, which will dramatically slow down your training process. You can use the following snippet to create a dilation convolution operation:

```
class DilConv(nn.Module):
    def __init__(self, C_in, C_out, kernel_size, stride, padding,
dilation, affine=True):
        super(DilConv, self).__init__()
        self.op = nn.Sequential(
            nn.ReLU(inplace=False),
            nn.Conv2d(C_in, C_in, kernel_size=kernel_size,
stride=stride, padding=padding, dilation=dilation, groups=C_in,
bias=False),
            nn.Conv2d(C_in, C_out, kernel_size=1, padding=0,
bias=False),
            nn.BatchNorm2d(C_out, affine=affine)
            )

    def forward(self, x):
        return self.op(x)
```

Normally, vanilla convolutions are already good enough. If your memory capacity is extremely limited, depthwise separable convolution would definitely be your best choice.

Choosing a downsampling operation method

It is often inevitable to increase or decrease the size of tensors (feature maps) in a network. The process of decreasing a tensor's size is called **downsampling** and the process of increasing a tensor's size is called **upsampling**. Downsampling is often trickier than upsampling since we don't want to lose too much useful information in the smaller tensors.

There are several ways to perform downsampling in neural networks, especially in CNNs. You may choose the most suitable one based on your needs:

- **Max-pooling** (for example, `nn.MaxPool2d`), which is where you select the maximum value in the sliding window. It is quite popular in the early shallow networks, such as LeNet-5. However, the maximum value is not necessarily the most significant feature in a feature map. For example, what happens to the minimum values? Apparently, the minimum value (-1.7) in the $[-0.1, -1.7, -0.5, 0.1]$ tensor gives us more information than the maximum value (0.1) about what kind of pattern this tensor contains.

- **Average-pooling** (for example, `nn.AvgPool2d` or `nn.AdaptiveAvgPool2d`), which is where you take the average value over the sliding window. It is becoming more popular than max-pooling. You should certainly choose average-pooling over max-pooling if you want to perform fast downsampling.

- **Strided convolution**, which is a convolution with a stride size larger than 1. This is actually what most of the models in this book use to perform downsampling since this approach can extract features and decrease the tensor size at the same time. It is worth pointing out that there can be a huge amount of information loss in this approach because the sliding window skips a lot of pixels while it's calculating. A decrease in the feature map size is often accompanied by an increase in the channel size. For example, a mini-batch tensor $[32, 8, 256, 256]$ (the four dimensions denote batch size, channel size, feature map height, and feature map width) is often downsampled to $[32, 16, 128, 128]$ so that the output tensor contains a similar amount of information to the input tensor.

- **Factorized reduction**, which is to perform two strided convolutions with a slight shift. In this approach, the second convolution covers the skipped pixels by the first convolution. Therefore, more information is reserved. It contains more parameters and so takes a longer time to train. You can use the following snippet to perform factorized reduction:

```
class FactorizedReduce(nn.Module):
    def __init__(self, C_in, C_out, affine=True):
        super(FactorizedReduce, self).__init__()
        assert C_out % 2 == 0
        self.relu = nn.ReLU(inplace=False)
        self.conv_1 = nn.Conv2d(C_in, C_out // 2, 1, stride=2,
padding=0, bias=False)
        self.conv_2 = nn.Conv2d(C_in, C_out // 2, 1, stride=2,
padding=0, bias=False)
        self.bn = nn.BatchNorm2d(C_out, affine=affine)

    def forward(self, x):
```

```
        x = self.relu(x)
        out = torch.cat([self.conv_1(x),
self.conv_2(x[:,:,1:,1:])], dim=1)
        out = self.bn(out)
        return out
```

If you have more than enough GPU memory to spare, use factorized reduction in your model. If not, using the strided convolution would save you a lot of memory.

More on model design

Feel free to check out PyTorch's official document at `torch.nn` to find out more about the various layers and operations that are available: `https://pytorch.org/docs/stable/nn.html`.

Model training cheat sheet

Designing a training strategy is just as important – if not more – than model design. Sometimes, a good training strategy can make a poorly designed model shine. Here, we will talk about the following topics:

- Parameter initialization
- Adjusting the loss function
- Choosing an optimization method
- Adjusting the learning rate
- Gradient clipping, weight clipping, and more

Parameter initialization

Sometimes, one of the most frustrating things about learning about an optimization method from a book/paper and implementing it with code is that the initial state of the machine learning system (initial values of the parameters) can have a great impact on the model's final performance. It is important to have knowledge of parameter initialization, especially while you're dealing with deep networks. A good parameter initialization also means that you won't always rely on Batch Normalization to keep your parameters in line during training. To quote from the PyTorch documentation, *"A PyTorch Tensor is basically the same as a numpy array: it does not know anything about deep learning or computational graphs or gradients and is just a generic n-dimensional array to be used for arbitrary numeric computation."* This is why there can be so many methods, and there will probably be more in the future.

There are several popular parameter initialization methods. We won't go into great detail about some of the methods since they are rather self-explanatory. Note that the uniform distributions are often used for fully-connected layers and normal distributions are often used for convolution layers. Let's go over some of these now:

- **Uniform** (`nn.init.uniform_(tensor, a, b)`): It initializes `tensor` with uniform distribution $\mathcal{U}(a, b)$.
- **Normal** (`nn.init.normal_(tensor, a, b)`): It initializes `tensor` with normal distribution $\mathcal{N}(a, b^2)$.
- **Xavier-uniform** (`nn.init.xavier_uniform_(tensor)`): It initializes `tensor` with uniform distribution $\mathcal{U}(-a, a)$, where we have the following equation:

$$a = \sqrt{\frac{6}{\text{in\_channels} + \text{out\_channels}}}$$

- **Xavier-normal** (`nn.init.xavier_normal_(tensor)`): It initializes `tensor` with normal distribution $\mathcal{N}(0, b^2)$, where we have the following equation:

$$b = \sqrt{\frac{2}{(\text{in\_channels} + \text{out\_channels}) \times \text{kernel\_size}^2}}$$

- **He-uniform** (that is, Kaiming-uniform or MSRA-uniform, `nn.init.kaiming_uniform_(tensor)`): It initializes `tensor` with uniform distribution $\mathcal{U}(-a, a)$, where we have the following equation:

$$a = \sqrt{\frac{6}{in\_channels}}$$

- **He-normal** (that is, Kaiming-normal or MSRA-normal, `nn.init.kaiming_normal_(tensor)`): It initializes `tensor` with normal distribution $\mathcal{N}(0, b^2)$, where we have the following equation:

$$b = \sqrt{\frac{2}{in\_channels \times kernel\_size^2}}$$

- **Truncated normal**: In this method, all the values that are larger (or smaller) than twice the standard deviation (or negative twice the standard deviation) are discarded and regenerated.

Besides using `torch.nn.init` to initialize your parameters, you can always create your own custom initializer. For example, here is an initializer that we can use for a convolution layer using `numpy` and `scipy.stats`:

```
import numpy as np
from scipy import stats

def initializer_conv(shape,
                     init='he',
                     dist='truncnorm',
                     dist_scale=1.0):
    w_width = shape[3]
    w_height = shape[2]
    size_in = shape[1]
    size_out = shape[0]

    limit = 0.
    if init == 'xavier':
        limit = math.sqrt(2. / (w_width * w_height * (size_in + size_out)))
* dist_scale
    elif init == 'he':
        limit = math.sqrt(2. / (w_width * w_height * size_in)) * dist_scale
    else:
        raise Exception('Arg `init` not recognized.')
    if dist == 'norm':
```

```
        var = np.array(stats.norm(loc=0,
scale=limit).rvs(shape)).astype(np.float32)
    elif dist == 'truncnorm':
        var = np.array(stats.truncnorm(a=-2, b=2,
scale=limit).rvs(shape)).astype(np.float32)
    elif dist == 'uniform':
        var = np.array(stats.uniform(loc=-limit,
scale=2*limit).rvs(shape)).astype(np.float32)
    else:
        raise Exception('Arg `dist` not recognized.')
    return var

class Conv2d(nn.Conv2d):
    def __init__(self, in_channels, out_channels, kernel_size,
            stride=1, padding=0, dilation=1, groups=1, bias=True,
            init='he', dist='truncnorm', dist_scale=1.0):
        super(Conv2d, self).__init__(
            in_channels, out_channels, kernel_size, stride,
            padding, dilation, groups, bias)
        self.weight = nn.Parameter(torch.Tensor(
            initializer_conv([out_channels, in_channels // groups,
kernel_size, kernel_size],
            init=init, dist=dist, dist_scale=dist_scale)))
```

There are times when different initialization methods don't make too much of a difference when it comes to the model's final performance, as long as the parameters' magnitudes are kept at a similar level. In those cases, we suggest you try different initialization methods when even the slightest improvement matters.

Adjusting the loss function

The loss function describes the objective of the training process. We have seen many forms of loss functions in different GAN models, depending on their different goals. Designing the right loss function is crucial for the success of your model's training. Typically, a GAN model comes with two loss functions: one generator loss function and one discriminator loss function. Of course, if there are more than two networks in your model, there can be more loss functions to deal with. Each loss function can have one or more regularization term. The three most common forms are as follows:

- $\mathop{\mathbb{E}}_{real}[\log D(x)] + \mathop{\mathbb{E}}_{fake}[\log(1 - D(x))]$

- $\mathop{\mathbb{E}}_{fake}[\log(1 - D(x))]$

- $\mathop{\mathbb{E}}_{fake}[-\log D(x)]$

In Chapter 7, *Image Restoration with GANs*, we will discuss different forms of loss functions in GANs at great length. Check it out to find out more.

The two most commonly used regularization terms are as follows:

- L1-loss, $\|e\|$
- L2-loss, $\|e\|^2$

In L1-loss and L2-loss, e can be many things, for example, the distance between two images or the gradients of an image. L2-loss tends to produce more dense results (where most values are closer to 0) and L1-loss produces more sparse results (where a few outliers with values larger than 0 are tolerated).

It is worth mentioning that L2-regularization (**L2-penalty**) on the parameters is essentially the same as **weight decay**. Here's why:

$$\mathcal{L} = \alpha \cdot f + \frac{\beta}{2} \sum_i w_i^2$$

$$\frac{\partial \mathcal{L}}{\partial w_i} = \alpha \cdot \frac{\partial f}{\partial w_i} + \beta \cdot w_i$$

The second term in the first equation is L2-penalty and the second term in the second equation is weight decay. Taking derivatives on both sides of the first equation gives us the second equation. Therefore, L2-penalty and weight decay in neural networks are essentially the same thing.

The loss function is also where you bring your algorithm's design to life. For example, if you have extra label information for your dataset, add it to your loss function. If you want your results to be as similar to something as possible, add their distance to your regularization term. If you want the generated images to be smooth, add their gradients to the regularization term.

Choosing an optimization method

Here, we will only discuss gradient-based optimization methods, which are most commonly used in GANs. Different gradient methods have their own strengths and weaknesses. There isn't a universal optimization method that can solve every problem. Therefore, we should choose them wisely when it comes to different practical problems. Let's have a look at some now:

1. **SGD** (calling `optim.SGD` with `momentum=0` and `nesterov=False`): It works fast and well for shallow networks. However, it can be very slow for deeper networks, and may not even converge for deep networks:

$$\theta_{t+1} = \theta_t - \eta \cdot \nabla J(\theta_t)$$

   In this equation, θ_t is the parameters at iteration step t, η is the learning rate, and ∇J is the gradient of the objective function, J.

2. **Momentm** (calling `optim.SGD` with the `momentum` argument when it's larger than 0 and `nestrov=False`): It is one of the most commonly used optimization methods. This method combines the updates of the previous step with the gradient at the current step so that it takes a smoother trajectory than SGD. The training speed of Momentum is often faster than SGD and it generally works well for both shallow and deep networks:

$$v_{t+1} = \mu \cdot v_t - \eta \cdot \nabla J(\theta_t)$$
$$\theta_{t+1} = \theta_t + v_{t+1}$$

   In this equation, μ is called the **momentum term**, which is usually set to a float value between 0.5~0.9.

3. **Nesterov** (calling `optim.SGD` with the `momentum` argument when it's larger than 0 and `nestrov=True`); This is a variant of the Momentum method. It calculates a "predicted" gradient of the objective function at iteration step $t+1$ when combining the momentum vector and the gradient vector. In theory, it has a faster convergence speed than Momentum. When your model is having trouble converging with Momentum, you should definitely give Nesterov a try:

$$v_{t+1} = \mu \cdot v_t - \eta \cdot \nabla J(\theta_t + \mu \cdot v_t)$$
$$\theta_{t+1} = \theta_t + v_{t+1}$$

4. **AdaGrad** (optim.Adagrad): This method updates parameters that are updated more frequently with a smaller learning rate and updates the less frequently updated parameters with a larger learning rate. It was used by Google's DistBelief in 2012. However, AdaGrad isn't widely used today because the learning rate keeps getting smaller, which is bad for long-term training in deep models:

$$\theta_{t+1} = \theta_t - \frac{\eta}{\sqrt{G_t + \epsilon}} \cdot \nabla J(\theta_t)$$

In this equation, G_t is the total sum of the square of gradients starting from iteration step 0 to t, which increases over time and decreases the learning rate, while ϵ is a very small value.

5. **RMSprop** (optim.RMSprop): This method is similar to AdaGrad, except that the moving average of squared gradients is taken instead of their sum. This method isn't very common among the various deep learning models. In Chapter 7, *Image Restoration with GANs*, we explicitly point out that RMSprop should be used in Wasserstein GAN:

$$\mathbb{E}[g^2]_t = \gamma\mathbb{E}[g^2]_{t-1} + (1 - \gamma)g_t^2, \quad g_t = \nabla J(\theta_t)$$
$$\theta_{t+1} = \theta_t - \frac{\eta}{\sqrt{\mathbb{E}[g^2]_t + \epsilon}} \cdot g_t$$

In this equation, $\mathbb{E}[g^2]_t$ is the moving average of g^2 until iteration step t, while γ is the smoothing term, which is usually set to a value very close to 1; for example, 0.99 or 0.999.

6. **Adam** (optim.Adam): This method, in a sense, combines Momentum and RMSprop via two moment terms. It is one of the most popular and effective optimization methods in deep models. If all of the previous methods don't perform well in your model, Adam is your best chance, especially when your model is very deep and the relationships between the parameters are very complex (for example, you have multiple branching structures in your model):

$$m_t = \beta_1 m_{t-1} + (1 - \beta_1)g_t, \quad g_t = \nabla J(\theta_t)$$
$$v_t = \beta_2 v_{t-1} + (1 - \beta_2)g_t^2$$
$$\hat{m}_t = \frac{m_t}{1 - \beta_1^t}, \quad \hat{v}_t = \frac{v_t}{1 - \beta_2^t}$$
$$\theta_{t+1} = \theta_t - \frac{\eta}{\sqrt{\hat{v}_t} + \epsilon} \cdot \hat{m}_t$$

In this equation, the moment coefficients (β_1 and β_2) are normally set to values very close to 1, for example, $\beta_1 = 0.9$ and $\beta_2 = 0.999$. The third line of the equation exists because we don't want the moment terms to be close to 0 at the beginning of the training, especially when they are normally initialized with zeros at $t = 0$. Note that the learning rate for Adam should be dramatically smaller than other methods (such as Momentum).

In summary, you should try using Momentum when you're trying out your training strategy for a new model since it has fewer adjustable hyperparameters and is faster to train. When you feel happy with the model's performance, it is always worth trying Adam to exploit its potential even more.

Adjusting the learning rate

Now that you have selected an optimization method, you need to set the proper learning rate for the gradient method and start training. Normally, the updates for the parameters are significant enough to be noticeable at the beginning of the training step. After training for a long time, the relations between the parameters are determined and it's time to adjust the parameters subtly with a smaller learning rate. We cannot simply rely on an optimization method (such as RMSprop or Adam) to gradually decrease the learning rate for us. It is far more efficient when we actively decrease the learning rate periodically during training.

You can use `optim.lr_scheduler` to set up a `scheduler` and call `scheduler.step()` after each epoch, as shown in the following code:

```
scheduler = optim.lr_scheduler.StepLR(optimizer, step_size=50, gamma=0.1)
for epoch in range(epochs):
    ...
    scheduler.step()
```

You can also create your own custom scheduler, as follows:

```
class LRScheduleCosine(object):
    def __init__(self, optimizer, epoch=0, epoch_start=0, lr_max=0.05,
lr_min=0.001, t_mul=10):
        self.optimizer = optimizer
        self.epoch = epoch
        self.lr_min = lr_min
        self.lr_max = lr_max
        self.t_start = epoch_start
        self.t_mul = t_mul
        self.lr = lr_max

    def step(self):
        self.epoch += 1
        self.lr = self.lr_min + 0.5*(self.lr_max-
self.lr_min)*(1.+math.cos(math.pi*(self.epoch-self.t_start)/self.t_mul))
        if self.optimizer is not None:
            for param_group in self.optimizer.param_groups:
                param_group['lr'] = self.lr
        if self.epoch == self.t_start + self.t_mul:
            self.t_start += self.t_mul
            self.t_mul *= 2
        return self.lr
```

This is an implementation of the cosine schedule with warm restarts. To use it in your training, simply call it, as follows:

```
scheduler = LRScheduleCosine(optimizer,
                                        lr_max=0.025,
                                        lr_min=0.001,
                                        t_mul=10)

for epoch in range(epochs):
    lr = scheduler.step()
    ...
```

The learning rate will decrease from 0.025 to 0.001 in the first 10 epochs, restart at 0.025 and decrease to 0.001 in the next 10 epochs, then restart back at 0.025 and decrease to 0.001 in the next 40 epochs, and so on.

 You can check out PyTorch's official documentation to find out more about other types of schedulers: https://pytorch.org/docs/stable/optim.html#how-to-adjust-learning-rate.

Gradient clipping, weight clipping, and more

In the very first chapter of this book, Chapter 1, *Generative Adversarial Networks Fundamentals*, we created a simple GAN with NumPy to generate sine signals using gradient clipping and weight clipping to make sure the training converged. Let's go over why these tricks can be useful for your models:

- **Gradient clipping**: The gradient basically tells us how to update our parameters. Normally, larger gradients lead to bigger changes being applied to our parameters. If, by chance, the loss surface around our search location is steep, large gradient values could mean that we will jump far away from this region at the next iteration step and we'll have to start looking for optimal solutions in a new region. Therefore, clipping gradients and setting limitations on their maximum/minimum values can make sure that we don't jeopardize our previous search results while spending a long time training. You can use nn.utils.clip_grad_norm_ to perform gradient clipping.

- **Vanishing Gradients**: When the change in the gradients is too small, this can cause problems as well. Often, this is because the inputs are simply too compressed to allow the system to learn correctly. If this seems to be happening, consider using **ReLU** or Leaky ReLU, which we introduced in Chapter 1, *Generative Adversarial Networks Fundamentals*.

- **Weight clipping**: This is not a widely used technique, besides its application in the Wasserstein GAN (Chapter 7, *Image Restoration with GANs*). It is an indirect way to perform gradient clipping. Therefore, it is not necessary to use both techniques in the same model. We only used both in the example in Chapter 1, *Generative Adversarial Networks Fundamentals*, to make sure that nothing went wrong in our model.

Efficient coding in Python

Most of the code you will see in this book is written in Python. Almost all of the popular deep learning tools (PyTorch, TensorFlow, Keras, MXNet, and so on) are also written in Python. Python is easy to learn and easy to use, especially compared to other **object-oriented programming (OOP)** languages such as C++ and Java. However, using Python does not excuse us from lazy coding. We should never settle with *it works*. In deep learning, efficient code may save us hours of training time. In this section, we will give you some tips and advice on writing efficient Python projects.

Reinventing the wheel wisely

Innovative developers are not enthusiastic about reinventing the wheel, that is, implementing every tiny component in the project that can be easily grabbed from GitHub or third-party libraries. Deep learning relies on being open source and anyone in the world can learn and do cool things with it. We encourage you to take advantage of any available tool you can find to solve your practical problems, as long as it saves your invaluable time. Some of the model implementations in this book come from other people's projects on GitHub. Imagine how long it would take us to figure out all the implementation details based on the papers that have already been published!

Here are some websites that may come in handy when you are looking for specific tools or code snippets:

- https://github.com
- https://stackoverflow.com
- https://stats.stackexchange.com
- https://discuss.pytorch.org
- https://www.reddit.com/r/MachineLearning
- https://www.kaggle.com/kernels
- Finally, the most important one: https://www.google.com

Advice for beginners in deep learning

The following is some advice that beginners in deep learning should definitely follow:

- **Set reasonable but solid goals and deadlines**: Give yourself plenty of time to research, learn, and experiment with a subject. Start with the goal and then create a series of steps that will achieve that goal. Keep a log of your progress.
- **Search the web to find information on the project you are working on**: The internet is often the fastest way to gather information about a particular subject. Start with simple but direct search text and then refine your searches to obtain the best resources.
- **Small steps are better than huge leaps**: As you read an article or chapter on your subject of choice, copy the code into your IDE and run the project. Don't move on until you understand the inputs, outputs, and the code that produces them.
- **Try to find pretrained models**: Once you have the basic information and understand the model process, use pretrained models to save time and hardware resources. Again, keep the results in your log.
- **Take the results from your searches and experiment on your own**: It's likely that you will gather ideas about the subject as you do your research and testing. Jot them down and test your ideas against what you have learned.
- **Get the best hardware that you can afford without breaking the bank**: This is probably the most important tip. A good computer with a good graphics card and GPU with as much memory as possible will potentially cut hours off your process.

Summary

In this chapter, we looked at the overall design of the model architecture and the steps that are required when it comes to choosing the best convolution operation.

In the next chapter, we will introduce a classic performant GAN model called DCGAN, which is used for generating 2D images.

Section 2: Typical GAN Models for Image Synthesis

2

In this section, the architectures, training strategies, and evaluation methods of typical GAN models for image generation, translation, and restoration will be introduced, along with actual working code.

This section contains the following chapters:

- Chapter 4, *Building Your First GAN with PyTorch*
- Chapter 5, *Generating Images Based on Label Information*
- Chapter 6, *Image-to-Image Translation and Its Applications*
- Chapter 7, *Image Restoration with GANs*
- Chapter 8, *Training Your GANs to Break Different Models*
- Chapter 9, *Image Generation from Description Text*
- Chapter 10, *Sequence Synthesis with GANs*
- Chapter 11, *Reconstructing 3D Models with GANs*

4
Building Your First GAN with PyTorch

In previous chapters, we covered the idea of using adversarial learning to generate simple signals with NumPy and learned about the new features and capabilities of PyTorch 1.3. It's time for us to use PyTorch to train a GAN model for generating interesting samples.

In this chapter, we will introduce you to a classic and well-performing GAN model, called DCGAN, to generate 2D images. You will learn the following:

- The architecture of DCGANs
- The training and evaluation of DCGANs
- Using a DCGAN to generate handwritten digits, human faces
- Having fun with the generator network by performing image interpolation and arithmetic calculation on the latent vectors to change the image attributes

By the end of this chapter, you will have grasped the core architecture design of GAN models for generating image data and have a better understanding of the relationship between latent vectors and generated samples.

Introduction to Deep Convolutional GANs

DCAGN (Deep Convolutional Generative Adversarial Network) is one of the early well-performing and stable approaches to generate images with adversarial training. Let's take a look back at the simple example in Chapter 1, *Generative Adversarial Networks Fundamentals*.

Here, even when we only train a GAN to manipulate 1D data, we have to use multiple techniques to ensure a stable training. A lot of things could go wrong in the training of GANs. For example, either a generator or a discriminator could overfit if one or the other does not converge. Sometimes, the generator only generates a handful of sample varieties. This is called **mode collapse**. The following is an example of mode collapse, where we want to train a GAN with some popular meme images in China called **Baozou**. We can see that our GAN is only capable of generating one or two memes at a time. Problems that commonly occur in other machine learning algorithms such as gradient vanishing/explosion and underfitting can also look familiar in the training of GANs. Therefore, just replacing 1D data with 2D images won't easily guarantee successful training:

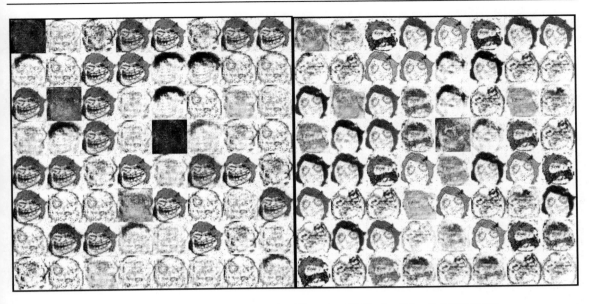

Mode collapse in GAN training (left: some training samples; middle: results at 492nd iteration; right: results at 500th iteration)

To ensure the stable training of GANs on image data like this, a DCGAN uses three techniques:

- Getting rid of fully connected layers and only using convolution layers
- Using strided convolution layers to perform downsampling, instead of using pooling layers
- Using ReLU/leakyReLU activation functions instead of Tanh between hidden layers

In this section, we will introduce the architectures of the generator and discriminator of the DCGAN and learn how to generate images with it. We'll use MNIST (http://yann.lecun.com/exdb/mnist) samples to illustrate the architecture of a DCGAN and use it to train the model in the next two sections.

The architecture of generator

The generator network of a DCGAN contains 4 hidden layers (we treat the input layer as the 1st hidden layer for simplicity) and 1 output layer. Transposed convolution layers are used in hidden layers, which are followed by batch normalization layers and ReLU activation functions. The output layer is also a transposed convolution layer and Tanh is used as the activation function. The architecture of the generator is shown in the following diagram:

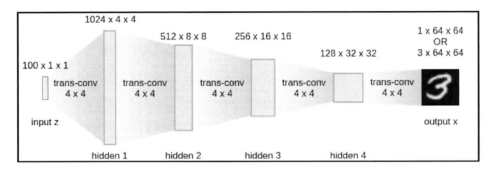

Generator architecture in DCGAN

The 2nd, 3rd, and 4th hidden layers and the output layer have a stride value of 2. The 1st layer has a padding value of 0 and the other layers have a padding value of 1. As the image (feature map) sizes increase by two in deeper layers, the numbers of channels are decreasing by half. This is a common convention in the architecture design of neural networks. All kernel sizes of transposed convolution layers are set to 4 x 4. The output channel can be either 1 or 3, depending on whether you want to generate grayscale images or color images.

 The transposed convolution layer can be considered as the **reverse process** of a normal convolution. It was once called by some a deconvolution layer, which is misleading because the transposed convolution is not the **inverse** of convolution. Most convolution layers are not invertible, because they are ill-conditioned (have extremely large condition numbers) from the linear algebra perspective, which makes their pseudoinverse matrices unfit for representing the inverse process. If you are interested in finding the inverse of a convolution kernel, you can search for numerical deconvolution methods on the internet.

The architecture of a discriminator

The discriminator network of a DCGAN consists of 4 hidden layers (again, we treat the input layer as the 1st hidden layer) and 1 output layer. Convolution layers are used in all layers, which are followed by batch normalization layers except that the first layer does not have batch normalization. LeakyReLU activation functions are used in the hidden layers and Sigmoid is used for the output layer. The architecture of the discriminator is shown in the following:

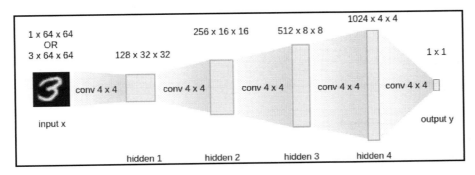

Discriminator architecture in DCGAN

The input channel can be either 1 or 3, depending on whether you are dealing with grayscale images or color images. All hidden layers have a stride value of 2 and a padding value of 1 so that their output image sizes will be half the input images. As image sizes increase in deeper layers, the numbers of channels are increasing by twice. All kernels in convolution layers are of a size of 4 x 4. The output layer has a stride value of 1 and a padding value of 0. It maps 4 x 4 feature maps to single values so that the Sigmoid function can transform the value into prediction confidence.

Creating a DCGAN with PyTorch

Let's start writing PyTorch code to create a DCGAN model. Here, we assume that you are using the Python 3.7 environment in Ubuntu 18.04. If not, please refer to Chapter 2, *Getting Started with PyTorch 1.3*, to learn how to create an Anaconda environment.

First, let's create a Python source file called `dcgan.py` and import the packages that we need:

```
import os
import sys

import numpy as np
import torch
import torch.nn as nn
import torch.nn.parallel
import torch.backends.cudnn as cudnn
import torch.optim as optim
import torch.utils.data
import torchvision.datasets as dset
import torchvision.transforms as transforms
import torchvision.utils as vutils

import utils
```

Here, NumPy is only used to initialize a random seed. If you don't have NumPy installed, simple replace `np.random` with `random` and insert the `import random` line after `import os`. In the last line of code, we import a module called `utils`, which is a custom utility package defined in the `utils.py` file. The full source code of `utils.py` is available under the code repository for this chapter.

In this book, we will put most of the PyTorch-independent helper functions (including file organization, learning rate adjustment, logging, tensor visualization, and so on) in this `utils.py` file. Therefore, we will also come across this module in future chapters. Don't forget to update this file as we move on to later chapters.

Then, we define the output path and hyperparameters. Note that here we set the minimal channel size of hidden layers in both the generator and discriminator to `64`, because we find that the value of `128` as we previously show could lead to the overfitting of the discriminator:

```
CUDA = True
DATA_PATH = '~/Data/mnist'
OUT_PATH = 'output'
LOG_FILE = os.path.join(OUT_PATH, 'log.txt')
BATCH_SIZE = 128
IMAGE_CHANNEL = 1
Z_DIM = 100
G_HIDDEN = 64
X_DIM = 64
D_HIDDEN = 64
```

```
EPOCH_NUM = 25
REAL_LABEL = 1
FAKE_LABEL = 0
lr = 2e-4
seed = 1
```

If you don't have a CUDA-enabled graphics card and want to train the networks on the CPU, you can change CUDA to False. DATA_PATH points to the root directory of the MNIST dataset. If you haven't downloaded and properly preprocessed MNIST yet, simply point it to any directory (such as '.') and we can download it later. BATCH_SIZE has a major impact on how much GPU memory your code will consume. If you are not sure what batch size is appropriate for your system, you can start at a small value, train your model for 1 epoch, and double the batch size until errors pop up.

For MNIST, setting BATCH_SIZE to 128 should be good enough and it costs less than 1 GB of GPU memory. IMAGE_CHANNEL describes the number of color channels of image samples. Since all images in MNIST are single-channel, we should set it to 1. EPOCH_NUM has a great impact on the training time of neural networks. If you want better results, setting a larger epoch number and small learning rates is almost always a good strategy. We set seed=1 so that your results should look exactly the same as what we get in this book.

Next, we need to do some preparation before creating the networks:

```
utils.clear_folder(OUT_PATH)
print("Logging to {}\n".format(LOG_FILE))
sys.stdout = utils.StdOut(LOG_FILE)
CUDA = CUDA and torch.cuda.is_available()
print("PyTorch version: {}".format(torch.__version__))
if CUDA:
    print("CUDA version: {}\n".format(torch.version.cuda))
if seed is None:
    seed = np.random.randint(1, 10000)
print("Random Seed: ", seed)
np.random.seed(seed)
torch.manual_seed(seed)
if CUDA:
    torch.cuda.manual_seed(seed)
cudnn.benchmark = True
device = torch.device("cuda:0" if CUDA else "cpu")
```

Here, `utils.clear_folder(OUT_PATH)` will empty the output folder for us and create one if it doesn't exist. `sys.stdout = utils.StdOut(LOG_FILE)` will redirect all messages from `print` to the log file and show these messages in the console at the same time. Refer to the `utils.py` file if you are interested in the implementations. `cudnn.benchmark = True` will tell cuDNN to choose the best set of algorithms for your model if the size of input data is fixed; otherwise, cuDNN will have to find the best algorithms at each iteration.

If you have previously done some training tasks on CNNs with PyTorch, you might notice that, sometimes, setting `cudnn.benchmark = True` will dramatically increase the GPU memory consumption, especially when your model architectures are changed during training and you are doing both training and evaluation in your code. Change it to `False` if you encounter strange **OOM (Out-Of-Memory)** issues.

Generator network

Now, let's define the generator network with PyTorch:

```python
class Generator(nn.Module):
    def __init__(self):
        super(Generator, self).__init__()
        self.main = nn.Sequential(
            # 1st layer
            nn.ConvTranspose2d(Z_DIM, G_HIDDEN * 8, 4, 1, 0, bias=False),
            nn.BatchNorm2d(G_HIDDEN * 8),
            nn.ReLU(True),
            # 2nd layer
            nn.ConvTranspose2d(G_HIDDEN * 8, G_HIDDEN * 4, 4, 2, 1,
bias=False),
            nn.BatchNorm2d(G_HIDDEN * 4),
            nn.ReLU(True),
            # 3rd layer
            nn.ConvTranspose2d(G_HIDDEN * 4, G_HIDDEN * 2, 4, 2, 1,
bias=False),
            nn.BatchNorm2d(G_HIDDEN * 2),
            nn.ReLU(True),
            # 4th layer
            nn.ConvTranspose2d(G_HIDDEN * 2, G_HIDDEN, 4, 2, 1,
bias=False),
            nn.BatchNorm2d(G_HIDDEN),
            nn.ReLU(True),
            # output layer
            nn.ConvTranspose2d(G_HIDDEN, IMAGE_CHANNEL, 4, 2, 1,
```

```
bias=False),
            nn.Tanh()
        )

    def forward(self, input):
        return self.main(input)
```

Note that the output layer does not have a batch normalization layer connected to it.

Let's create a `helper` function to initialize the network parameters:

```
def weights_init(m):
    classname = m.__class__.__name__
    if classname.find('Conv') != -1:
        m.weight.data.normal_(0.0, 0.02)
    elif classname.find('BatchNorm') != -1:
        m.weight.data.normal_(1.0, 0.02)
        m.bias.data.fill_(0)
```

There are only two types of layers in the generator network that contain trainable parameters: transposed convolution layers and batch normalization layers. Here, we initialize the convolution kernels based on the Gaussian distribution (normal distribution) with a mean of 0 and a standard deviation of 0.02. We also need to initialize the affine parameters (scaling factors) in batch normalization.

Now, we can create a `Generator` object, as follows:

```
netG = Generator().to(device)
netG.apply(weights_init)
print(netG)
```

We can check what modules are contained in the generator network by directly printing it. We won't show the output of it considering its length.

Discriminator network

Now, let's define the discriminator network:

```
class Discriminator(nn.Module):
    def __init__(self):
        super(Discriminator, self).__init__()
        self.main = nn.Sequential(
            # 1st layer
            nn.Conv2d(IMAGE_CHANNEL, D_HIDDEN, 4, 2, 1, bias=False),
            nn.LeakyReLU(0.2, inplace=True),
            # 2nd layer
```

```
            nn.Conv2d(D_HIDDEN, D_HIDDEN * 2, 4, 2, 1, bias=False),
            nn.BatchNorm2d(D_HIDDEN * 2),
            nn.LeakyReLU(0.2, inplace=True),
            # 3rd layer
            nn.Conv2d(D_HIDDEN * 2, D_HIDDEN * 4, 4, 2, 1, bias=False),
            nn.BatchNorm2d(D_HIDDEN * 4),
            nn.LeakyReLU(0.2, inplace=True),
            # 4th layer
            nn.Conv2d(D_HIDDEN * 4, D_HIDDEN * 8, 4, 2, 1, bias=False),
            nn.BatchNorm2d(D_HIDDEN * 8),
            nn.LeakyReLU(0.2, inplace=True),
            # output layer
            nn.Conv2d(D_HIDDEN * 8, 1, 4, 1, 0, bias=False),
            nn.Sigmoid()
        )

    def forward(self, input):
        return self.main(input).view(-1, 1).squeeze(1)
```

Note that the input layer does not have a batch normalization layer connected to it. This is because, when applying batch normalization to all layers, it could lead to sample oscillation and model instability, as pointed out in the original paper.

Similarly, we can create a Discriminator object as follows:

```
netD = Discriminator().to(device)
netD.apply(weights_init)
print(netD)
```

Model training and evaluation

We will use Adam as the training method for both the generator and discriminator networks. If you are interested in the details of gradient descent methods, please refer to Chapter 3, *Best Practices for Model Design and Training,* to learn more about the common training methods.

Let's first define the loss function for the discriminator network and `optimizers` for both of the networks:

```
criterion = nn.BCELoss()

optimizerD = optim.Adam(netD.parameters(), lr=lr, betas=(0.5, 0.999))
optimizerG = optim.Adam(netG.parameters(), lr=lr, betas=(0.5, 0.999))
```

Here, `nn.BCELoss()` represents the Binary Cross-Entropy loss function, which we previously used in `Chapter 1`, *Generative Adversarial Networks Fundamentals*.

Next, let's load the MNIST dataset to the GPU memory:

```
dataset = dset.MNIST(root=DATA_PATH, download=True,
                 transform=transforms.Compose([
                 transforms.Resize(X_DIM),
                 transforms.ToTensor(),
                 transforms.Normalize((0.5,), (0.5,))
                 ]))
assert dataset
dataloader = torch.utils.data.DataLoader(dataset, batch_size=BATCH_SIZE,
                                 shuffle=True, num_workers=4)
```

You can also add a `pin_memory=True` argument when calling `torch.utils.data.DataLoader()` on small datasets, which will make sure data is stored at fixed GPU memory addresses and thus increase the data loading speed during training.

Training iteration

The training procedure is basically the same as in the simple example in `Chapter 1`, *Generative Adversarial Networks Fundamentals*:

1. Train the discriminator with the real data and recognize it as real.
2. Train the discriminator with the fake data and recognize it as fake.
3. Train the generator with the fake data and recognize it as real.

The first two steps let the discriminator learn how to tell the difference between real data and fake data. The third step teaches the generator how to confuse the discriminator with generated samples:

```python
viz_noise = torch.randn(BATCH_SIZE, Z_DIM, 1, 1, device=device)
for epoch in range(EPOCH_NUM):
    for i, data in enumerate(dataloader):
        x_real = data[0].to(device)
        real_label = torch.full((x_real.size(0),), REAL_LABEL,
device=device)
        fake_label = torch.full((x_real.size(0),), FAKE_LABEL,
device=device)

        # Update D with real data
        netD.zero_grad()
        y_real = netD(x_real)
        loss_D_real = criterion(y_real, real_label)
        loss_D_real.backward()

        # Update D with fake data
        z_noise = torch.randn(x_real.size(0), Z_DIM, 1, 1, device=device)
        x_fake = netG(z_noise)
        y_fake = netD(x_fake.detach())
        loss_D_fake = criterion(y_fake, fake_label)
        loss_D_fake.backward()
        optimizerD.step()

        # Update G with fake data
        netG.zero_grad()
        y_fake_r = netD(x_fake)
        loss_G = criterion(y_fake_r, real_label)
        loss_G.backward()
        optimizerG.step()

        if i % 100 == 0:
            print('Epoch {} [{}/{}] loss_D_real: {:.4f} loss_D_fake:
                {:.4f} loss_G: {:.4f}'.format(
                epoch, i, len(dataloader),
                loss_D_real.mean().item(),
                loss_D_fake.mean().item(),
                loss_G.mean().item()
            ))
```

Here, we create the `real_label` and `fake_label` tensors in real time because there is no guarantee that all sample batches will have the same size (the last batch is often smaller depending on the batch size and the total number of training samples).

Visualizing generated samples

It's better if we can check how well the generator is trained. Therefore, we need to export the generated images during training. Add these lines at the end of the `if` scope:

```
if i % 100 == 0:
    ...
            vutils.save_image(x_real, os.path.join(OUT_PATH,
'real_samples.png'), normalize=True)
            with torch.no_grad():
                viz_sample = netG(viz_noise)
                vutils.save_image(viz_sample, os.path.join(OUT_PATH,
'fake_samples_{}.png'.format(epoch)), normalize=True)
        torch.save(netG.state_dict(), os.path.join(OUT_PATH,
'netG_{}.pth'.format(epoch)))
        torch.save(netD.state_dict(), os.path.join(OUT_PATH,
'netD_{}.pth'.format(epoch)))
```

Now, your DCGAN is ready for training. Open the Terminal, `activate` the Anaconda environment and start training DCGAN:

```
$ conda activate torch
(torch) $ python dcgan.py
```

The training takes about 13 minutes on a GTX 1080Ti graphics card. If you don't like the generated samples even before the training is finished, you can always press *Ctrl + C* to cancel the training. The generated images after the 1st and 25th epoch are shown in the following. Note that we only show halves of the generated images (that is, 64 samples).

We can see that the DCGAN does a good job at generating handwritten digits:

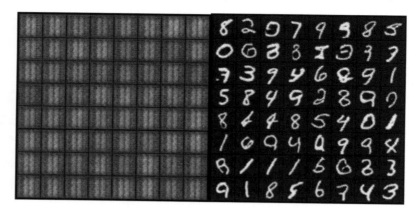

Generated images by the DCGAN from MNIST after the 1st and 25th epoch

For your reference, here is a list of GPU memory consumption with different BATCH_SIZE values. Note that no matter how large the batch size is, the total training time is almost unchanged, since the total workload of the computation is basically the same:

Batch size	128	256	512	1024	2048
GPU memory	939 MB	1283 MB	1969 MB	3305 MB	6011 MB

Checking GPU usage information

Here, we will talk about how to check GPU usage along with other hardware usage information in Windows 10 and Ubuntu 18.04.

In Windows 10, the easiest way to check hardware usage (including GPU usage) is using Task Manager. You can open it by pressing *Ctrl + Shift + Esc*, and switch to the **Performance** panel. All hardware usage information is available to you now.

In Ubuntu 18.04, you can check CPU, RAM, and drive usage with **GNOME System Monitor**, which is shipped with the system. You can search for the system monitor in the **Application** menu, or run gnome-system-monitor in a Terminal to open it.

Alternatively, you can install a GNOME extension to illustrate the usage graphs in the status bar. We recommend that you use the **system-monitor extension** (`https://extensions.gnome.org/extension/120/system-monitor`) for this purpose. To install it, you first need to install several prerequisites:

```
$ sudo apt-get install gir1.2-gtop-2.0 gir1.2-networkmanager-1.0 gir1.2-
clutter-1.0 gir1.2-clutter-gst-3.0 gir1.2-gtkclutter-1.0
```

Then, open a Firefox browser and navigate to this site, `https://addons.mozilla.org/en-US/firefox/addon/gnome-shell-integration`, to install the browser extension for easy installation of GNOME extensions provided by `http://gnome.org`. You also need to run `sudo apt-get install chrome-gnome-shell` in Terminal.

Next, open the web page, `https://extensions.gnome.org/extension/120/system-monitor`, with the Firefox browser; you'll see a switch button on the right side of the extension title. Click it to switch it to ON and you will be prompted to install the system-monitor extension.

Finally, press *Alt + F2*, type in `r`, and then press *Enter*. This will restart the GNOME shell so that the system-monitor extension will be activated.

To check GPU usage in Ubuntu, you can run this script in the Terminal to show it in real time:

```
watch -n 0.5 nvidia-smi
```

You can also create a `.sh` file in a convenient directory, for example, `~/gpu.sh`: copy the script into this file, then run `chmod +x ~/.gpu.sh`. Then, you can simply run `./gpu.sh` in the Terminal whenever you need to check GPU usage.

Alternatively, there are many other tools you can use on Ubuntu, for example, NVTOP (`https://github.com/Syllo/nvtop`).

Moving to larger datasets

Generating digits is fun. We can have way more fun generating other stuff, such as human faces and bedroom photos. To generate good complex images like these, we need more training samples than the 60,000 samples that MNIST offers. In this section, we will download two much larger datasets (CelebA and LSUN) and train the DCGAN on them to get more complex generated samples.

Generating human faces from the CelebA dataset

The CelebFaces Attributes (**CelebA**, `http://mmlab.ie.cuhk.edu.hk/projects/CelebA.html`) dataset is a large-scale face attributes dataset with more than 200,000 celebrity images, each with 40 attribute annotations. We need to download the cropped and aligned images. We won't need any attribute annotation here so we only need to download the file named `img_align_celeba.zip`, which is no more than 2 GB in size.

If you can't download the CelebA dataset from official links, try these links provided by Kaggle and the official PyTorch tutorial: `https://www.kaggle.com/jessicali9530/celeba-dataset` and `https://drive.google.com/drive/folders/0B7EVK8r0v71pWEZsZE9oNnFzTm8`. Note that you only need to download `Img/img_align_celeba.zip` from the Google Drive link.

Extract the downloaded images to a directory, for example, `~/Data/CelebA`. Make sure all your images are contained in an individual directory inside this root directory so that the images are stored at a location such as `~/Data/CelebA/img_align_celeba/000001.png`.

If you have a **Solid-State Drive (SSD)** with enough space plugged in your machine, we highly recommend you move all of your training samples to the SSD, especially when you have a powerful graphics card. Because when you are training neural networks on a very large dataset, which cannot fit in the GPU memory, the reading speed from physical drives could be the bottleneck of your training performance. Sometimes, the speed-up of SSD (reading samples at 50 MB/s) over the traditional hard drive (5 MB/s) can save you a big chunk of training time.

We only need to alter 3 different parts of code in the previous section to train the DCGAN on the CelebA dataset:

1. Change the dataset root directory:

   ```
   DATA_PATH = '/media/john/FastData/CelebA'    # Load data from SSD
   ```

   If you are not sure what absolute path you're currently at in the file manager on Ubuntu, simply press *Ctrl + L* and the full path will show up.

2. Change the image channel number:

   ```
   IMAGE_CHANNEL = 3
   ```

3. Redefine the `dataset` object:

```
dataset = dset.ImageFolder(root=DATA_PATH,
                        transform=transforms.Compose([
                        transforms.Resize(X_DIM),
                        transforms.CenterCrop(X_DIM),
                        transforms.ToTensor(),
                        transforms.Normalize((0.5, 0.5, 0.5),
                                    (0.5, 0.5, 0.5)),
                        ]))
```

Now, let's run `python dcgan.py` in the Terminal and wait for a while. It takes about 88 minutes to finish 25 epochs of training on a GTX 1080Ti graphics card. The generated images after the 1st epoch and the 25th epoch are shown in the following. Again, we only show 64 generated samples:

Generated images by the DCGAN from CelebA after the 1st and 25th epoch

Here is a list of GPU memory consumption with different `BATCH_SIZE` values:

Batch size	64	128	256	512	1024	2048
GPU memory	773 MB	963 MB	1311 MB	2029 MB	3441 MB	6283 MB

Generating bedroom photos from the LSUN dataset

LSUN (Large-scale Scene Understanding, `https://www.yf.io/p/lsun`) is a large image dataset with 10 scene categories and 20 object categories. You can get the downloading toolkit from `https://github.com/fyu/lsun`. We will use the `bedroom` category to train our DCGAN, which has more than 3 million bedroom photos:

```
$ git clone https://github.com/fyu/lsun.git
$ cd lsun
$ python download.py -c bedroom
```

 You can also export the images as individual files with `python data.py export bedroom_train_lmdb --out_dir bedroom_train_img` so that you can easily use these images for other projects. But try not to directly open the image folder with your file manager. It will take a lot of RAM and time.

The dataset is contained in an **LMDB (Lightning Memory-Mapped Database Manager)** database file, which is about 54 GB in size. Make sure the database files are located in the `bedroom_train_lmdb` directory so that PyTorch's data loader can recognize it when the root directory is specified.

Similarly, we only need to change 3 parts of the code to use the LSUN dataset for our model:

1. Change the dataset root directory:

   ```
   DATA_PATH = '/media/john/FastData/lsun'    # Load data from SSD
   ```

2. Change the image channel number:

   ```
   IMAGE_CHANNEL = 3
   ```

3. Redefine the `dataset` object:

   ```
   dataset = dset.LSUN(root=DATA_PATH, classes=['bedroom_train'],
               transform=transforms.Compose([
               transforms.Resize(X_DIM),
               transforms.CenterCrop(X_DIM),
               transforms.ToTensor(),
               transforms.Normalize((0.5, 0.5, 0.5),
                                     (0.5, 0.5, 0.5)),
               ]))
   ```

And don't forget to install the `lmdb` library for Python so that we can read the database file:

```
$ pip install lmdb
```

Now, let's save the source file and run `python dcgan.py` in the Terminal. Since there are way more samples in the LSUN dataset, we don't have to train the model for 25 epochs. Some of the generated images are already impressive even after the 1st epoch of training. It takes about 5 hours to train for 5 epochs on a GTX 1080Ti graphics card. The generated images after the 1st epoch and the 25th epoch are shown in the following. Here, we only show 64 generated samples. We will not show the GPU memory consumption for LSUN because it's almost the same as CelebA since the input images are both 3-channel and the network structure is not changed:

Generated images by the DCGAN from LSUN after the 1st and 5th epochs

Again, we'd like to point out that if you plan on training GANs on a large dataset, always consider using powerful GPUs and putting your dataset on an SSD. Here, we give two sets of performance comparisons. In the first configuration, we use an NVIDIA GTX 960 graphics card and put the training set on an **HDD (hard disk drive)**. In the second configuration, we use an NVIDIA GTX 1080Ti graphics card and put the training set on an SSD. We can see the speedup of the powerful platform is life changing:

Dataset	CelebA	LSUN
GTX 960 + HDD	2 hours/epoch	16.6 hours/epoch
GTX 1080Ti + SSD	3.5 minutes/epoch	53 minutes/epoch
Speedup	34X	19X

Having fun with the generator network

Now that our first image generator is trained, aren't you curious about what it is capable of and how images are generated from random noise vectors? In this section, we will have some fun with the generator network. First, we will choose two random vectors and calculate the interpolation between them to see what images will be generated. Second, we will choose some exemplary vectors and perform arithmetic calculations on them to find out what changes appear in the generated samples.

First, we need a test version of the DCGAN code.

Copy your original `dcgan.py` file to `dcgan_test.py`. Next, we need to make some changes to our new file. First, we need to replace these lines of just the `Generator` class:

```
netG = Generator().to(device)
netG.apply(weights_init)
print(netG)
```

We replace them with the following lines (you can either delete them or simply comment them out):

```
netG = Generator()
negG.load_state_dict(torch.load(os.path.join(OUT_PATH, 'netG_24.pth')))
netG.to(device)
```

Next, we need to remove (or comment out) the `weights_init`, `Discriminator`, `dataset`, `dataloader`, `criterion`, and `optimizer` objects.

Next, we need to replace the entire training iteration section with this:

```
if VIZ_MODE == 0:
    viz_tensor = torch.randn(BATCH_SIZE, Z_DIM, 1, 1, device=device)
elif VIZ_MODE == 1:
    load_vector = np.loadtxt('vec_20190317-223131.txt')
    xp = [0, 1]
    yp = np.vstack([load_vector[2], load_vector[9]]) # choose two exemplar
vectors
    xvals = np.linspace(0, 1, num=BATCH_SIZE)
    sample = interp1d(xp, yp, axis=0)
    viz_tensor = torch.tensor(sample(xvals).reshape(BATCH_SIZE, Z_DIM, 1,
1), dtype=torch.float32, device=device)
elif VIZ_MODE == 2:
    load_vector = np.loadtxt('vec_20190317-223131.txt')
    z1 = (load_vector[0] + load_vector[6] + load_vector[8]) / 3.
    z2 = (load_vector[1] + load_vector[2] + load_vector[4]) / 3.
    z3 = (load_vector[3] + load_vector[4] + load_vector[6]) / 3.
```

```
        z_new = z1 - z2 + z3
        sample = np.zeros(shape=(BATCH_SIZE, Z_DIM))
        for i in range(BATCH_SIZE):
            sample[i] = z_new + 0.1 * np.random.normal(-1.0, 1.0, 100)
        viz_tensor = torch.tensor(sample.reshape(BATCH_SIZE, Z_DIM, 1, 1),
    dtype=torch.float32,  device=device)
```

We're almost done. We need to add the following code at the end:

```
with torch.no_grad():
    viz_sample = netG(viz_tensor)
    viz_vector = utils.to_np(viz_temsor).reshape(BATCH_SIZE, Z_DIM)
    cur_time = datetime.now().strftime("%Y%m%d-%H%M%S")
    np.savetxt('vec_{}.txt'.format(cur_time), viz_vector)
    vutils.save_image(viz_sample, 'img_{}.png'.format(cur_time), nrow=10,
    normalize=True
```

Now, go back to the top of the code file and add a line in the `import` section:

```
from datetime import datetime
```

And finally, we need to add a line to the variable definitions. Just after the line that says `CUDA = True`, add this:

```
VIZ_MODE = 0
```

The values for `VIZ_MODE` are 0 for random, 1 for interpolation, and 2 for semantic calculation. This will be used as we move forward through the three sets of code.

We need to export the input vector and the generated images to file. The full code for the DCGAN testing is available under the code repository for this chapter, which is called `dcgan_test.py`. And don't forget to delete or comment out the `utils.clear_folder(OUT_PATH)` line; otherwise, all your training results will be deleted, which would be a bad thing.

Image interpolation

The generator network maps the input random vector (the latent vector) to a generated image. If we perform linear interpolation on the latent vectors, the corresponding output images also obey the interpolation relation. Let's take the trained model on CelebA, for example.

First, let's randomly choose two vectors that generate clean images. Here, we set `BATCH_SIZE=10` for simplicity. We'll also add the beginnings of an `if` conditional to allow easy selection of what parts of the code to run:

```
if VIZ_MODE == 0:
    viz_tensor = torch.randn(BATCH_SIZE, Z_DIM, 1, 1, device=device)
```

The generated images may look like the following. And the latent vectors for these images are exported to a file (for example, `vec_20190317-223131.txt`):

Randomly generated images

Assume that we choose the 3rd and the last images for interpolation. Now, let's perform linear interpolation on their latent vectors with SciPy (replace the previous line starting with `viz_tensor = ...` with the following lines). Be sure to change the filename to the one that was just generated on your system:

```
elif VIZ_MODE == 1:
    load_vector = np.loadtxt('vec_20190317-223131.txt')
    xp = [0, 1]
    yp = np.vstack([load_vector[2], load_vector[9]])
    xvals = np.linspace(0, 1, num=BATCH_SIZE)
    sample = interp1d(xp, yp, axis=0)
    viz_tensor = torch.tensor(sample(xvals).reshape(BATCH_SIZE, Z_DIM, 1,
1), dtype=torch.float32, device=device)
```

You will also need to change the `VIZ_MODE` flag from 0 to 1 for interpolation:

```
VIZ_MODE = 1
```

Now, run your changed source code. The corresponding generated images are as follows:

Image interpolation

We can see that the image on the left is smoothly transformed into the one on the right. Therefore, we know that the interpolation of the latent vectors leads to the interpolation of generated images.

Semantic vector arithmetic

Linear interpolation is one of the basic methods in linear algebra. We can do a lot more with arithmetic calculations on the latent vectors.

Take the randomly generated images from previous steps. We notice that some images are of smiling women (the 1st, 7th, and 9th images), some women's images are not smiling (the 2nd, 3rd, and 5th images), and none of the men in the images are smiling. Man, aren't they serious! How do we put a smile on a man's face without regenerating a new set of random vectors?

Well, imagine we can solve it with arithmetic calculations:

[smiling woman] - [woman] = [smile]

[smile] + [man] = [smiling man]

Can we do that? Let's try it!

First, set the VIS_MODE flag again, this time to 2 for semantic calculations:

```
VIZ_MODE = 2
```

Next, continue the if conditional with the following code. Once again, use the filename that was created earlier:

```
elif VIZ_MODE == 2:
    load_vector = np.loadtxt('vec_20190317-223131.txt')
    z1 = (load_vector[0] + load_vector[6] + load_vector[8]) / 3.
    z2 = (load_vector[1] + load_vector[2] + load_vector[4]) / 3.
    z3 = (load_vector[3] + load_vector[4] + load_vector[6]) / 3.
    z_new = z1 - z2 + z3
    sample = np.zeros(shape=(BATCH_SIZE, Z_DIM))
    for i in range(BATCH_SIZE):
        sample[i] = z_new + 0.1 * np.random.normal(-1.0, 1.0, 100)
    viz_tensor = torch.tensor(sample.reshape(BATCH_SIZE, Z_DIM, 1, 1),
dtype=torch.float32, device=device)
```

Here, by performing $z1-z2$, we get a smiling vector. And $z3$ gives us a man vector. Adding them together will give us the following results. We use the mean vector of 3 different latent vectors for more stable results and we add small random values to the arithmetic results to introduce a slight randomness:

Vector arithmetic on latent vectors

The vector arithmetic calculation process can be described as follows:

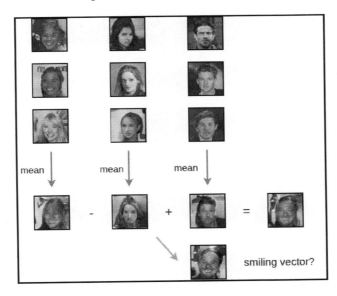

Vector arithmetic

Out of curiosity, we directly generate images based on *z1-z2*, which gives us the sample at the bottom right in the previous screenshot. We can tell it's a smiling face, but the rest of the face is rather unnatural. It looks like the face of a strange dude.

Now, we have unlocked the potential of GANs on manipulating the attributes of the generated images. However, the results are not natural and authentic enough. In the next chapter, we will learn how to generate samples with the exact attributes we desire.

Summary

We spent a tremendous amount of time learning about Deep Convolutional GANs in this chapter. We dealt with the MNIST dataset as well as two huge datasets in the form of the CelebA and LSUN datasets. We also consumed a large number of computing cycles. Hopefully, you have a good grasp of DCGANs at this point.

Next, we'll look at a **Conditional GAN (CGAN)** and how to add label information during the training process. Let's get going!

References and useful reading list

Hui J. (2018, Jun 21). GAN—*Why it is so hard to train Generative Adversarial Networks!*. Retrieved from https://medium.com/@jonathan_hui/gan-why-it-is-so-hard-to-train-generative-advisory-networks-819a86b3750b.

5

Generating Images Based on Label Information

In the previous chapter, we got the first taste of the potential of GANs to learn the connections between latent vectors and generated images and made a vague observation that latent vectors somehow manipulate the attributes of images. In this chapter, we will officially make use of the label and attribute information commonly seen in open datasets to properly establish the bridge between latent vectors and image attributes.

In this chapter, you will learn how to use **conditional GANs (CGANs)** to generate images based on a given label and how to implement adversarial learning with autoencoders and age human faces from young to old. Following this, you will be shown how to efficiently organize your source code for easy adjustments and extensions.

After reading this chapter, you will have learned both supervised and unsupervised approaches to improve the quality of the images generated by GANs with label and attribute information. This chapter also introduces the basic source code hierarchy throughout this book, which can be very useful for your own projects.

The following topics will be covered in this chapter:

- CGANs – how are labels used?
- Generating images from labels with CGANs
- Working with Fashion-MNIST
- InfoGAN – unsupervised attribute extraction
- References and useful reading list

CGANs – how are labels used?

In the previous chapter, we learned that a relation between the latent vector and the generated images can be established by the training process of GANs and certain manipulation of the latent vectors is reflected by the changes in the generated images. But we have no control over what part or what kinds of latent vectors would give us images with the attributes we want. To address this issue, we will use a CGAN to add label information in the training process so that we can have a say in what kinds of images the model will generate.

The idea of CGANs was proposed by Mehdi Mirza and Simon Osindero in their paper, *Conditional Generative Adversarial Nets*. The core idea was to integrate the label information into both generator and discriminator networks so that the label vector would alter the distribution of latent vectors, which leads to images with different attributes.

Compared to the vanilla GAN model, CGAN makes a small change to the objective function to make it possible to include extra information by replacing the real data, x, and generated data, x^*, with $x|\gamma$ and $x^*|\gamma$, respectively, in which γ represents auxiliary information such as label and attribute:

$$\min_{G} \max_{D} V(D, G) = \mathbb{E}_x[\log D(x|\gamma)] + \mathbb{E}_{x^*}[\log(1 - D(x^*|\gamma))]$$

In this equation, $D(x|\gamma)$ borrows the form of conditional probability that describes how data x is distributed under the condition of γ. To calculate the new object function, we need the generator network to be able to generate data given certain conditions and the discriminator network to tell whether the input image obeys the given condition. Therefore, in this section, we will talk about how to design the generator and discriminator to achieve this purpose.

We will create two different models in this chapter and, in order to write reusable code, we will put our source codes in separate files instead of putting all the code in to one single file as we did in previous chapters.

Combining labels with the generator

The architecture of the generator network of the CGAN is illustrated as follows. As described in the original paper, all data is generated through an MLP-like network. Unlike in the original paper, however, we use a much deeper structure and techniques such as batch normalization and LeakyReLU to ensure better-looking results:

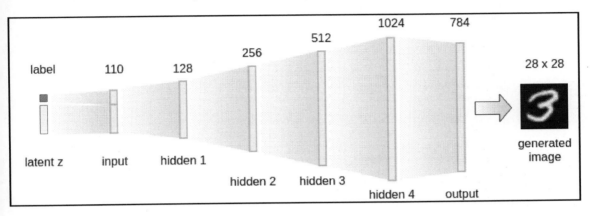

The generator network architecture of the CGAN

The label value is transformed into a vector with a length of 10, which is concatenated with the latent vector z. All data in the generator network is stored in the form of a vector. The length of the output vector equals the multiplication of width and height of the generated image, which is $28 \times 28 = 784$ for the MNIST dataset. We can, of course, change the size of the output image to other values we want (we will set the image size to 64 x 64 later in the source code).

Let's organize the codes differently from previous chapters and create a `cgan.py` file for model definition.

First, we import the PyTorch and NumPy modules at the beginning of the source file:

```
import torch
import torch.nn as nn
import torch.nn.functional as F
import numpy as np
```

Then, we define the `Generator` network:

```
class Generator(nn.Module):
    def __init__(self, classes, channels, img_size, latent_dim):
        super(Generator, self).__init__()
        self.classes = classes
        self.channels = channels
        self.img_size = img_size
        self.latent_dim = latent_dim
        self.img_shape = (self.channels, self.img_size, self.img_size)
        self.label_embedding = nn.Embedding(self.classes, self.classes)

        self.model = nn.Sequential(
            *self._create_layer(self.latent_dim + self.classes, 128,
    False),
            *self._create_layer(128, 256),
            *self._create_layer(256, 512),
            *self._create_layer(512, 1024),
            nn.Linear(1024, int(np.prod(self.img_shape))),
            nn.Tanh()
        )

    def _create_layer(self, size_in, size_out, normalize=True):
        layers = [nn.Linear(size_in, size_out)]
        if normalize:
            layers.append(nn.BatchNorm1d(size_out))
        layers.append(nn.LeakyReLU(0.2, inplace=True))
        return layers

    def forward(self, noise, labels):
        z = torch.cat((self.label_embedding(labels), noise), -1)
        x = self.model(z)
        x = x.view(x.size(0), *self.img_shape)
        return x
```

The generator network consists of 5 linear layers, 3 of which are connected to batch normalization layers, and the first 4 linear layers have `LeakyReLU` activation functions while the last has a `Tanh` activation function. The label information is processed by the `nn.Embedding` module, which behaves as a lookup table. Say we have 10 labels at hand for training samples. The embedding layer transforms the 10 different labels into 10 predefined embedding vectors, which are initialized based on normal distribution by default. The embedding vector of labels is then concatenated with the random latent vector to serve as the input vector of the first layer. Finally, we need to reshape the output vector into 2D images as the final results.

Integrating labels into the discriminator

The architecture of the discriminator network of the CGAN is illustrated as follows. Again, the discriminator architecture is different from the one used in the original paper. You are, of course, more than welcome to make adjustments to the networks and see whether your models can generate better results:

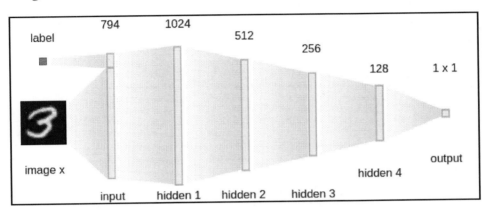

Discriminator network architecture of CGAN

Similar to the generator network, the label value is also part of the input of the discriminator network of the CGAN. The input image (with a size of 28 x 28) is transformed into a vector with a length of 784, therefore, the total length of the input vector of the discriminator network is 794. There are 4 hidden layers in the discriminator network. Unlike common CNN models for image classification, the discriminator network outputs a single value instead of a vector with the length as the number of classes. It is because we already include the label information in the network input and we only want the discriminator network to tell us how close an image is to the real images, given the label condition.

Now, let's define the discriminator network in the `cgan.py` file:

```
class Discriminator(nn.Module):
    def __init__(self, classes, channels, img_size, latent_dim):
        super(Discriminator, self).__init__()
        self.classes = classes
        self.channels = channels
        self.img_size = img_size
        self.latent_dim = latent_dim
        self.img_shape = (self.channels, self.img_size, self.img_size)
        self.label_embedding = nn.Embedding(self.classes, self.classes)
        self.adv_loss = torch.nn.BCELoss()
```

```
        self.model = nn.Sequential(
            *self._create_layer(self.classes +
  int(np.prod(self.img_shape)), 1024, False, True),
            *self._create_layer(1024, 512, True, True),
            *self._create_layer(512, 256, True, True),
            *self._create_layer(256, 128, False, False),
            *self._create_layer(128, 1, False, False),
            nn.Sigmoid()
        )

    def _create_layer(self, size_in, size_out, drop_out=True,
  act_func=True):
        layers = [nn.Linear(size_in, size_out)]
        if drop_out:
            layers.append(nn.Dropout(0.4))
        if act_func:
            layers.append(nn.LeakyReLU(0.2, inplace=True))
        return layers

    def forward(self, image, labels):
        x = torch.cat((image.view(image.size(0), -1),
  self.label_embedding(labels)), -1)
        return self.model(x)

    def loss(self, output, label):
        return self.adv_loss(output, label)
```

Similarly, the labels are passed by another nn.Embedding module before being concatenated with the image vector. The discriminator network consists of 5 linear layers, 2 of which are connected to Dropout layers to enhance the generalization capability. Since we cannot always guarantee that the output values of the last layer lie within a range of [0, 1], we need a Sigmoid activation function to make sure of that.

A Dropout layer with a dropout rate of 0.4 means that, at each iteration during training, each neuron has a probability of 0.4 of not participating in the calculation of the final results. Therefore, different submodels are trained at different training steps, which makes it harder for the whole model to overfit the training data compared to the one without Dropout layers. Dropout layers are often deactivated during evaluation.

The choice of which layer has a `Dropout` or `LeakyReLU` activation function is rather subjective. You can try out other combinations and find out which configuration yields the best results.

Generating images from labels with the CGAN

In the previous section, we defined the architecture of both generator and discriminator networks of the CGAN. Now, let's write the code for model training. In order to make it easy for you to reproduce the results, we will use MNIST as the training set to see how the CGAN performs in image generation. What we want to accomplish here is that, after the model is trained, it can generate the correct digit image we tell it to, with extensive variety.

One-stop model training API

First, let's create a new `Model` class that serves as a wrapper for different models and provides the one-stop training API. Create a new file named `build_gan.py` and import the necessary modules:

```
import os

import numpy as np
import torch
import torchvision.utils as vutils

from cgan import Generator as cganG
from cgan import Discriminator as cganD
```

Then, let's create the `Model` class. In this class, we will initialize the `Generator` and `Discriminator` modules and provide `train` and `eval` methods so that users can simply call `Model.train()` (or `Model.eval()`) somewhere else to complete the model training (or evaluation):

```
class Model(object):
    def __init__(self,
                 name,
                 device,
                 data_loader,
                 classes,
                 channels,
                 img_size,
                 latent_dim):
        self.name = name
        self.device = device
        self.data_loader = data_loader
        self.classes = classes
        self.channels = channels
        self.img_size = img_size
        self.latent_dim = latent_dim
        if self.name == 'cgan':
            self.netG = cganG(self.classes, self.channels,
                self.img_size, self.latent_dim)
        self.netG.to(self.device)
        if self.name == 'cgan':
            self.netD = cganD(self.classes, self.channels,
                self.img_size, self.latent_dim)
        self.netD.to(self.device)
        self.optim_G = None
        self.optim_D = None
```

Here, the generator network, `netG`, and the discriminator network, `netD`, are initialized based on the class number (`classes`), image channel (`channels`), image size (`img_size`), and length of the latent vector (`latent_dim`). These arguments will be given later. For now, let's assume that these values are already known. Since we need to initialize all tensors and functions in this class, we need to define the `device` our model is running on (`self.device`). The `optim_G` and `optim_D` objects are optimizers for the two networks. They are initialized with the following:

```
def create_optim(self, lr, alpha=0.5, beta=0.999):
    self.optim_G = torch.optim.Adam(filter(lambda p: p.requires_grad,
                                     self.netG.parameters()),
                                     lr=lr,
                                     betas=(alpha, beta))
    self.optim_D = torch.optim.Adam(filter(lambda p: p.requires_grad,
```

```
                                    self.netD.parameters()),
                                    lr=lr,
                                    betas=(alpha, beta))
```

The first argument of the `Adam` **optimizer,** `filter(lambda p:`
`p.requires_grad, self.netG.parameters())`, **is to grab all**
`Tensor` whose `requires_grad` **flag is set to** `True`. It is pretty useful
when part of the model is untrained (for example, fine-tuning the last
layer after transferring a trained model to a new dataset), even though it's
not necessary in our case.

Next, let's define a method called `train` for model training. Arguments of `train` include
the number of training epochs (`epochs`), the iteration interval between logging messages
(`log_interval`), the output directory for results (`out_dir`), and whether to print training
messages to the Terminal (`verbose`):

```
def train(self,
          epochs,
          log_interval=100,
          out_dir='',
          verbose=True):
    self.netG.train()
    self.netD.train()
    viz_noise = torch.randn(self.data_loader.batch_size,
self.latent_dim, device=self.device)
    viz_label = torch.LongTensor(np.array([num for _ in range(nrows)
for num in range(8)])).to(self.device)
    for epoch in range(epochs):
        for batch_idx, (data, target) in enumerate(self.data_loader):
            data, target = data.to(self.device), target.to(self.device)
            batch_size = data.size(0)
            real_label = torch.full((batch_size, 1), 1.,
device=self.device)
            fake_label = torch.full((batch_size, 1), 0.,
device=self.device)

            # Train G
            self.netG.zero_grad()
            z_noise = torch.randn(batch_size, self.latent_dim,
device=self.device)
            x_fake_labels = torch.randint(0, self.classes,
(batch_size,), device=self.device)
            x_fake = self.netG(z_noise, x_fake_labels)
            y_fake_g = self.netD(x_fake, x_fake_labels)
            g_loss = self.netD.loss(y_fake_g, real_label)
            g_loss.backward()
```

```
                        self.optim_G.step()

                        # Train D
                        self.netD.zero_grad()
                        y_real = self.netD(data, target)
                        d_real_loss = self.netD.loss(y_real, real_label)

                        y_fake_d = self.netD(x_fake.detach(), x_fake_labels)
                        d_fake_loss = self.netD.loss(y_fake_d, fake_label)
                        d_loss = (d_real_loss + d_fake_loss) / 2
                        d_loss.backward()
                        self.optim_D.step()
```

In train, we first switch the networks to train mode (for example, self.netG.train()). It mostly affects the behaviors of Dropout and the batch normalization layers. Then, we define a set of fixed latent vectors (viz_noise) and labels (viz_label). They are used to occasionally produce images during training so that we can track how the model is trained, otherwise, we may only realize the training has gone south after the training is done:

```
                        if verbose and batch_idx % log_interval == 0 and batch_idx
    > 0:
                                print('Epoch {} [{}/{}] loss_D: {:.4f} loss_G:
    {:.4f}'.format(
                                        epoch, batch_idx, len(self.data_loader),
                                        d_loss.mean().item(),
                                        g_loss.mean().item()))
                                vutils.save_image(data, os.path.join(out_dir,
    'real_samples.png'), normalize=True)
                                with torch.no_grad():
                                        viz_sample = self.netG(viz_noise, viz_label)
                                        vutils.save_image(viz_sample, os.path.join(out_dir,
    'fake_samples_{}.png'.format(epoch)), nrow=8, normalize=True)
                                self.save_to(path=out_dir, name=self.name, verbose=False)
```

Here, we omitted some parts of the code (including the evaluation API and model exporting and loading). You can get the full source code from the code repository for this chapter.

Argument parsing and model training

Now, the only thing left for us to do is to create and define the main entry for the project. In this file, we will need to define the arguments we previously have assumed to be known. These hyper-parameters are essential when we create any network, and we will elegantly parse these values. Let's create a new file called main.py and import the necessary modules:

```
import argparse
import os
import sys

import numpy as np
import torch
import torch.backends.cudnn as cudnn
import torch.utils.data
import torchvision.datasets as dset
import torchvision.transforms as transforms

import utils

from build_gan import Model
```

Have you noticed that the only Python module that's related to our model is `build_gan.Model`? We can easily create another project and copy most of the content in this file without major revisions.

Then, let's define the `main` function:

```
FLAGS = None

def main():
    device = torch.device("cuda:0" if FLAGS.cuda else "cpu")

    if FLAGS.train:
        print('Loading data...\n')
        dataset = dset.MNIST(root=FLAGS.data_dir, download=True,
                             transform=transforms.Compose([
                             transforms.Resize(FLAGS.img_size),
                             transforms.ToTensor(),
                             transforms.Normalize((0.5,), (0.5,))
                             ]))
        assert dataset
        dataloader = torch.utils.data.DataLoader(dataset,
batch_size=FLAGS.batch_size,
                                                 shuffle=True,
num_workers=4, pin_memory=True)
        print('Creating model...\n')
        model = Model(FLAGS.model, device, dataloader, FLAGS.classes,
FLAGS.channels, FLAGS.img_size, FLAGS.latent_dim)
        model.create_optim(FLAGS.lr)

        # Train
        model.train(FLAGS.epochs, FLAGS.log_interval, FLAGS.out_dir, True)

        model.save_to('')
```

```
        else:
            model = Model(FLAGS.model, device, None, FLAGS.classes,
    FLAGS.channels, FLAGS.img_size, FLAGS.latent_dim)
            model.load_from(FLAGS.out_dir)
            model.eval(mode=0, batch_size=FLAGS.batch_size)
```

Since we have already defined the networks and training schedule in separate files, the initialization and training of the model are accomplished with only 3 lines of codes: `model = Model()`, `model.create_optim()`, and `model.train()`. This way, our code is easy to read, modify, and maintain, and we can easily use most of the code in other projects.

The `FLAGS` object stores all the arguments and hyper-parameters needed for model definition and training. To make the configuration of the arguments more user-friendly, we will use the `argparse` module provided by Python.

Note that if you would like to use a different dataset, you can change the definition of the `dataset` object in the same way as in the previous chapter.

The `main` entry of the source code and the definitions of arguments are as follows:

```
    if __name__ == '__main__':
        from utils import boolean_string
        parser = argparse.ArgumentParser(description='Hands-On GANs - Chapter
    5')
        parser.add_argument('--model', type=str, default='cgan', help='one of
    `cgan` and `infogan`.')
        parser.add_argument('--cuda', type=boolean_string, default=True,
    help='enable CUDA.')
        parser.add_argument('--train', type=boolean_string, default=True,
    help='train mode or eval mode.')
        parser.add_argument('--data_dir', type=str, default='~/Data/mnist',
    help='Directory for dataset.')
        parser.add_argument('--out_dir', type=str, default='output',
    help='Directory for output.')
        parser.add_argument('--epochs', type=int, default=200, help='number of
    epochs')
        parser.add_argument('--batch_size', type=int, default=128, help='size
    of batches')
        parser.add_argument('--lr', type=float, default=0.0002, help='learning
    rate')
        parser.add_argument('--latent_dim', type=int, default=100, help='latent
    space dimension')
        parser.add_argument('--classes', type=int, default=10, help='number of
    classes')
        parser.add_argument('--img_size', type=int, default=64, help='size of
    images')
        parser.add_argument('--channels', type=int, default=1, help='number of
```

```
image channels')
    parser.add_argument('--log_interval', type=int, default=100,
help='interval between logging and image sampling')
    parser.add_argument('--seed', type=int, default=1, help='random seed')

    FLAGS = parser.parse_args()
```

A new argument is created by `parser.add_argument(ARG_NAME, ARG_TYPE, DEFAULT_VALUE, HELP_MSG)`, in which `ARG_NAME` is the argument name, `ARG_TYPE` is the value type of argument (for example, `int`, `float`, `bool`, or `str`), `DEFAULT_VALUE` is the default argument value when none is given, and `HELP_MSG` is the message printed when running `python main.py --help` in the Terminal. The argument value is specified by `python main.py --ARG_NAME ARG_VALUE`, or you can change the default value in the source code and simply run `pythin main.py`. Here, our model is to be trained for 200 epochs with a batch size of 128. The learning rate is set to 0.0002, because a small learning rate value is suitable for the `Adam` method. The length of the latent vector is 100 and the size of the generated image is set to 64. We also set the random seed to 1 so that you can produce the exact same results as in this book.

`boolean_string` is defined in the `utils.py` file, which is as follows (reference visit `https://stackoverflow.com/a/44561739/3829845` for more information). Otherwise, passing `--train False` in the Terminal will not affect the script:

```
def boolean_string(s):
    if s not in {'False', 'True'}:
        raise ValueError('Not a valid boolean string')
    return s == 'True'
```

We still need to do some preprocessing on the arguments:

```
FLAGS.cuda = FLAGS.cuda and torch.cuda.is_available()

if FLAGS.seed is not None:
    torch.manual_seed(FLAGS.seed)
    if FLAGS.cuda:
        torch.cuda.manual_seed(FLAGS.seed)
    np.random.seed(FLAGS.seed)

cudnn.benchmark = True

if FLAGS.train:
    utils.clear_folder(FLAGS.out_dir)

log_file = os.path.join(FLAGS.out_dir, 'log.txt')
print("Logging to {}\n".format(log_file))
sys.stdout = utils.StdOut(log_file)
```

```
print("PyTorch version: {}".format(torch.__version__))
print("CUDA version: {}\n".format(torch.version.cuda))

print(" " * 9 + "Args" + " " * 9 + "| " + "Type" + \
        " | " + "Value")
print("-" * 50)
for arg in vars(FLAGS):
    arg_str = str(arg)
    var_str = str(getattr(FLAGS, arg))
    type_str = str(type(getattr(FLAGS, arg)).__name__)
    print(" " + arg_str + " " * (20-len(arg_str)) + "|" + \
            " " + type_str + " " * (10-len(type_str)) + "|" + \
            " " + var_str)

main()
```

Here, we first make sure that CUDA is indeed available to PyTorch. Then, we manually set the random seed to the NumPy, PyTorch, and CUDA backend. We need to clear the output directory each time we retrain the model and all output messages are redirected to an external file, log.txt. Finally, we print all of the arguments taken before running the main function so that we may have a chance to check whether we have configured the model correctly.

Now, open a Terminal and run the following script. Remember to change DATA_DIRECTORY to the path of the MNIST dataset on your machine:

```
$ conda activate torch
(torch)$ python main.py --model cgan --train True --data_dir DATA_DIRECTORY
```

The output message may look like this (the order of the arguments might be different):

```
Logging to output/log.txt

PyTorch version: 1.0.1.post2
CUDA version: 10.0.130
```

Args	Type	Value
model	str	cgan
cuda	bool	True
train	bool	True
data_dir	str	~/Data/mnist
out_dir	str	output
epochs	int	200
batch_size	int	128
lr	float	0.0002
latent_dim	int	100

```
classes             | int    | 10
img_size            | int    | 64
channels            | int    | 1
log_interval        | int    | 100
seed                | int    | 1
Loading data...

Creating model...

Epoch 0 [100/469] loss_D: 0.6747 loss_G: 0.6119
Epoch 0 [200/469] loss_D: 0.4745 loss_G: 0.8135
...
```

It takes about 22 minutes to train for 200 epochs on a GTX 1080Ti graphics card and costs about 729 MB of GPU memory. The generated images from the MNIST dataset are shown here:

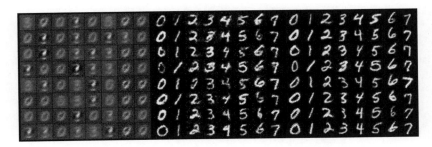

Generated images from MNIST by the CGAN (left: 1st epoch; middle: 25th epoch; right: 200th epoch)

We can see that the digit images are correctly generated for the corresponding labels while maintaining realistic variety in appearance. Because we treat the images as very long vectors in the model, it is hard to generate smoothness in both vertical and horizontal directions and it is easy to spot speckle noise in the generated images after only 25 epochs of training. However, the quality of the images gets a lot better after 200 epochs.

Working with Fashion-MNIST

So you know by now that the MNIST dataset is comprised of a bunch of handwritten numbers. It is the defacto standard for the Machine Learning community, and it is often used to validate processes. Another group has decided to create another dataset that could be a better replacement. This project is named **Fashion-MNIST** and is designed to be a simple drop-in replacement. You can get a deeper understanding of the project at https://www.kaggle.com/zalando-research/fashionmnist/data#.

Fashion-MNIST consists of a training set of 60,000 images and labels and a test set of 10,000 images and labels. All images are grayscale and set to 28x28 pixels, and there are 10 classes of images, namely: T-shirt/top, Trouser, Pullover, Dress, Coat, Saldal, Shirt, Sneaker, Bag, and Ankle boot. You can already begin to see that this replacement dataset should work the algorithms harder.

To demonstrate the use of the dataset, we will use the program that we just created for the standard MNIST dataset, and make a few changes.

1. Copy the main.py file to `fashion-main.py` to keep the original safe. Now in the `fashion-main.py` file find the following portion of code:

```
dataset = dset.MNIST(root=FLAGS.data_dir, download=True,
                      transform=transforms.Compose([
                      transforms.Resize(FLAGS.img_size),
                      transforms.ToTensor(),
                      transforms.Normalize((0.5,), (0.5,))
                      ]))
```

It's the fourth line in the `main()` function.

2. Now, all you need to change is the the `dset.MNIST(` to `dset.FashionMNIST(` like this:

```
dataset = dset.FashionMNIST(root=FLAGS.data_dir, download=True,
                      transform=transforms.Compose([
                      transforms.Resize(FLAGS.img_size),
                      transforms.ToTensor(),
                      transforms.Normalize((0.5,), (0.5,))
                      ]))
```

Luckily, torchvision already has a built-in class for Fashion-MNIST. We'll point out a few others in a few minutes.

3. Now save your source file.

4. Now, to make sure that your dataset from the first example is safe, rename the Data folder that was used last time. The new dataset will automatically be downloaded for you. One other thing you should do is to rename your output folder, again to keep that safe.

5. As we did with the last program, we'll start it with a command line entry:

```
(torch)$ python fashion_main.py --model cgan --train True --
data_dir DATA_DIRECTORY
```

The output in the Terminal will look pretty much like that of the last program, except for the lines showing the download of the new dataset information:

```
Downloading
http://fashion-mnist.s3-website.eu-central-1.amazonaws.com/train-images-idx
3-ubyte.gz to ./Data/fashion/FashionMNIST/raw/train-images-idx3-ubyte.gz
26427392it [00:06, 4212673.42it/s]
Extracting ./Data/fashion/FashionMNIST/raw/train-images-idx3-ubyte.gz to
./Data/fashion/FashionMNIST/raw
...
```

Here is an example of the output images you can expect:

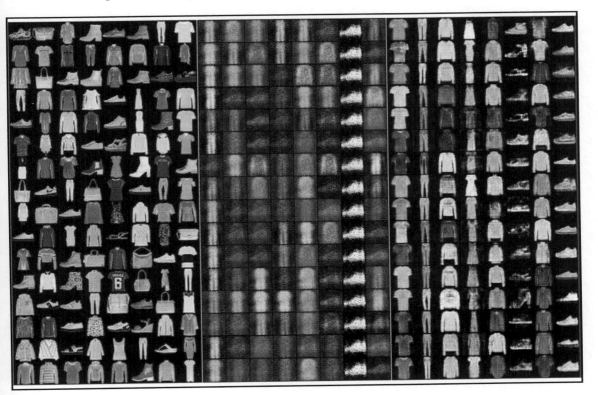

On the left is the real sample data, in the middle is the result from epoch 0, and finally on the right is the result from epoch 199. While not perfect, you can see that the output is getting quite good.

Earlier, I said that we would look at other classes that torchvision supports. There are too many to discuss here, but if you go to: `https://pytorch.org/docs/stable/torchvision/datasets.html`, you can see the large list of each supported class and the API parameters. Many of them can be used as-is with our code, with the exception of modifying the dataset line in your code, and even allow the program to download the dataset for you.

InfoGAN – unsupervised attribute extraction

In the previous sections, we have learned how to use auxiliary information such as the labels of data to improve the image quality generated by GANs. However, it is not always possible to prepare accurate labels of training samples beforehand. Sometimes, it is even difficult for us to accurately describe the labels of extremely complex data. In this section, we will introduce another excellent model from the GAN family, **InfoGAN**, which is capable of extracting data attributes during training in an unsupervised manner. InfoGAN was proposed by Xi Chen, Yan Duan, Rein Houthooft, et. al. in their paper, *InfoGAN: Interpretable Representation Learning by Information Maximizing Generative Adversarial Nets*. It showed that GANs could not only learn to generate realistic samples but also learn semantic features, which are essential to sample generation.

Similar to CGANs, InfoGAN also replaces the original distribution of data with conditional distribution (with auxiliary information as conditions). The main difference is that InfoGAN does not need to feed label and attribute information into the discriminator network; instead, it uses another classifier, Q, to measure how auxiliary features are learned. The objective function of InfoGAN is as follows. You may notice that it adds another objective, $-\lambda L_I$, at the end of the formula:

$$\min_{G,Q} \max_D V(D,G,Q) = \mathbb{E}_x[\log D(x)] + \mathbb{E}_{x^*}[\log(1 - D(x^*))] - \lambda L_I(G,Q)$$

$$L_I(G,Q) = \mathbb{E}_{\gamma \sim P(\gamma), x \sim G(z,\gamma)}[\log Q(\gamma|x)] + H(\gamma)$$

In this formula, $x^* = G(z,\gamma)$ is the generated sample, z is the latent vector, γ and represent auxiliary information. $P(\gamma)$ describes the actual distribution of γ, which is rather hard to find. Therefore, we use the posterior distribution, $Q(\gamma|x)$, to ate, and this process is done with a neural network classifier. $P(\gamma)$

In the preceding formula, $L_I(G, Q)$ is, in fact, an approximation of **mutual information**, $I(\gamma; G(z, \gamma))$, between the auxiliary vector and generated sample. Mutual information, $I(X; Y)$, describes how much we know about random variable X based on knowledge of Y— $I(X; Y) = H(X) - H(X|Y)$, in which $H(X)$ is **entropy** and $H(X|Y)$ is **conditional entropy**. It can also be described by the **Kullback–Leibler divergence**, $D_{KL}(p(x, y) \| p(x)p(y))$, which describes the information loss when we use marginal distributions to approximate the joint distribution of X and Y. You can refer to the original InfoGAN paper for detailed mathematical derivation. For now, you only need to know that L_I tells us whether the generation of x^* based on γ goes as desired.

Network definitions of InfoGAN

The architecture of the generator network of InfoGAN is illustrated as follows. The reproduction of results from the original paper is rather tricky to handle. Therefore, we present a model architecture based on this GitHub repository, `https://github.com/` `eriklindernoren/PyTorch-GAN/blob/master/implementations/infogan/infogan.py`:

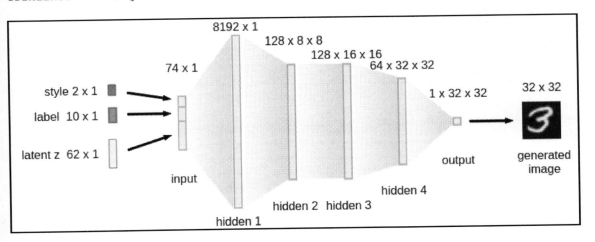

Generator architecture of InfoGAN

The generator network of InfoGAN consists of 4 hidden layers. The first hidden layer transforms the input vector with a length of 74 (*62+10+2*) into a length of 8,192 (*128*8*8*), which is then directly turned into tensor with the dimensionality of *128*8*8*. The feature maps are then gradually up-scaled to 32*32 images. The scaling of feature maps is done with `torch.nn.functional.interpolate`. We need to define a derived `Module` class for upsampling so that we can treat it as other `torch.nn` layers.

Let's create a new source file called `infogan.py` and import the same Python modules as in `cgan.py` and define the `Upsample` class as follows:

```
class Upsample(nn.Module):
    def __init__(self, scale_factor):
        super(Upsample, self).__init__()
        self.scale_factor = scale_factor

    def forward(self, x):
        return F.interpolate(x, scale_factor=self.scale_factor,
mode='bilinear', align_corners=False)
```

We use the `bilinear` method to up-scale the images because it's the best fit compared to other choices. Since we derive this class from `torch.nn.Module` and only use the functions from `torch` to perform the calculation in the forward pass, our custom class will have no trouble performing the gradient back-propagation in training.

 In PyTorch 1.0, calling `nn.Upsample` will give a deprecated warning and it is now, in fact, implemented with `torch.nn.functional.interpolate`. Therefore, our custom `Upsample` layer is the same as `nn.Upsample`, but without warning message.

The generator network is defined as follows:

```
class Generator(nn.Module):
    def __init__(self, classes, channels, img_size, latent_dim, code_dim):
        super(Generator, self).__init__()
        self.classes = classes
        self.channels = channels
        self.img_size = img_size
        self.img_init_size = self.img_size // 4
        self.latent_dim = latent_dim
        self.code_dim = code_dim
        self.img_init_shape = (128, self.img_init_size, self.img_init_size)
        self.img_shape = (self.channels, self.img_size, self.img_size)
        self.stem_linear = nn.Sequential(
            nn.Linear(latent_dim + classes + code_dim,
```

```
                        int(np.prod(self.img_init_shape)))
        )
        self.model = nn.Sequential(
            nn.BatchNorm2d(128),
            *self._create_deconv_layer(128, 128, upsample=True),
            *self._create_deconv_layer(128, 64, upsample=True),
            *self._create_deconv_layer(64, self.channels, upsample=False,
normalize=False),
            nn.Tanh()
        )

    def _create_deconv_layer(self, size_in, size_out, upsample=True,
        normalize=True):
        layers = []
        if upsample:
            layers.append(Upsample(scale_factor=2))
        layers.append(nn.Conv2d(size_in, size_out, 3, stride=1,
          padding=1))
        if normalize:
            layers.append(nn.BatchNorm2d(size_out, 0.8))
            layers.append(nn.LeakyReLU(0.2, inplace=True))
        return layers

    def forward(self, noise, labels, code):
        z = torch.cat((noise, labels, code), -1)
        z_vec = self.stem_linear(z)
        z_img = z_vec.view(z_vec.shape[0], *self.img_init_shape)
        x = self.model(z_img)
        return x
```

In this class, we use a helper function, `_create_deconv_layer`, to create the convolutional hidden layers. Since we will use the custom `Upsample` layer to increase the size of feature maps, we only need to use `nn.Conv2d`, whose input size equals, output size, rather than `nn.ConvTranspose2d` as in the DCGAN in the last chapter.

In our configuration of InfoGAN, `torch.nn.functional.interpolate` combined with `nn.Conv2d` performs better than `nn.ConvTranspose2d` with stride. Although you are welcome to try out different configurations and see whether they produce better results.

The architecture of the discriminator network of InfoGAN is illustrated as follows. Again, we use a different structure than in the original paper:

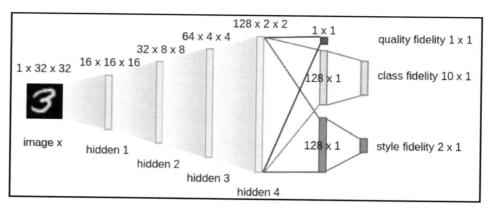

Discriminator architecture of InfoGAN

The discriminator network consists of 4 hidden layers. As explained before, InfoGAN uses an additional classifier network to measure the validity of the auxiliary vector. In fact, this additional classifier shares most of its weights (the first 4 hidden layers) with the discriminator. Therefore, the quality measure on the image is represented by a 1 x 1 tensor, which is a result of a linear layer at the end of the 4 hidden layers. The measurement of auxiliary information, which includes class fidelity and style fidelity, is obtained from two different groups of linear layers, in which the *128*2*2* feature maps are first mapped to 128-length vectors then mapped to output vectors with lengths of 10 and 2, respectively.

The definition of the discriminator in PyTorch code is as follows:

```
class Discriminator(nn.Module):
  def __init__(self, classes, channels, img_size, latent_dim, code_dim):
  super(Discriminator, self).__init__()
  self.classes = classes
  self.channels = channels
  self.img_size = img_size
  self.latent_dim = latent_dim
  self.code_dim = code_dim
  self.img_shape = (self.channels, self.img_size, self.img_size)
  self.model = nn.Sequential(
  *self._create_conv_layer(self.channels, 16, True, False),
  *self._create_conv_layer(16, 32, True, True),
  *self._create_conv_layer(32, 64, True, True),
  *self._create_conv_layer(64, 128, True, True),
  )
  out_linear_dim = 128 * (self.img_size // 16) * (self.img_size // 16)
```

```python
self.adv_linear = nn.Linear(out_linear_dim, 1)
self.class_linear = nn.Sequential(
nn.Linear(out_linear_dim, 128),
nn.BatchNorm1d(128),
nn.LeakyReLU(0.2, inplace=True),
nn.Linear(128, self.classes)
)
self.code_linear = nn.Sequential(
nn.Linear(out_linear_dim, 128),
nn.BatchNorm1d(128),
nn.LeakyReLU(0.2, inplace=True),
nn.Linear(128, self.code_dim)
)
self.adv_loss = torch.nn.MSELoss()
self.class_loss = torch.nn.CrossEntropyLoss()
self.style_loss = torch.nn.MSELoss()

def _create_conv_layer(self, size_in, size_out, drop_out=True,
normalize=True):
layers = [nn.Conv2d(size_in, size_out, 3, 2, 1)]
if drop_out:
layers.append(nn.LeakyReLU(0.2, inplace=True))
layers.append(nn.Dropout(0.4))
if normalize:
layers.append(nn.BatchNorm2d(size_out, 0.8))
return layers

def forward(self, image):
y_img = self.model(image)
y_vec = y_img.view(y_img.shape[0], -1)
y = self.adv_linear(y_vec)
label = F.softmax(self.class_linear(y_vec), dim=1)
code = self.code_linear(y_vec)
return y, label, code
```

Here, we treat the quality fidelity (self.adv_loss) as in an ordinary GAN model, the class fidelity (self.class_loss) as a classification problem (because label values are hard-coded, often in one-hot codes) and the style fidelity (self.style_loss) as an expectation maximization problem (because we want style vectors to obey certain random distribution). Therefore, cross-entropy (torch.nn.CrossEntropyLoss) and mean squared (torch.nn.MSELoss) loss functions are used for them.

We'd like explain why mean squared error is used for expectation maximization. We assume that the style vectors obey a normal distribution with a mean of 0 and a standard deviation of 1. In the calculation of entropy, the logarithm of the probability of random variable is taken. The logarithm of **probability density function (pdf)** of the normal distribution $\log\left((1/\sqrt{2\pi\sigma^2})\exp(-(x-\mu)^2/2\sigma^2)\right)$ is deduced to $-x^2/2 - \log\sqrt{2\pi}$. Therefore, mean squared error is suited for such a purpose.

Training and evaluation of InfoGAN

We need to make some adjustments to the training API so that we can make use of the class and style vectors for attribute extraction and image generation.

First, we add several imported modules in the `build_gan.py` file:

```
import itertools

from infogan import Generator as infoganG
from infogan import Discriminator as infoganD
```

The default weight initialization provided by PyTorch easily leads to saturation, so we need a custom `weight` initializer:

```
def _weights_init(m):
    classname = m.__class__.__name__
    if classname.find('Conv') != -1:
        torch.nn.init.normal_(m.weight.data, 0.0, 0.02)
    elif classname.find('BatchNorm') != -1:
        torch.nn.init.normal_(m.weight.data, 1.0, 0.02)
        torch.nn.init.constant_(m.bias.data, 0.0)
```

Let's add the following lines in the definition of the `Model` class:

```
        self.style_dim = 2
        self.infogan = self.name == 'infogan'
        self.optim_info = None
```

And we need to change the definitions of `self.netG` and `self.netD`:

```
    if self.name == 'cgan':
        self.netG = cganG(self.classes, self.channels, self.img_size,
self.latent_dim)
    elif self.name == 'infogan':
        self.netG = infoganG(self.classes, self.channels,
self.img_size, self.latent_dim, self.style_dim)
        self.netG.apply(_weights_init)
    self.netG.to(self.device)
    if self.name == 'cgan':
        self.netD = cganD(self.classes, self.channels, self.img_size,
self.latent_dim)
    elif self.name == 'infogan':
        self.netD = infoganD(self.classes, self.channels,
self.img_size, self.latent_dim, self.style_dim)
        self.netD.apply(_weights_init)
    self.netD.to(self.device)
```

Then, we add an optimizer for mutual information at the end of the `create_optim` method:

```
    if self.infogan:
        self.optim_info =
torch.optim.Adam(itertools.chain(self.netG.parameters(),
self.netD.parameters()),
                                        lr=lr, betas=(alpha, beta))
```

Next, we need to make some adjustments to `train` method, in which we first train the generator and discriminator networks and update the two networks again based on auxiliary information. Here, we omit all of the `if self.infogan` statements and only show the training procedure for InfoGAN. Full source code can be referred to in the code repository for this chapter.

Initialize the fixed latent vectors for result visualization:

```
    viz_noise = torch.randn(self.data_loader.batch_size,
self.latent_dim, device=self.device)
        nrows = self.data_loader.batch_size // 8
        viz_label = torch.LongTensor(np.array([num for _ in range(nrows)
for num in range(8)])).to(self.device)
        viz_onehot = self._to_onehot(viz_label, dim=self.classes)
        viz_style = torch.zeros((self.data_loader.batch_size,
self.style_dim), device=self.device)
```

Here, the `self._to_onehot` method is responsible for transforming the label values to one-hot coding:

```
def _to_onehot(self, var, dim):
    res = torch.zeros((var.shape[0], dim), device=self.device)
    res[range(var.shape[0]), var] = 1.
    return res
```

A training iteration for InfoGAN includes the following:

- Training the generator with fake data and letting the discriminator see them as real ones
- Training the discriminator with both real and fake data to increase its ability to distinguish them
- Training both generator and discriminator so that the generator can produce samples with good quality based on given auxiliary information and the discriminator can tell whether the generated samples obey the distribution of given auxiliary information:

```
for epoch in range(epochs):
    for batch_idx, (data, target) in enumerate(self.data_loader):
        data, target = data.to(self.device), target.to(self.device)
        batch_size = data.size(0)
        real_label = torch.full((batch_size, 1), 1.,
            device=self.device)
        fake_label = torch.full((batch_size, 1), 0.,
            device=self.device)

        # Train G
        self.netG.zero_grad()
        z_noise = torch.randn(batch_size, self.latent_dim,
            device=self.device)
        x_fake_labels = torch.randint(0, self.classes,
            (batch_size,), device=self.device)
        labels_onehot = self._to_onehot(x_fake_labels,
            dim=self.classes)
        z_style = torch.zeros((batch_size, self.style_dim),
            device=self.device).normal_()
        x_fake = self.netG(z_noise, labels_onehot, z_style)
        y_fake_g, _, _ = self.netD(x_fake)
        g_loss = self.netD.adv_loss(y_fake_g, real_label)
        g_loss.backward()
        self.optim_G.step()

        # Train D
        self.netD.zero_grad()
```

```
y_real, _, _ = self.netD(data)
d_real_loss = self.netD.adv_loss(y_real, real_label)
y_fake_d, _, _ = self.netD(x_fake.detach())
d_fake_loss = self.netD.adv_loss(y_fake_d, fake_label)
d_loss = (d_real_loss + d_fake_loss) / 2
d_loss.backward()
self.optim_D.step()

# Update mutual information
self.optim_info.zero_grad()
z_noise.normal_()
x_fake_labels = torch.randint(0, self.classes,
    (batch_size,), device=self.device)
labels_onehot = self._to_onehot(x_fake_labels,
    dim=self.classes)
z_style.normal_()
x_fake = self.netG(z_noise, labels_onehot, z_style)
_, label_fake, style_fake = self.netD(x_fake)
info_loss = self.netD.class_loss(label_fake,
    x_fake_labels) +\
            self.netD.style_loss(style_fake, z_style)
info_loss.backward()
self.optim_info.step()
```

We don't need to change anything in the `main.py` file at all, and we can simply run the following script in the Terminal:

```
(torch)$ python main.py --model infogan --latent_dim 62 --img_size 32 --batch_size 64 --data_dir DATA_DIRECTORY
```

It takes about 2 hours to finish 200 epochs of training and costs about 833 MB GPU memory on a GTX 1080Ti graphics card. The results produced during training are shown here:

Generated images from MNIST by the CGAN (left: 1st epoch; middle: 25th epoch; right: 200th epoch)

After the training is done, run the following script to perform the model evaluation:

```
(torch)$ python main.py --model infogan --latent_dim 62 --img_size 32 --
batch_size 64 --train False
```

Calling `model.eval()` with `mode=0` or `mode=1` will tell us what the two values in the style vector are responsible for, as shown here:

The first style bit (mode=0) controls the digit angle, and the second style bit (mode=1) controls the width of strokes.

One of the style vector values is responsible for the angle of digits, and the other is responsible for the width of strokes, just as the original InfoGAN paper proclaims. Imagine what this technique is capable of on complex datasets and an elaborate training configuration.

We can do a lot more with CGANs and similar. For example, the labels can be more than for images. An individual pixel in the image can certainly have its own label. In the next chapter, we will look into how GANs perform on pixel-wise labels and we can do interesting things, more than hand-written digits and human faces.

References and useful reading list

1. Mirza M and Osindero S. (2014). *Conditional Generative Adversarial Nets.* arXiv preprint arXiv:1411.1784.

2. Hui J. (Jun 3, 2018). *GAN — CGAN & InfoGAN (using labels to improve GAN).* Retrieved from https://medium.com/@jonathan_hui/gan-cgan-infogan-using-labels-to-improve-gan-8ba4de5f9c3d.

3. Zhang Z and Song Y and Qi H. (2017). *Age Progression/Regression by Conditional Adversarial Autoencoder.* CVPR.

4. Chen X, Duan Y, Houthooft R. (2016). *InfoGAN: Interpretable Representation Learning by Information Maximizing Generative Adversarial Nets.* arXiv preprint arXiv:1606.03657.

Summary

In this chapter, we discovered **Conditional Generative Adversarial Networks (CGANs)**, which worked with MNIST and Fashion-MNIST, and we learned about using the InfoGAN model, which again, worked with MNIST.

In our next chapter, we will learn about image-to-image translation, which I truly believe you will find exciting and very relevant in today's world.

6

Image-to-Image Translation and Its Applications

In this chapter, we will push the label-based image generation to the next level: we will use pixel-wise labeling to perform image-to-image translation and transfer image styles.

You will learn how to use pixel-wise label information to perform image-to-image translation with pix2pix and translate high-resolution images with pix2pixHD. Following this, you will learn how to perform style transfer between unpaired image collections with CycleGAN.

By the end of this chapter, combined with the knowledge from the previous chapter, you will have grasped the core methodology of using image-wise and pixel-wise label information to improve the quality, or manipulate the attributes, of generated images. You will also know how to flexibly design model architectures to accomplish your goals, including generating larger images or transferring textures between different styles of images.

The following topics will be covered in this chapter:

- Using pixel-wise labels to translate images with pix2pix
- Pix2pixHD – high-resolution image translation
- CycleGAN – image-to-image translation from unpaired collections

ng pixel-wise labels to translate images
h pix2pix

In the previous chapter, we learned how to use auxiliary information such as labels and attributes to improve the quality of images that are generated by GANs. The labels we used in the previous chapter were image-wise, which means that each image has only one or several labels. Labels can be assigned to specific pixels, which are known as pixel-wise labels. Pixel-wise labels are playing an increasingly important role in the realm of deep learning. For example, one of the most famous online image classification contests, the **ImageNet Large Scale Visual Recognition Challenge** (**ILSVRC**, http://www.image-net. org/challenges/LSVRC), is no longer being hosted since its last event in 2017, whereas object detection and segmentation challenges such as COCO (http://cocodataset.org) are receiving more attention.

An iconic application of pixel-wise labeling is semantic segmentation. **Semantic segmentation** (or image/object segmentation) is a task in which every pixel in the image must belong to one object. The most promising application of semantic segmentation is autonomous cars (or self-driving cars). If each and every pixel that's captured by the camera that's mounted on the self-driving car is correctly classified, all of the objects in the image will be easily recognized, which makes it much easier for the vehicle to properly analyze the current environment and make the right decision upon whether it should, for example, turn or slow down to avoid other vehicles and pedestrians. To understand more about semantic segmentation, please refer to the following link: https://devblogs.nvidia. com/image-segmentation-using-digits-5.

Transforming the original color image into a segmentation map (as shown in the following diagram) can be considered as an image-to-image translation problem, which is a much larger field and includes style transfer, image colorization, and more. Image **style transfer** is about moving the iconic textures and colors from one image to another, such as combining your photo with a Vincent van Gogh painting to create a unique artistic portrait of you. **Image colorization** is a task where we feed a 1-channel grayscale image to the model and let it predict the color information for each pixel, which leads to a 3-channel color image.

GANs can be used in image-to-image translation as well. In this section, we will use a classic image-to-image translation model, pix2pix, to transform images from one domain to another. Pix2pix was proposed by Phillip Isola, Jun-Yan Zhu, and Tinghui Zhou, et. al. in their paper *Image-to-Image Translation with Conditional Adversarial Networks*. Pix2pix was designed to learn of the connections between paired collections of images, for example, ing an aerial photo taken by a satellite into a regular map, or a sketch image into a ge, and vice versa.

The authors of the paper have kindly provided the full source code for their work, which runs perfectly on PyTorch 1.3. The source code is also well organized. Therefore, we will use their code directly in order to train and evaluate the pix2pix model and learn how to organize our models in a different way.

First, open a Terminal and download the code for this section using the following command. This is also available under the `pix2pix` directory in this chapter's code repository:

```
$ git clone https://github.com/junyanz/pytorch-CycleGAN-and-pix2pix.git
```

Then, `install` the prerequisites to be able to visualize the results during training:

```
$ pip install dominate visdom
```

Generator architecture

The architecture of the generator network of pix2pix is as follows:

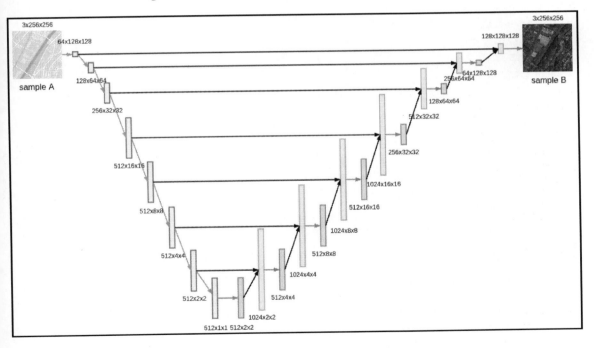

Generator architecture of pix2pix

Here, we assume that both the input and output data are 3-channel 256x256 images. In order to illustrate the generator structure of pix2pix, feature maps are represented by colored blocks and convolution operations are represented by gray and blue arrows, in which gray arrows are convolution layers for reducing the feature map sizes and blue arrows are for doubling the feature map sizes. Identity mapping (including skip connections) is represented by black arrows.

We can see that the first half layers of this network gradually transform the input image into 1x1 feature maps (with wider channels) and the last half layers transform these very small feature maps into an output image with the same size of the input image. It compresses the input data into much lower dimensions and changes them back to their original dimensions. Therefore, this U-shaped kind of network structure is often known as U-Net. There are also many skip connections in the U-Net that connect the mirrored layers in order to help information (including details coming from previous layers in the forward pass and gradients coming from the latter layers in the backward pass) flow through the network. Without these skip connections, the network is also known as an encoder-decoder model, meaning that we stack a decoder at the end of an encoder.

The pix2pix model is defined in the `models.pix2pix_model.Pix2PixModel` class, which is derived from an **abstract base class (ABC)** known as `models.base_model.BaseModel`.

 An **abstract base class** in Python is a class containing at least one **abstract method** (that's declared and not implemented). It cannot be instantiated. You can only create objects with its subclasses after providing the implementations for all the abstract methods.

The generator network, `netG`, is created by the `models.networks.define_G` method. By default, it takes `'unet_256'` as the `netG` argument value (which is specified at line 32 in `models/pix2pix_model.py` and overrides the initialized value, that is, `"resnet_9blocks"`, at line 34 in `options/base_options.py`). Therefore, `models.networks.UnetGenerator` is used to create the U-Net. In order to show how the U-Net is created in a recursive manner, we replace the arguments with their actual values, as shown in the following code:

```
import torch.nn as nn
class UnetGenerator(nn.Module):
    def __init__(self):
        super(UnetGenerator, self).__init__()
        unet_block = UnetSkipConnectionBlock(64 * 8, 64 * 8,
submodule=None, innermost=True)
        for i in range(8 - 5):
            unet_block = UnetSkipConnectionBlock(64 * 8, 64 * 8,
submodule=unet_block, use_dropout=True)
        unet_block = UnetSkipConnectionBlock(64 * 4, 64 * 8,
```

```
submodule=unet_block)
        unet_block = UnetSkipConnectionBlock(64 * 2, 64 * 4,
submodule=unet_block)
        unet_block = UnetSkipConnectionBlock(64, 64 * 2,
submodule=unet_block)
        self.model = UnetSkipConnectionBlock(3, 64, input_nc=3,
submodule=unet_block, outermost=True)

    def forward(self, input):
        return self.model(input)
```

At the fourth line in the preceding code snippet, the innermost block is defined, which creates the layers in the middle of the U-Net. The innermost block is defined as follows. Note that the following code should be treated as pseudocode since it's simply to show you how different blocks are designed:

```
class UnetSkipConnectionBlock(nn.Module):
    # Innermost block */
    def __init__(self):
        down = [nn.LeakyReLU(0.2, inplace=True),
                nn.Conv2d(64 * 8, 64 * 8, kernel_size=4,
                        stride=2, padding=1, bias=False)]
        up = [nn.ReLU(inplace=True),
                nn.ConvTranspose2d(64 * 8, 64 * 8,
                                kernel_size=4, stride=2,
                                padding=1, bias=False),
                nn.BatchNorm2d(64 * 8)]
        model = down + up
        self.model = nn.Sequential(*model)

    def forward(self, x):
        return torch.cat([x, self.model(x)], 1)
```

The nn.Conv2d layer in down transforms 2x2 input feature maps into 1x1 ones (because kernel_size=4 and padding=1), and the nn.ConvTranspose2d layer transforms them back so that they're 2x2 in size.

Remember the calculation formula of the output size for nn.Conv2d and nn.ConvTranspose2d? The output size of the convolution is $size\_out = 1 + (size\_in + 2 * padding - dilation * (kernel\_size - 1))/stride$, while the output size of the transposed convolution is $size\_out = (size\_in - 1) * stride - 2 * padding + kernel\_size + out\_padding$.

In the forward pass, it concatenates the output with a skip connection (that is, the input *x* itself) along the depth channel, which doubles the number of channels (and leads to the first 1,024-channel feature maps in the preceding diagram).

 When designing complex networks, it's been observed that the concatenation of the feature maps from two branches is better than their sum because the concatenation reserves more information. Of course, this concatenation costs a little more memory as well.

Then, the rest of the layers are built recursively, as follows:

```python
class UnetSkipConnectionBlock(nn.Module):
    # Other blocks */
    def __init__(self, out_channels, in_channels, submodule, use_dropout):
        down = [nn.LeakyReLU(0.2, inplace=True),
                nn.Conv2d(out_channels, in_channels, kernel_size=4,
                        stride=2, padding=1, bias=False),
                nn.BatchNorm2d(in_channels)]
        up = [nn.ReLU(inplace=True),
                nn.ConvTranspose2d(in_channels * 2, out_channels,
                                kernel_size=4, stride=2,
                                padding=1, bias=False),
                nn.BatchNorm2d(out_channels)]
        if use_dropout:
            model = down + [submodule] + up + [nn.Dropout(0.5)]
        else:
            model = down + [submodule] + up
        self.model = nn.Sequential(*model)

    def forward(self, x):
        return torch.cat([x, self.model(x)], 1)
```

Although in `models.networks.UnetGenerator`, the `unet_block` object is recursively passed as a `submodule` to a new `unet_block`, thanks to the compact design to the implementation of tensors, the actual modules will be created and saved on memory properly.

Finally, the first and last layers (which can be seen in the outermost block) are defined as follows:

```python
class UnetSkipConnectionBlock(nn.Module):
    # Outermost block */
    def __init__(self):
        down = [nn.Conv2d(3, 64, kernel_size=4,
                        stride=2, padding=1, bias=False)]
        up = [nn.ReLU(inplace=True),
                nn.ConvTranspose2d(64 * 2, 3,
```

```
                                kernel_size=4, stride=2,
                                padding=1),
                nn.Tanh()]
        model = down + [submodule] + up
        self.model = nn.Sequential(*model)

    def forward(self, x):
        return self.model(x)
```

All the convolution kernels in the generator network are initialized based on a normal distribution with a mean of 0 and a standard deviation of 0.02. The scale factors in all the batch normalization layers are initialized based on the normal distribution with a mean of 1 and a standard deviation of 0.02.

Discriminator architecture

The architecture of the discriminator network of pix2pix is as follows:

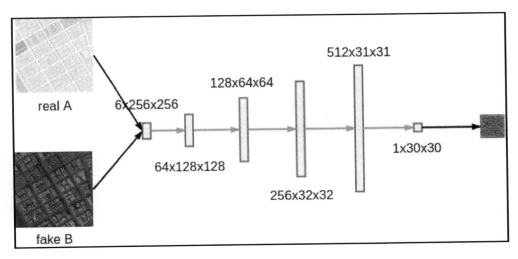

Discriminator architecture of pix2pix

A pair of samples (one from each collection) are concatenated along the depth channel, and this 6-channel image is treated as the actual input of the discriminator network.
The discriminator network maps the 6-channel 256x256 image to a 1-channel 30x30 image, which is used to calculate the discriminator loss.

The discriminator network, `netD`, is created by the `models.networks.define_G` method. By default, it takes `"basic"` as the argument value of `netD`, which is defined at line 33 in `options/base_options.py`. The `models.networks.NLayerDiscriminator` module, which has `n_layer=3`, is initialized so that it can serve as the discriminator network. Again, we've simplified the code so that it's easy to read. You may refer to the full code in the `models/networks.py` file:

```
class NLayerDiscriminator(nn.Module):
    def __init__(self, n_layers=3):
        super(NLayerDiscriminator, self).__init__()
        sequence = [nn.Conv2d(3 + 3, 64, kernel_size=4, stride=2,
padding=1),
                        nn.LeakyReLU(0.2, True)]
        channel_scale = 1
        channel_scale_prev = 1
        for n in range(1, n_layers):
            channel_scale_prev = channel_scale
            channel_scale = 2**n
            sequence += [
                nn.Conv2d(64 * channel_scale_prev, 64 * channel_scale,
kernel_size=4, stride=2, padding=1, bias=False),
                nn.BatchNorm2d(64 * channel_scale),
                nn.LeakyReLU(0.2, True)
            ]
        channel_scale_prev = channel_scale
        sequence += [
            nn.Conv2d(64 * channel_scale_prev, 64 * 8, kernel_size=4,
stride=1, padding=1, bias=False),
            nn.BatchNorm2d(64 * 8),
            nn.LeakyReLU(0.2, True)
        ]
        sequence += [nn.Conv2d(64 * 8, 1, kernel_size=4, stride=1,
padding=1)]
        self.model = nn.Sequential(*sequence)

    def forward(self, input):
        return self.model(input)
```

Here, we provide a short snippet so that we can print the sizes of all the feature maps if the model is created, as follows:

```
class SomeModel(nn.Module):
    def __init__(self):
        super(SomeModel, self).__init__()
        sequence = [layer1, layer2, ...]
        self.model = nn.Sequential(*sequence)
```

```
def forward(self, input):
    return self.model(input)
```

You can replace the line `return self.model(input)` with the following code to check the feature map sizes in all the layers (including the normalization and activation function layers):

```
def forward(self, input):
x = input
for i in range(len(self.model)):
print(x.shape)
x = self.model[i](x)
print(x.shape)
return x
```

Alternatively, you can always use TensorBoard or other tools, which we will introduce in the last chapter of this book, so that you can easily examine the architectures of your models.

The discriminator network creates a 30x30 feature map to represent the loss. This kind of architecture is called **PatchGAN**, which means that every small image patch in the original image is mapped to a pixel in the final loss map. A big advantage of PatchGAN is that it can handle the arbitrary sizes of input images as long as the labels have been transformed so that they're the same size as the loss map. It also evaluates the quality of the input image according to the quality of the local patches, rather than their global property. Here, we will show you how the size of the image patch (that is, 70) is calculated.

First, let's consider a single convolution layer with a kernel size of k and a stride size of s. For each pixel in the output feature map, its value is only determined by a small patch of pixels in the input image, whose size is the same as the convolution kernel.

When there are more than two convolution layers, the size of the input patch is calculated with the following formula:

$$input\_patch\_size = k + s \cdot (output\_patch\_size - 1)$$

Therefore, the size of the input patch corresponding to a single pixel in the output feature map in each layer of the discriminator network can be obtained:

- 5th layer (k=4, s=1): Input patch size is 4 (which is the size of the kernel)
- 4th layer (k=4, s=1): Input patch size is 4+1*(4-1)=7
- 3rd layer (k=4, s=2): Input patch size is 4+2*(7-1)=16
- 2nd layer (k=4, s=2): Input patch size is 4+2*(16-1)=34
- 1st layer (k=4, s=2): Input patch size is 4+2*(34-1)=70

This means that all of these 70x70 overlapping image patches are transformed by convolution layers into individual pixels in the 30x30 loss map. Any pixel outside this 70x70 image patch has no influence over the corresponding pixel in the loss map.

Training and evaluation of pix2pix

The training of pix2pix is very similar to conditional GANs, which we introduced in the previous chapter. When training the discriminator network, a pair of real data and a label should be mapped to 1, whereas a pair of generated data and a label (that fake data is generated from) is mapped to 0. When training the generator network, the gradients are passed through both of the discriminator and generator networks when the parameters in the generator network are updated. This generated data and the label should be mapped to 1 by the discriminator network. The major difference is that the labels are image-wise in CGAN and are pixel-wise in pix2pix. This process is described in the following diagram:

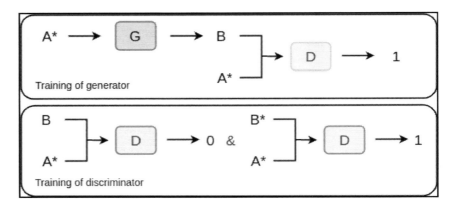

Basic training process of image-wise and pixel-wise labeled GANs. A* and B* denote real samples. Networks in red boxes are actually updated.

Note that, when training pix2pix, in order to let the generated samples be as similar to the real ones as possible, an additional term is added to the loss function when training the generator network, as follows:

$$V_{pix2pix} = \min_{G} \max_{D} V(D, G) + \lambda \mathcal{L}_{L1}(G)$$

Here, $\mathcal{L}_{L1}(G)$ represents the L1-loss between the generated samples and the real ones from the paired collection. The purpose of the L1-loss is to reserve the low-frequency information in the images for better image quality.

It is worth mentioning that using L1-norm or L2-norm alone will generate blurry or blocky images. A short explanation of this can be found here: `https://wiseodd.github.io/techblog/2017/02/09/why-12-blurry`. It is also common to use them as regularization terms in the traditional image restoration methods, in which the gradients of the restored images control the sharpness. If you are interested in the roles of L1-loss and L2-loss in the field of image processing, feel free to check out the famous paper, *Total variation blind deconvolution* by Tony F. Chan and C.K. Wong in 1998.

Now, we can define the training procedure of pix2pix, as follows (pseudocode):

```
class Pix2PixModel(BaseModel):
    def __init__(self):
        BaseModel.__init__(self)
        self.netG = networks.define_G()
        self.netD = networks.define_D()

        self.criterionGAN = torch.nn.BCEWithLogitsLoss()
        self.criterionL1 = torch.nn.L1Loss()
        self.optimizer_G = torch.optim.Adam(self.netG.parameters(),
lr=0.0002, betas=(0.5, 0.999))
        self.optimizer_D = torch.optim.Adam(self.netD.parameters(),
lr=0.0002, betas=(0.5, 0.999))
        self.optimizers.append(self.optimizer_G)
        self.optimizers.append(self.optimizer_D)

    def forward(self):
        self.fake_B = self.netG(self.real_A)

    def backward_D(self):
        fake_AB = torch.cat((self.real_A, self.fake_B), 1)
        pred_fake = self.netD(fake_AB.detach())
        self.loss_D_fake = self.criterionGAN(pred_fake, False)

        real_AB = torch.cat((self.real_A, self.real_B), 1)
        pred_real = self.netD(real_AB)
        self.loss_D_real = self.criterionGAN(pred_real, True)

        self.loss_D = (self.loss_D_fake + self.loss_D_real) * 0.5
        self.loss_D.backward()

    def backward_G(self):
        fake_AB = torch.cat((self.real_A, self.fake_B), 1)
        pred_fake = self.netD(fake_AB)
        self.loss_G_GAN = self.criterionGAN(pred_fake, True)
```

```
        self.loss_G_L1 = self.criterionL1(self.fake_B, self.real_B)

        self.loss_G = self.loss_G_GAN + self.loss_G_L1 * 100.0
        self.loss_G.backward()

    def optimize_parameters(self):
        self.forward()
        # update D
        self.set_requires_grad(self.netD, True)
        self.optimizer_D.zero_grad()
        self.backward_D()
        self.optimizer_D.step()
        # update G
        self.set_requires_grad(self.netD, False)
        self.optimizer_G.zero_grad()
        self.backward_G()
        self.optimizer_G.step()
```

The `Pix2PixModel` class serves a similar purpose to the `Model` class in `build_gan.py` from the previous chapter, which creates the generator and discriminator networks, defines their optimizers, and controls the training procedures of the networks.

Now, let's download some images and train the pix2pix model to perform image-to-image translation.

Run the `datasets/download_pix2pix_dataset.sh` script to download the dataset files, as follows:

```
$ ./datasets/download_pix2pix_dataset.sh maps
```

Alternatively, you can go to `http://efrosgans.eecs.berkeley.edu/pix2pix/datasets/` to download the dataset files manually and extract them to any location you like (for example, an external hard drive such as `/media/john/HouseOfData/image_transfer/maps`). The maps dataset file is approximately 239 MB in size and contains a few more than 1,000 images in the collections of the train, validation, and test sets.

 Note that collection A in the maps dataset contains satellite photos and that collection B contains map images, which is opposite to what was shown in the diagrams in the previous subsections.

Next, open a Terminal and run the following script to start training. Make sure you modify the `dataroot` argument so that it specifies your own location. You may also try other datasets and change `direction` from `BtoA` to `AtoB` to change the translation direction between two image collections:

```
$ python train.py --dataroot /media/john/HouseOfData/image_transfer/maps --
name maps_pix2pix --model pix2pix --direction BtoA
```

For the first time of training, you may encounter an error stating `Could not connect to Visdom server`. This is because the training script calls the `Visdom` module to dynamically update the generated results so that we can monitor the training process via web browsers. You can manually open the `checkpoints/maps_pix2pix/web/index.html` file with your favorite browser to keep an eye on the generated images as the model is being trained. Note that there is a chance that closing the `index.html` page in the web browser could cause the training process to freeze.

It takes about 6.7 hours to finish 200 epochs of training and costs about 1,519 MB GPU memory on a GTX 1080Ti graphics card.

The results are also saved in the `checkpoints/maps_pix2pix/web/images` directory. The images that are generated by doing this are as follows:

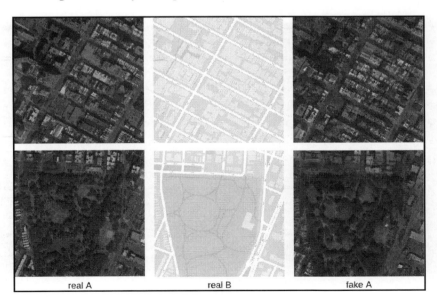

Generated images by pix2pix

can see, the generated satellite photos look pretty convincing on their own. ....red to real satellite photos, they do a good job of organizing the trees along the trails in the park.

In this section, we managed to translate and generate 256 x 256 images. In the next section, we will learn how to generate high-resolution images with an upgraded version of pix2pix: pix2pixHD.

Pix2pixHD – high-resolution image translation

Pix2pixHD was proposed by Ting-Chun Wang, Ming-Yu Liu, and Jun-Yan Zhu, et. al. in their paper, *High-Resolution Image Synthesis and Semantic Manipulation with Conditional GANs*, which was an upgraded version of the pix2pix model. The biggest improvement of pix2pixHD over pix2pix is that it supports image-to-image translation at 2,048x1,024 resolution and with high quality.

Model architecture

To make this happen, they designed a two-stage approach to gradually train and refine the networks, as shown in the following diagram. First, a lower resolution image of 1,024x512 is generated by a generator network, G_1, called the **global generator** (the red box). Second, the image is enlarged by a generator network, G_2, called the **local enhancer network** so that it's around 2,048x1,024 in size (the black box). It is also viable to put another local enhancer network at the end to generate 4,096x2,048 images. Note that the last feature map in G_1 is also inserted into G_2 (before the residual blocks) via an element-wise sum to introduce more global information into higher resolution images:

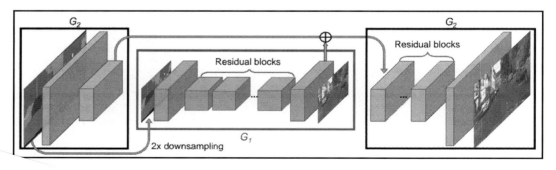

Architecture of the generator model in pix2pixHD (image retrieved from the paper by T. C. Wang, et. al., 2018)

The discriminator network in pix2pixHD is also designed in a multi-scale fashion. Three identical discriminator networks work on different image scales (original size, 1/2 size, and 1/4 size) and their loss values are added together. It is reported by the authors that, without multi-scale design in the discriminator, repeated patterns are often observed in the generated images. Also, an additional term, called the **feature matching loss**, is added to the final discriminator loss, as shown the following formula:

$$V_{pix2pixHD} = \min_{G} \max_{D_1,D_2} \sum_{k=1,2} V(D_k, G) + \lambda \mathcal{L}_{FM}(D_k, G)$$

Here, $\lambda \mathcal{L}_{FM}(D_k, G)$ measures the L1-loss between the feature maps of the generated and real images at multiple layers in the discriminator networks. It forces the generator to approximate the real data at different scales, thereby generating more realistic images.

Sometimes, several objects with the same label may find their way together, which makes it difficult for the generator to correctly distinguish these objects. It would help if the generator knew which pixels belong to which object compared to which class they belong to. Therefore, in pix2pixHD, an **instance boundary map** (which is a binary map denoting the boundaries of all the objects) is channel-wise concatenated to the semantic label map before it's fed into the generator. Similarly, the instance boundary map is also concatenated to the semantic label map and the image (the generated one or the real one), before being fed into the discriminator.

Furthermore, in order to make it easier to manipulate the attributes of the generated images, pix2pixHD uses an additional **encoder** to extract features from the real images and performs instance-wise average pooling (averages all the pixels in one object and then broadcasts back to these pixels) on the features. These features are also part of the input to the generator. K-means clustering is performed on the features of all the objects in each class, and several available textures or colors can be chosen for the objects during inference.

We will not dive deep into the specific architecture designs of pix2pixHD since the main structure of its source code is similar to pix2pix. You can check out the source code if you're interested.

Model training

The training of pix2pixHD is both time- and memory-consuming. It requires about 24 GB GPU memory to train 2,048x1,024 images. Therefore, we will only train on a 1,024x512 resolution in order to fit this on a single graphic card.

has already open-sourced the full source code of pix2pixHD for PyTorch. All we
o is download the source code and dataset to produce our own high resolution
ed images. Let's do this now:

1. Install the prerequisites (dominate and apex). We previously installed
   the `dominate` library. **Apex** is a mixed precision and distributed training library
   that's developed by NVIDIA.

2. Use **Automatic Mixed Precision (AMP)** to reduce the GPU memory
   consumption (or even the training time) during training by replacing the
   standard floating-point values with lower bit floats.

3. Open a Terminal in Ubuntu and type in the following scripts to install `apex`:

   ```
   $ git clone https://github.com/NVIDIA/apex
   $ cd apex
   $ pip install -v --no-cache-dir --global-option="--cpp_ext" --
   global-option="--cuda_ext" .
   ```

4. Download the source code of pix2pixHD (also available under the code
   repository for this chapter):

   ```
   $ git clone https://github.com/NVIDIA/pix2pixHD
   ```

5. Use the **Cityscapes** dataset to train the pix2pixHD model. It is available
   at `https://www.cityscapes-dataset.com` and you'll need to register first before
   being granted access to the download links. We need to download
   the `gtFine_trainvaltest.zip` (241
   MB) and `leftImg8bit_trainvaltest.zip` (11 GB) files for this experiment.

6. When the download is finished, we need to reorganize the images so that the
   training script can pick up the images correctly:

   - Put all the image files in the `gtFine/train/*` folders that end with
     `_gtFine_instanceIds.png` into
     the `datasets/cityscapes/train_inst` directory.
   - Put all the image files in the `gtFine/train/*` folders that end with
     `_gtFine_labelIds.png` into the `datasets/cityscapes/train_label`
     directory.
   - Put all the image files in the `leftImg8bit/train/*` folders that end with
     `_leftImg8bit.png` into the `datasets/cityscapes/train_img`
     directory.

7. The test and validation sets can be ignored since we only need the training images. There should be 2,975 images in each of the training folders.
8. Run `scripts/train_512p.sh` to start the training process or simply type the following in the Terminal:

```
$ python train.py --name label2city_512p
```

All the intermediate results (arguments taken, generated images, logging information, and model files) will be saved in the `checkpoints/label2city_512p` folder. You can always check the `checkpoints/label2city_512p/web/index.html` file in your favorite browser or directly check out the images in the `checkpoints/label2city_512p/web/images` folder to monitor the training process.

Here are the results after 35 epochs of training (about 20 hours):

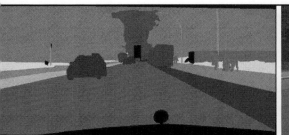

Generated image after 35 epochs of training by pix2pixHD

Here, we can see that the model has already figured out where to put vehicles, trees, buildings, and pedestrians based on the label information from the instance map, although the objects themselves still have much to improve on in terms of appearance. It is interesting to observe that the model is trying to put road lines in the correct positions and that the badge of the car that the images have been captured from has an almost perfect reflection on the front hood (which makes sense since the badge and the hood appear in every image).

If you are willing to wait long enough (approximately 110 hours), the results are pretty impressive:

Generated image by pix2pixHD (images retrieved from https://github.com/NVIDIA/pix2pixHD)

It costs about 8,077 MB GPU memory to train on a 1,024x512 resolution. When AMP is enabled (trained with `--fp16`), the GPU memory consumption starts with 7,379 MB at first and gradually increases to 7,829 MB after a few epochs, which is indeed lower than before. However, the training time is almost half as long than it is without AMP. Therefore, you should go without AMP for now, until its performance is improved in the future.

CycleGAN – image-to-image translation from unpaired collections

You may have noticed that, when training pix2pix, we need to determine a direction (`AtoB` or `BtoA`) that the images are translated to. Does this mean that, if we want to freely translate from image set A to image set B and vice versa, we need to train two models separately? Not with CycleGAN, we say!

CycleGAN was proposed by Jun-Yan Zhu, Taesung Park, and Phillip Isola, et. al. in their paper, *Unpaired Image-to-Image Translation using Cycle-Consistent Adversarial Networks*. It is a bidirectional generative model based on unpaired image collections. The core idea of CycleGAN is built on the assumption of cycle consistency, which means that if we have two generative models, G and F, that translate between two sets of images, X and Y, in which $Y=G(X)$ and $X=F(Y)$, we can naturally assume that $F(G(X))$ should be very similar to X and $G(F(Y))$ should be very similar to Y. This means that we can train two sets of generative models at the same time that can freely translate between two sets of images.

CycleGAN is specifically designed for unpaired image collections, which means that the training samples are not necessarily strictly paired like they were in the previous sections when we looked at pix2pix and pix2pixHD (for example, semantic segmentation maps versus street views from the same perspective, or regular maps versus satellite photos of the same location). This makes CycleGAN more than just an image-to-image translation tool. It unlocks the potential to **transfer style** from any kind of images to your own images, for example, turning apples into oranges, horses into zebras, photos into oil paintings, and vice versa. Here, we'll perform image-to-image translation on landscape photos and Vincent van Gogh's paintings as an example to show you how CycleGAN is designed and trained.

Note that, in this section, the code layout is similar to CGAN in the previous chapter. The full source code is available under the code repository for this chapter. The models are defined in `cyclegan.py`, the training process is defined in `build_gan.py`, and the main entry is located at `main.py`. The source code is based on the implementation provided by `https://github.com/eriklindernoren/PyTorch-GAN`. It is worth mentioning that our implementation trains 1.2x faster and costs 28% less GPU memory than that implementation. Also, in the source code of pix2pix, which can be found in the first section of this chapter, an implementation of CycleGAN was provided. You may choose whichever implementation you like since there isn't much of a difference between the two.

Cycle consistency-based model design

Two pairs of generator and discriminator networks are used, with each being responsible for a translation direction. In order to understand why CycleGAN is designed as such, we need to understand how the cycle consistency is constructed.

In the following diagram, the generator, G_{AB} maps sample A to sample B and its performance is measured by the discriminator, D_B. At the same time, another generator, G_{BA}, is trained to map sample B back to sample A, whose performance is measured by the discriminator, D_A. In this process, the distance between a generated sample, $A = G_{BA}(B) = G_{BA}(G_{AB}(A^*))$, and the corresponding original real sample, A^*, tells us whether a cycle consistency exists in our model, as shown in the dotted box in the following diagram. The distance between $G_{BA}(G_{AB}(A^*))$ and A^* is measured by the **cycle consistency loss**, which takes the form of the L1-norm.

Besides the traditional **adversarial loss** (distance between $D_B(G_{AB}(A^*))$ and 1), the **identity loss** (which means that $G_{BA}(A^*)$ should be very close to A^* itself) is also added to help maintain the color style of the images:

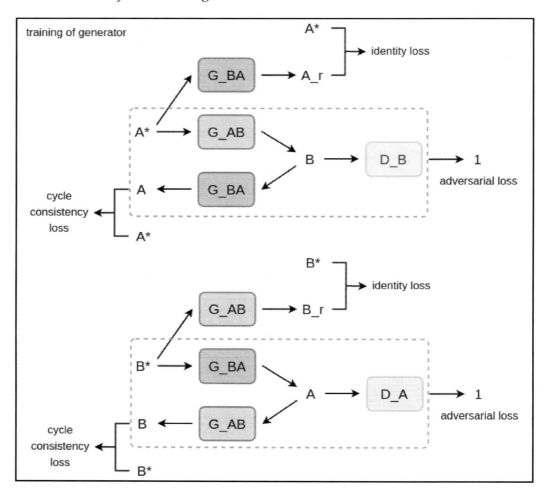

The calculation of loss in CycleGAN. A* and B* denote real samples. Networks denoted by red boxes are updated while training the generators.

The two generator networks, G_{AB} and, are identical. The architecture of the generator network can be seen in the following diagram. The 256x256 input image is downsampled by multiple convolution layers to 64x64, processed by nine successive residual blocks, and finally upsampled by convolutions back to 256x256:

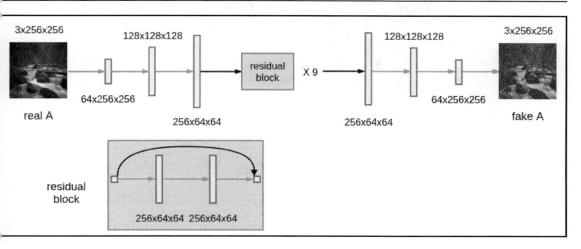

Generator architecture in CycleGAN

We'll start the code with a blank file named `cyclegan.py`, as we mentioned previously. Let's start with the imports:

```
import torch
import torch.nn as nn
import torch.nn.functional as F
import numpy as np
```

Next, we'll create the code for the definition of the residual block, as follows:

```
class ResidualBlock(nn.Module):
    def __init__(self, channels):
        super(ResidualBlock, self).__init__()

        block = [nn.ReflectionPad2d(1),
                 nn.Conv2d(channels, channels, 3),
                 nn.InstanceNorm2d(channels),
                 nn.ReLU(inplace=True),
                 nn.ReflectionPad2d(1),
                 nn.Conv2d(channels, channels, 3),
                 nn.InstanceNorm2d(channels)]
        self.block = nn.Sequential(*block)

    def forward(self, x):
        return x + self.block(x)
```

Now, we can define the generator network, as follows:

```python
class Generator(nn.Module):
    def __init__(self, channels, num_blocks=9):
        super(Generator, self).__init__()
        self.channels = channels

        model = [nn.ReflectionPad2d(3)]
        model += self._create_layer(self.channels, 64, 7, stride=1,
padding=0, transposed=False)
        # downsampling
        model += self._create_layer(64, 128, 3, stride=2, padding=1,
transposed=False)
        model += self._create_layer(128, 256, 3, stride=2, padding=1,
transposed=False)
        # residual blocks
        model += [ResidualBlock(256) for _ in range(num_blocks)]
        # upsampling
        model += self._create_layer(256, 128, 3, stride=2, padding=1,
transposed=True)
        model += self._create_layer(128, 64, 3, stride=2, padding=1,
transposed=True)
        # output
        model += [nn.ReflectionPad2d(3),
                  nn.Conv2d(64, self.channels, 7),
                  nn.Tanh()]

        self.model = nn.Sequential(*model)

    def _create_layer(self, size_in, size_out, kernel_size, stride=2,
padding=1, transposed=False):
        layers = []
        if transposed:
            layers.append(nn.ConvTranspose2d(size_in, size_out,
kernel_size, stride=stride, padding=padding, output_padding=1))
        else:
            layers.append(nn.Conv2d(size_in, size_out, kernel_size,
stride=stride, padding=padding))
        layers.append(nn.InstanceNorm2d(size_out))
        layers.append(nn.ReLU(inplace=True))
        return layers

    def forward(self, x):
        return self.model(x)
```

As you may have noticed, here, we used `torch.nn.InstanceNorm2d` instead of `torch.nn.BatchNorm2d`. The former normalization layer is more suitable for style transfer.

Similarly, two identical discriminator networks are used in CycleGAN and their relationship can be seen in the following diagram:

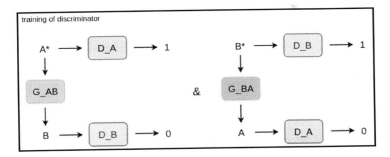

Relationship between two discriminator networks in CycleGAN. Networks denoted by red boxes are updated during training.

The architecture of the discriminator network is almost the same as it is in pix2pix (which is called PatchGAN), except that the input image has a depth channel of 3, instead of 6, and `torch.nn.BatchNorm2d` is replaced with `torch.nn.InstanceNorm2d`.

The code for the definition of the discriminator network is as follows:

```python
class Discriminator(nn.Module):
    def __init__(self, channels):
        super(Discriminator, self).__init__()
        self.channels = channels

        self.model = nn.Sequential(
            *self._create_layer(self.channels, 64, 2, normalize=False),
            *self._create_layer(64, 128, 2),
            *self._create_layer(128, 256, 2),
            *self._create_layer(256, 512, 1),
            nn.Conv2d(512, 1, 4, stride=1, padding=1)
        )

    def _create_layer(self, size_in, size_out, stride, normalize=True):
        layers = [nn.Conv2d(size_in, size_out, 4, stride=stride,
padding=1)]
        if normalize:
            layers.append(nn.InstanceNorm2d(size_out))
        layers.append(nn.LeakyReLU(0.2, inplace=True))
        return layers

    def forward(self, x):
        return self.model(x)
```

Now, let's learn how the model can be trained and evaluated.

Model training and evaluation

Now, we'll create the `build_gan.py` file. As usual, we'll begin with the imports:

```python
import itertools
import os
import time

from datetime import datetime

import numpy as np
import torch
import torchvision.utils as vutils
import utils

from cyclegan import Generator as cycG
from cyclegan import Discriminator as cycD
```

We'll need a function to initialize the weights:

```python
def _weights_init(m):
    classname = m.__class__.__name__
    if classname.find('Conv') != -1:
        torch.nn.init.normal_(m.weight.data, 0.0, 0.02)
    elif classname.find('BatchNorm') != -1:
        torch.nn.init.normal_(m.weight.data, 1.0, 0.02)
        torch.nn.init.constant_(m.bias.data, 0.0)
```

Now, we will create the `Model` class:

```python
class Model(object):
    def __init__(self,
                 name,
                 device,
                 data_loader,
                 test_data_loader,
                 channels,
                 img_size,
                 num_blocks):
        self.name = name
        self.device = device
        self.data_loader = data_loader
        self.test_data_loader = test_data_loader
        self.channels = channels
        self.img_size = img_size
        self.num_blocks = num_blocks
        assert self.name == 'cyclegan'
        self.netG_AB = cycG(self.channels, self.num_blocks)
```

```python
        self.netG_AB.apply(_weights_init)
        self.netG_AB.to(self.device)
        self.netG_BA = cycG(self.channels, self.num_blocks)
        self.netG_BA.apply(_weights_init)
        self.netG_BA.to(self.device)
        self.netD_A = cycD(self.channels)
        self.netD_A.apply(_weights_init)
        self.netD_A.to(self.device)
        self.netD_B = cycD(self.channels)
        self.netD_B.apply(_weights_init)
        self.netD_B.to(self.device)
        self.optim_G = None
        self.optim_D_A = None
        self.optim_D_B = None
        self.loss_adv = torch.nn.MSELoss()
        self.loss_cyc = torch.nn.L1Loss()
        self.loss_iden = torch.nn.L1Loss()

    @property
    def generator_AB(self):
        return self.netG_AB

    @property
    def generator_BA(self):
        return self.netG_BA

    @property
    def discriminator_A(self):
        return self.netD_A

    @property
    def discriminator_B(self):
        return self.netD_B

    def create_optim(self, lr, alpha=0.5, beta=0.999):
        self.optim_G =
torch.optim.Adam(itertools.chain(self.netG_AB.parameters(),
self.netG_BA.parameters()),
                                        lr=lr,
                                        betas=(alpha, beta))
        self.optim_D_A = torch.optim.Adam(self.netD_A.parameters(),
                                          lr=lr,
                                          betas=(alpha, beta))
        self.optim_D_B = torch.optim.Adam(self.netD_B.parameters(),
                                          lr=lr,
                                          betas=(alpha, beta))
```

The training processes for the generator and discriminator networks were shown previously. Here, we will dive into the implementation of `build_gan.train()`.

First, we need to train the generator networks:

```
def train(self,
          epochs,
          log_interval=100,
          out_dir='',
          verbose=True):
    self.netG_AB.train()
    self.netG_BA.train()
    self.netD_A.train()
    self.netD_B.train()
    lambda_cyc = 10
    lambda_iden = 5
    real_label = torch.ones((self.data_loader.batch_size, 1,
self.img_size//2**4, self.img_size//2**4), device=self.device)
    fake_label = torch.zeros((self.data_loader.batch_size, 1,
self.img_size//2**4, self.img_size//2**4), device=self.device)
    image_buffer_A = utils.ImageBuffer()
    image_buffer_B = utils.ImageBuffer()
    total_time = time.time()
    for epoch in range(epochs):
        batch_time = time.time()
        for batch_idx, data in enumerate(self.data_loader):
            real_A = data['trainA'].to(self.device)
            real_B = data['trainB'].to(self.device)

            # Train G
            self.optim_G.zero_grad()

            # adversarial loss
            fake_B = self.netG_AB(real_A)
            _loss_adv_AB = self.loss_adv(self.netD_B(fake_B),
              real_label)
            fake_A = self.netG_BA(real_B)
            _loss_adv_BA = self.loss_adv(self.netD_A(fake_A),
              real_label)
            adv_loss = (_loss_adv_AB + _loss_adv_BA) / 2

            # cycle loss
            recov_A = self.netG_BA(fake_B)
            _loss_cyc_A = self.loss_cyc(recov_A, real_A)
            recov_B = self.netG_AB(fake_A)
            _loss_cyc_B = self.loss_cyc(recov_B, real_B)
            cycle_loss = (_loss_cyc_A + _loss_cyc_B) / 2
```

```
# identity loss
_loss_iden_A = self.loss_iden(self.netG_BA(real_A), real_A)
_loss_iden_B = self.loss_iden(self.netG_AB(real_B), real_B)
iden_loss = (_loss_iden_A + _loss_iden_B) / 2

g_loss = adv_loss + lambda_cyc * cycle_loss +
  lambda_iden * iden_loss
g_loss.backward()
self.optim_G.step()
```

hen, we need to train the discriminator networks:

```
# Train D_A
self.optim_D_A.zero_grad()

_loss_real = self.loss_adv(self.netD_A(real_A), real_label)
fake_A = image_buffer_A.update(fake_A)
_loss_fake = self.loss_adv(self.netD_A(fake_A.detach()),
 fake_label)
d_loss_A = (_loss_real + _loss_fake) / 2

d_loss_A.backward()
self.optim_D_A.step()

# Train D_B
self.optim_D_B.zero_grad()

_loss_real = self.loss_adv(self.netD_B(real_B), real_label)
fake_B = image_buffer_B.update(fake_B)
_loss_fake = self.loss_adv(self.netD_B(fake_B.detach()),
  fake_label)
d_loss_B = (_loss_real + _loss_fake) / 2

d_loss_B.backward()
self.optim_D_B.step()

d_loss = (d_loss_A + d_loss_B) / 2
```

he last variable, d_loss, is simply for logging and has been omitted here. You can refer to
he source code file for this chapter if you want to find out more about logging printing and
nage exporting:

```
if verbose and batch_idx % log_interval == 0 and batch_idx
 > 0:
            print('Epoch {} [{}/{}] loss_D: {:.4f} loss_G: {:.4f}
time: {:.2f}'.format(
            epoch, batch_idx, len(self.data_loader),
            d_loss.mean().item(),
```

```
                        g_loss.mean().item(),
                        time.time() - batch_time))
                with torch.no_grad():
                    imgs = next(iter(self.test_data_loader))
                    _real_A = imgs['testA'].to(self.device)
                    _fake_B = self.netG_AB(_real_A)
                    _real_B = imgs['testB'].to(self.device)
                    _fake_A = self.netG_BA(_real_B)
                    viz_sample = torch.cat(
                        (_real_A, _fake_B, _real_B, _fake_A), 0)
                    vutils.save_image(viz_sample,
                                    os.path.join(
                                        out_dir,
'samples_{}_{}.png'.format(epoch, batch_idx)),
nrow=self.test_data_loader.batch_size,
                                        normalize=True)
                    batch_time = time.time()

        self.save_to(path=out_dir, name=self.name, verbose=False)
        if verbose:
            print('Total train time: {:.2f}'.format(time.time() -
total_time))
    def eval(self,
             batch_size=None):
        self.netG_AB.eval()
        self.netG_BA.eval()
        self.netD_A.eval()
        self.netD_B.eval()
        if batch_size is None:
            batch_size = self.test_data_loader.batch_size

        with torch.no_grad():
            for batch_idx, data in enumerate(self.test_data_loader):
                _real_A = data['testA'].to(self.device)
                _fake_B = self.netG_AB(_real_A)
                _real_B = data['testB'].to(self.device)
                _fake_A = self.netG_BA(_real_B)
                viz_sample = torch.cat((_real_A, _fake_B, _real_B,
_fake_A), 0)
                vutils.save_image(viz_sample,
                                'img_{}.png'.format(batch_idx),
                                nrow=batch_size,
                                normalize=True)

    def save_to(self,
                path='',
                name=None,
                verbose=True):
```

```
        if name is None:
            name = self.name
        if verbose:
            print('\nSaving models to {}_G_AB.pt and such
...'.format(name))
            torch.save(self.netG_AB.state_dict(), os.path.join(
                path, '{}_G_AB.pt'.format(name)))
            torch.save(self.netG_BA.state_dict(), os.path.join(
                path, '{}_G_BA.pt'.format(name)))
            torch.save(self.netD_A.state_dict(), os.path.join(
                path, '{}_D_A.pt'.format(name)))
            torch.save(self.netD_B.state_dict(), os.path.join(
                path, '{}_D_B.pt'.format(name)))

    def load_from(self,
                    path='',
                    name=None,
                    verbose=True):
        if name is None:
            name = self.name
        if verbose:
            print('\nLoading models from {}_G_AB.pt and such
...'.format(name))
            ckpt_G_AB = torch.load(os.path.join(path,
'{}_G_AB.pt'.format(name)))
            if isinstance(ckpt_G_AB, dict) and 'state_dict' in ckpt_G_AB:
                self.netG_AB.load_state_dict(ckpt_G_AB['state_dict'],
strict=True)
            else:
                self.netG_AB.load_state_dict(ckpt_G_AB, strict=True)
            ckpt_G_BA = torch.load(os.path.join(path,
'{}_G_BA.pt'.format(name)))
            if isinstance(ckpt_G_BA, dict) and 'state_dict' in ckpt_G_BA:
                self.netG_BA.load_state_dict(ckpt_G_BA['state_dict'],
strict=True)
            else:
                self.netG_BA.load_state_dict(ckpt_G_BA, strict=True)
            ckpt_D_A = torch.load(os.path.join(path, '{}_D_A.pt'.format(name)))
            if isinstance(ckpt_D_A, dict) and 'state_dict' in ckpt_D_A:
                self.netD_A.load_state_dict(ckpt_D_A['state_dict'],
strict=True)
            else:
                self.netD_A.load_state_dict(ckpt_D_A, strict=True)
            ckpt_D_B = torch.load(os.path.join(path, '{}_D_B.pt'.format(name)))
            if isinstance(ckpt_D_B, dict) and 'state_dict' in ckpt_D_B:
                self.netD_B.load_state_dict(ckpt_D_B['state_dict'],
strict=True)
            else:                   self.netD_B.load_state_dict(ckpt_D_B, strict=True)
```

Here, as suggested in the paper, we update the discriminators by randomly picking an image from the history of generated images, rather than the fake samples in real-time. The history of generated images is maintained by the `ImageBuffer` class, which is defined as follows. Copy the `utils.py` file from the previous chapter and add the `ImageBuffer` class to it:

```python
class ImageBuffer(object):
    def __init__(self, depth=50):
        self.depth = depth
        self.buffer = []

    def update(self, image):
        if len(self.buffer) == self.depth:
            i = random.randint(0, self.depth-1)
            self.buffer[i] = image
        else:
            self.buffer.append(image)
        if random.uniform(0,1) > 0.5:
            i = random.randint(0, len(self.buffer)-1)
            return self.buffer[i]
        else:
            return image
```

We also need to write a custom dataset reader that picks up unpaired images from separate folders. Place the following content into a new file called `datasets.py`:

```python
import glob
import random
import os

import torchvision

from torch.utils.data import Dataset
from PIL import Image


class ImageDataset(Dataset):
    def __init__(self, root_dir, transform=None, unaligned=False,
mode='train'):
        self.transform = torchvision.transforms.Compose(transform)
        self.unaligned = unaligned
        self.train = (mode == 'train')

        self.files_A = sorted(glob.glob(os.path.join(root_dir, '%sA' %
mode) + '/*.*'))
        self.files_B = sorted(glob.glob(os.path.join(root_dir, '%sB' %
mode) + '/*.*'))
```

```
    def __getitem__(self, index):
        item_A = self.transform(Image.open(self.files_A[index %
len(self.files_A)]))

        if self.unaligned:
            item_B =
self.transform(Image.open(self.files_B[random.randint(0, len(self.files_B)
- 1)]))
        else:
            item_B = self.transform(Image.open(self.files_B[index %
len(self.files_B)]))

        if self.train:
            return {'trainA': item_A, 'trainB': item_B}
        else:
            return {'testA': item_A, 'testB': item_B}

    def __len__(self):
        return max(len(self.files_A), len(self.files_B))
```

The shapes of the paintings and photos are not always square. Therefore, we need to crop 256x256 patches from the original images. We preprocess the data (**data augmentation**) in main.py. Here, we're only showing a part of the code. You can find the rest of the code in the main.py file:

```
def main():
    device = torch.device("cuda:0" if FLAGS.cuda else "cpu")

    if FLAGS.train:
        print('Loading data...\n')
        transform = [transforms.Resize(int(FLAGS.img_size*1.12),
Image.BICUBIC),
                        transforms.RandomCrop((FLAGS.img_size,
FLAGS.img_size)),
                        transforms.RandomHorizontalFlip(),
                        transforms.ToTensor(),
                        transforms.Normalize((0.5,0.5,0.5), (0.5,0.5,0.5))]
        dataloader = DataLoader(ImageDataset(os.path.join(FLAGS.data_dir,
FLAGS.dataset),
                                                transform=transform,
unaligned=True, mode='train'),
                                batch_size=FLAGS.batch_size, shuffle=True,
num_workers=2)
        test_dataloader =
DataLoader(ImageDataset(os.path.join(FLAGS.data_dir, FLAGS.dataset),
                                                transform=transform,
unaligned=True, mode='test'),
                                    batch_size=FLAGS.test_batch_size,
```

```
shuffle=True, num_workers=2)

        print('Creating model...\n')
        model = Model(FLAGS.model, device, dataloader, test_dataloader,
FLAGS.channels, FLAGS.img_size, FLAGS.num_blocks)
        model.create_optim(FLAGS.lr)

        # Train
        model.train(FLAGS.epochs, FLAGS.log_interval, FLAGS.out_dir, True)
```

Don't forget to adjust the argument parsing for CycleGAN. Remember, you should change the `--data_dir` default so that it matches your own setup, so be sure to include the following on the command line:

```
    parser.add_argument('--data_dir', type=str,
default='/media/john/HouseOfData/image_transfer', help='Directory for
dataset.')
    parser.add_argument('--dataset', type=str, default='vangogh2photo',
help='Dataset name.')
    ...
    parser.add_argument('--num_blocks', type=int, default=9, help='number
of residual blocks')
```

Now, it's time to download the datasets and start having fun! Go to `https://people.eecs.berkeley.edu/~taesung_park/CycleGAN/datasets` to manually download the dataset files. Alternatively, you can use the `datasets/download_cyclegan_dataset.sh` script that's located in the source code of pix2pix to download the `vangogh2photo.zip` file, which is about 292 MB in size and contains 400 Van Gogh paintings and 7,038 photos (6,287 in train and 751 in test). When the download is finished, extract the images to a folder (for example, an external hard drive such as `/media/john/HouseOfData/image_transfer`).

Open a Terminal and type the following script to start training:

```
$ python main.py --dataset vangogh2photo
```

takes about 10 hours to train CycleGAN for 20 epochs and costs about 4,031 MB GPU memory on a GTX 1080Ti graphics card. Some of the results can be seen in the following image. Here, we can see that the style transfer capability of CycleGAN is pretty amazing. You can also check out this site to learn about more applications of CycleGAN: `https://junyanz.github.io/CycleGAN`:

Generated images by CycleGAN. Top two rows: Painting to photo; Bottom two rows: Photo to painting.

Summary

We have been getting familiar with image generation for several chapters now. Although it is always challenging and fulfilling to successfully train GANs to generate amazing images, we should recognize that GANs can also be used to fix things and restore images.

In the next chapter, we will explore the generative power of GANs to address some of the challenging problems in image restoration.

Furthering reading

1. Le J. (May 3, 2018) *How to do Semantic Segmentation using Deep learning*. Retrieved from `https://medium.com/nanonets/how-to-do-image-segmentation-using-deep-learning-c673cc5862ef`.

2. Rainy J. (Feb 12, 2018) *Stabilizing neural style-transfer for video*. Retrieved from `https://medium.com/element-ai-research-lab/stabilizing-neural-style-transfer-for-video-62675e203e42`.

3. Isola P, Zhu JY, Zhou T, Efros A. (2017) *Image-to-Image Translation with Conditional Adversarial Networks*. CVPR.

4. Agustinus K. (Feb 9, 2017) *Why does L2 reconstruction loss yield blurry images?* Retrieved from `https://wiseodd.github.io/techblog/2017/02/09/why-l2-blurry`.

5. Chan T F, Wong C K. (1998) *Total Variation Blind Deconvolution. IEEE Transactions on Image Processing*. 7(3): 370-375.

6. Wang T C, Liu M Y, Zhu J Y, et. al. (2018) *High-Resolution Image Synthesis and Semantic Manipulation with Conditional GANs*. CVPR.

7. Zhu J Y, Park T, Isola P, et. al. (2017) *Unpaired Image-to-Image Translation using Cycle-Consistent Adversarial Networks*. ICCV.

Image Restoration with GANs 7

Have you ever stumbled upon an image (or meme) you really love from the internet that has poor quality and is blurry, and even Google couldn't help you to find a high-resolution version of it? Unless you are one of the few who have spent years learning math and coding, knowing exactly which fractional-order regularization term in your objective equation can be solved by which numerical method, we might as well give GANs a shot!

This chapter will help you to perform image super-resolution with SRGAN to generate high-resolution images from low-resolution ones and use a data prefetcher to speed up data loading and increase your GPU's efficiency during training. You will also learn how to implement your own convolution with several methods, including the direct approach, the FFT-based method, and the im2col method. Later on, we will get to see the disadvantages of vanilla GAN loss functions and how to improve them by using Wasserstein loss (the Wasserstein GAN). By the end of this chapter, you will have learned how to train a GAN model to perform image inpainting and fill in the missing parts of an image.

The following topics will be covered in this chapter:

- Image super-resolution with SRGAN
- Generative image inpainting

Image super-resolution with SRGAN

Image restoration is a vast field. There are three main processes involved in image restoration:

- Image super-resolution: Expanding an image to a higher resolution
- Image deblur: Turning a blurry image into a sharp one
- Image inpainting: Filling in holes or removing watermarks in an image

All of these processes involve estimating pixel information from existing pixels. The term **restoration** of the pixels actually refers to estimating the way they should have looked. Take image super-resolution, for example: to expand the image size by 2, we need to estimate 3 additional pixels to form a 2 x 2 region with the current pixel. Image restoration has been studied by researchers and organizations for decades and many profound mathematical methods have been developed, which kind of discourages non-mathematicians from having fun with it. Now, intriguingly enough, GANs are starting to gain popularity.

In this section, we will introduce another member of the GAN family, SRGAN, to upscale our images to a higher resolution.

SRGAN (Super-Resolution Generative Adversarial Network) was proposed by Christian Ledig, Lucas Theis, Ferenc Huszar, et al. in their paper, *Photo-Realistic Single Image Super-Resolution Using a Generative Adversarial Network*. It is considered the first method to successfully upscale images by four. Its structure is very straightforward. Like many other GANs, it consists of one generator network and one discriminator network. Their architectures are shown in the following sections.

Creating a generator

Let's take a look at the components of the generator network:

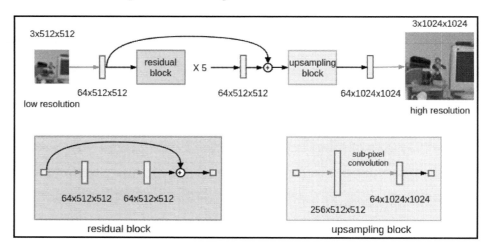

Generator architecture of SRGAN (2X)

n the preceding diagram, we upscale a 512*512 image by 2x (to 1,024*1,024) as an example. he size of the input image is rather arbitrary since the design of each component in the generator network is independent of the size of feature maps. The **upsampling block** is responsible for expanding the image size by two. If we want to upscale by four, we simply need to append another upsampling block to the end of the existing one. Using three upsampling blocks will, of course, expand the image size by eight.

n the generator network, the high-level features are extracted by the five residual blocks, which are combined with the less-processed detail information from a raw image (via the ong skip-connection crossing over the residual blocks). The combined feature map is xpanded to r^2C channels (in which r stands for scale factor and C stands for the number of hannels in the residual blocks) with the size of $W \times H$. The upsampling block transforms his $[B, r^2C, H, W]$ Tensor (B stands for batch size) into $[B, C, rH, rW]$. This is done by **ub-pixel convolution**, which was proposed by Wenzhe Shi, Jose Caballero, Ferenc Huszár, t al. in their paper, *Real-Time Single Image and Video Super-Resolution Using an Efficient Sub-Pixel Convolutional Neural Network*.

An example of sub-pixel convolution is shown in the following. For every r^2 channel in the ow-resolution feature map, each channel is only responsible for one pixel inside the $r \times r$ block in the high-resolution output. A big advantage of this approach is that it only performs $1/r^2$ of the convolution operations compared to the vanilla convolution layer, which makes it easier and faster to train.

n PyTorch, the upscaling step in sub-pixel convolution can be done by he nn.PixelShuffle layer, which is essentially reshaping the input tensor. You can check out the source code in C++ here, pytorch/aten/src/ATen/native/PixelShuffle.cpp, to see ow the reshaping is performed.

How do we check out the source code of a PyTorch operation? It is easy when using VS Code. We can just keep repeatedly double-clicking the class name and press *F12* until we reach the class definition inside the source tree of the torch module under the Python environment. We then look for what other method is called inside this class (normally, we can find it in self.forward), which will lead us to its C++ implementation.

Here are the steps to reach the C++ source code for implementation of `nn.PixelShuffle`:

1. Double-click the name, `PixelShuffle`, and press *F12*. It leads us to this line in `site-packages/torch/nn/modules/__init__.py`:

   ```
   from .pixelshuffle import PixelShuffle
   ```

2. Double-clicking and pressing *F12* on `PixelShuffle` inside this line brings us to the class definition of `PixelShuffle` in `site-packages/torch/nn/modules/pixelshuffle.py`. Inside its `forward` method, we can see that `F.pixel_shuffle` is called.

3. Again, double-click and press *F12* on `pixel_shuffle`. We reach a snippet like this in `site-packages/torch/nn/functional.py`:

   ```
   pixel_shuffle = _add_docstr(torch.pixel_shuffle, r"""
   ...
   """)
   ```

   This is where the C++ part of the code is registered as a Python object in PyTorch. The C++ counterpart of a PyTorch operation is sometimes also called from the `torch._C._nn` module. Hovering the mouse over `torch.pixel_shuffle` will show us `pixel_shuffle(self: Tensor, upscale_factor: int) -> Tensor`, depending on what extensions are used in VS Code. Unfortunately, we cannot find anything useful by pressing *F12* on it.

4. To find the C++ implementation of this `pixel_shuffle` function, we can simply search for the `pixel_shuffle` keyword inside the PyTorch repository on GitHub. If you have cloned the source code of PyTorch locally, you can type in the following command in the Terminal to search for a keyword in the `*.cpp` files:

   ```
   $ grep -r --include \*.cpp pixel_shuffle .
   ```

   Hence, we can find the function definition, `Tensor pixel_shuffle(const Tensor& self, int64_t upscale_factor)`, inside `pytorch/aten/src/ATen/native/PixelShuffle.cpp`.

 If you are interested in how PyTorch was made and how C++ and Python are working together (on CPU and GPU) to deliver such a flexible and easy-to-use interface, you can check out this lone essay written by one of the developers of PyTorch, Edward Z. Yang: `http://blog.ezyang.com/2019/05/pytorch-internals`.

Now, let's take a look at the code for defining the generator network. Our implementation of SRGAN is mostly based on this repository: `https://github.com/leftthomas/SRGAN`. The full working source code for PyTorch 1.3 is also available under the code repository for this chapter. We'll start by creating a new Python file. We'll call it `srgan.py`:

1. Define the residual block (after, of course, importing the necessary modules).

```python
import math
import torch
import torch.nn.functional as F
from torch import nn
import torchvision.models as models


class ResidualBlock(nn.Module):
    def __init__(self, channels):
        super(ResidualBlock, self).__init__()
        self.conv1 = nn.Conv2d(channels, channels, kernel_size=3,
            padding=1)
        self.bn1 = nn.BatchNorm2d(channels)
        self.prelu = nn.PReLU()
        self.conv2 = nn.Conv2d(channels, channels, kernel_size=3,
            padding=1)
        self.bn2 = nn.BatchNorm2d(channels)

    def forward(self, x):
        residual = self.conv1(x)
        residual = self.bn1(residual)
        residual = self.prelu(residual)
        residual = self.conv2(residual)
        residual = self.bn2(residual)
        return x + residual
```

Here, **Parametric ReLU (PReLU)** is used as an activation function. PReLU is very similar to LeakyReLU, except that the slope factor for negative values is a learnable parameter.

2. Define the upsampling block:

```python
class UpsampleBLock(nn.Module):
    def __init__(self, in_channels, up_scale):
        super(UpsampleBLock, self).__init__()
        self.conv = nn.Conv2d(in_channels, in_channels * up_scale
** 
            2, kernel_size=3, padding=1)
        self.pixel_shuffle = nn.PixelShuffle(up_scale)
        self.prelu = nn.PReLU()
```

```
def forward(self, x):
    x = self.conv(x)
    x = self.pixel_shuffle(x)
    x = self.prelu(x)
    return x
```

Here, we use one `nn.Conv2d` layer and one `nn.PixelShuffle` layer to perform the sub-pixel convolution, for reshaping the low-resolution feature map to high-resolution. It is a recommended method by the PyTorch official example: `https://github.com/pytorch/examples/blob/master/super_resolution/model.py`.

3. Define the generator network with the residual and upsampling blocks:

```
class Generator(nn.Module):
    def __init__(self, scale_factor):
        upsample_block_num = int(math.log(scale_factor, 2))

        super(Generator, self).__init__()
        self.block1 = nn.Sequential(
            nn.Conv2d(3, 64, kernel_size=9, padding=4),
            nn.PReLU()
        )
        self.block2 = ResidualBlock(64)
        self.block3 = ResidualBlock(64)
        self.block4 = ResidualBlock(64)
        self.block5 = ResidualBlock(64)
        self.block6 = ResidualBlock(64)
        self.block7 = nn.Sequential(
            nn.Conv2d(64, 64, kernel_size=3, padding=1),
            nn.BatchNorm2d(64)
        )
        block8 = [UpsampleBLock(64, 2) for _ in
            range(upsample_block_num)]
        block8.append(nn.Conv2d(64, 3, kernel_size=9, padding=4))
        self.block8 = nn.Sequential(*block8)

    def forward(self, x):
        block1 = self.block1(x)
        block2 = self.block2(block1)
        block3 = self.block3(block2)
        block4 = self.block4(block3)
        block5 = self.block5(block4)
        block6 = self.block6(block5)
        block7 = self.block7(block6)
        block8 = self.block8(block1 + block7)

        return (torch.tanh(block8) + 1) / 2
```

Don't forget the long skip-connection at the end (`self.block8(block1 + block7)`). Finally, the output of the generator network is scaled to [0,1] from the range of [-1,1] by a tanh activation function. It is because the pixel values of the training images lie within the range of [0,1] and we should make it comfortable for the discriminator network to distinguish the differences between real and fake images when we put their values in the same range.

> We haven't talked about how we should watch out for the trap of value range when training GANs. In the previous chapters, we pretty much always scale the input images to [-1,1] with `transforms.Normalize((0.5,), (0.5,))` during the pre-processing of training data. Since the output of `torch.tanh` is also [-1,1], there's no need to rescale the generated samples before feeding them to the discriminator network or loss function.

Creating the discriminator

The architecture of the discriminator network is shown in the following:

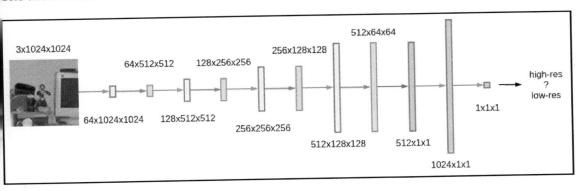

Discriminator architecture of SRGAN

The discriminator of SRGAN takes a VGG-like structure that gradually decreases the sizes of feature maps and expands the depth channel, in the hope that each layer contains a similar amount of information. Unlike in the vanilla VGG networks, the discriminator uses a pooling layer to transform the last VGG's feature map to 1 x 1. The final output of the discriminator network is a single value, which indicates whether the input image is high-resolution or low-resolution.

Here, we give the definition code of the discriminator network of SRGAN:

```python
class Discriminator(nn.Module):
    def __init__(self):
        super(Discriminator, self).__init__()
        self.net = nn.Sequential(
            nn.Conv2d(3, 64, kernel_size=3, padding=1),
            nn.LeakyReLU(0.2),

            nn.Conv2d(64, 64, kernel_size=3, stride=2, padding=1),
            nn.BatchNorm2d(64),
            nn.LeakyReLU(0.2),

            nn.Conv2d(64, 128, kernel_size=3, padding=1),
            nn.BatchNorm2d(128),
            nn.LeakyReLU(0.2),

            nn.Conv2d(128, 128, kernel_size=3, stride=2, padding=1),
            nn.BatchNorm2d(128),
            nn.LeakyReLU(0.2),

            nn.Conv2d(128, 256, kernel_size=3, padding=1),
            nn.BatchNorm2d(256),
            nn.LeakyReLU(0.2),

            nn.Conv2d(256, 256, kernel_size=3, stride=2, padding=1),
            nn.BatchNorm2d(256),
            nn.LeakyReLU(0.2),

            nn.Conv2d(256, 512, kernel_size=3, padding=1),
            nn.BatchNorm2d(512),
            nn.LeakyReLU(0.2),

            nn.Conv2d(512, 512, kernel_size=3, stride=2, padding=1),
            nn.BatchNorm2d(512),
            nn.LeakyReLU(0.2),

            nn.AdaptiveAvgPool2d(1),
            nn.Conv2d(512, 1024, kernel_size=1),
            nn.LeakyReLU(0.2),
            nn.Conv2d(1024, 1, kernel_size=1)
        )

    def forward(self, x):
        batch_size = x.size(0)
        return torch.sigmoid(self.net(x).view(batch_size))
```

Defining training loss

The loss of SRGAN consists of 4 parts. Here, we let z denote the low-resolution (**LR**) image, $= G(z)$ denote the super-resolution (**SR**) image given by the generator, and y denote the real high-resolution (**HR**) image:

- Adversarial loss l_{adv}, as similar to previous GAN models
- Pixel-wise content loss l_{pixel}, which is the MSE loss between the SR and HR images
- VGG loss l_{vgg}, which is the MSE loss between the last feature maps of a pre-trained VGG network from the SR and HR images
- Regularization loss l_{reg}, which is the sum of average L2-norm of pixel gradients in horizontal and vertical directions

The final training loss is as follows:

$$l_{\text{pixel}} + 10^{-3} \cdot l_{\text{adv}} + 6 \cdot 10^{-3} \cdot l_{\text{vgg}} + 2 \cdot 10^{-8} \cdot l_{\text{reg}}$$

It is called **perceptual loss**, which means that it takes both pixel-wise similarities and high-level features into consideration when judging the quality of the SR images.

Note that the L2-norm regularization term in the perceptual loss will actually make images blurry since it adds strong restraints to the pixel gradients. If you feel puzzled by the assertion, imagine a normal distribution in your head, in which the x axis represents the pixel gradient and the y axis tells us how likely a pixel gradient value would appear in the image. In a normal distribution, $\mathcal{N}(0, 1)$, most of the elements are very close to the y axis, which means that most of the pixels have very small gradients. It indicates that the changes between the neighboring pixels are mostly smooth. Therefore, we don't want the regularization term to dominate the final loss. In fact, the regularization term is deleted from the updated version of the SRGAN paper. You can safely get rid of it as well.

Here is the definition code of the perceptual `loss` function:

```
class GeneratorLoss(nn.Module):
    def __init__(self):
        super(GeneratorLoss, self).__init__()
        vgg = models.vgg16(pretrained=True)
        loss_network = nn.Sequential(*list(vgg.features)[:31]).eval()
        for param in loss_network.parameters():
            param.requires_grad = False
        self.loss_network = loss_network
        self.mse_loss = nn.MSELoss()
```

```
        self.l2_loss = L2Loss()

    def forward(self, out_labels, out_images, target_images):
        # adversarial Loss
        adversarial_loss = torch.mean(1 - out_labels)
        # vgg Loss
        vgg_loss = self.mse_loss(self.loss_network(out_images),
            self.loss_network(target_images))
        # pixel-wise Loss
        pixel_loss = self.mse_loss(out_images, target_images)
        # regularization Loss
        reg_loss = self.l2_loss(out_images)
        return pixel_loss + 0.001 * adversarial_loss + 0.006 * vgg_loss
        + 2e-8 * reg_loss
```

And the regularization term is calculated as follows:

```
class L2Loss(nn.Module):
    def __init__(self, l2_loss_weight=1):
        super(L2Loss, self).__init__()
        self.l2_loss_weight = l2_loss_weight

    def forward(self, x):
        batch_size = x.size()[0]
        h_x = x.size()[2]
        w_x = x.size()[3]
        count_h = self.tensor_size(x[:, :, 1:, :])
        count_w = self.tensor_size(x[:, :, :, 1:])
        h_l2 = torch.pow((x[:, :, 1:, :] - x[:, :, :h_x - 1, :]), 2).sum()
        w_l2 = torch.pow((x[:, :, :, 1:] - x[:, :, :, :w_x - 1]), 2).sum()
        return self.l2_loss_weight * 2 * (h_l2 / count_h + w_l2 / count_w)
        / batch_size

    @staticmethod
    def tensor_size(t):
        return t.size()[1] * t.size()[2] * t.size()[3]
```

Now, we need to modify the existing `train.py` file to support our new functions:

```
# from loss import GeneratorLoss
# from model import Generator, Discriminator
from srgan1 import GeneratorLoss, Discriminator, Generator
```

The training script provided by https://github.com/leftthomas/SRGAN works fine with a few other minor fixes by replacing every .data[0] instance with .item().

Training SRGAN to generate high-resolution images

Of course, we need to have some data to work with. We simply need to download the training images from the links in the README.md file. You can always use any image collection you like since the training of SRGAN only requires low-resolution images (which can be easily acquired by resizing to smaller scales) besides the original images.

Create a folder named data and place the training images into a folder called DIV2K_train_HR and the valid images into DIV2K_valid_HR. Next, create a folder named epochs to hold the epoch data. Finally, create a folder named training_results.

To train SRGAN, execute the following command in a Terminal:

```
$ pip install tqdm, pandas
$ python train.py
```

The image collection provided by leftthomas is sampled from the VOC2012 dataset and contains 16,700 images. With a batch size of 64, it takes about 6.6 hours to train for 100 epochs on a GTX 1080Ti graphics card. The GPU memory usage is about 6433 MB with a batch size of 88 and 7509 MB when the batch size is 96.

However, during the training of SRGAN, the GPU usage lies below 10% most of the time (observed via nvtop), which indicates that the loading and pre-processing of data take up too much time. This issue can be solved by two different solutions:

- Putting the dataset on an SSD (preferably, via an NVMe interface)
- Using a data prefetcher to preload the data into GPU memory before the next iteration begins

e, we will talk about how to carry out the second solution. The code for a data prefetcher is borrowed from the ImageNet example of NVIDIA's `apex` project: `https://github.com/NVIDIA/apex/blob/master/examples/imagenet/main_amp.py`. Follow these steps:

1. Define the data prefetcher somewhere in your source tree (for example, the `data_utils.py` file in SRGAN):

```
class data_prefetcher():
 def __init__(self, loader):
 self.loader = iter(loader)
 self.stream = torch.cuda.Stream()
 self.preload()

 def preload(self):
 try:
 self.next_input, self.next_target = next(self.loader)
 except StopIteration:
 self.next_input = None
 self.next_target = None
 return
 with torch.cuda.stream(self.stream):
 self.next_input = self.next_input.cuda(non_blocking=True)
 self.next_target = self.next_target.cuda(non_blocking=True)
 self.next_input = self.next_input.float()

 def next(self):
 torch.cuda.current_stream().wait_stream(self.stream)
 input = self.next_input
 target = self.next_target
 self.preload()
 return input, target
```

2. Use the data `prefetcher` to load samples during training:

```
for epoch in range(1, NUM_EPOCHS + 1):
    train_bar = tqdm(train_loader)
    prefetcher = data_prefetcher(train_bar)
    data, target = prefetcher.next()
    ...
    while data is not None:
        // train D
        ...
        // train G
        ...
        data, target = prefetcher.next()
```

Here, the `tqdm` module is for printing the progress bar in the Terminal during training and can be treated as its original iterable object. In the training of SRGAN, the data `prefetcher` makes a huge difference in GPU efficiency, as shown here:

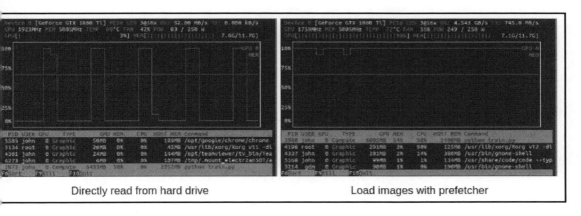

Directly read from hard drive   Load images with prefetcher

GPU usage before and after using prefetcher to load images into GPU memory

The data prefetcher can be adjusted to another form of data, which is also included in the source code under the repository for this chapter.

Some super-resolution results are shown in the following. We can see that SRGAN is doing a good job sharpening the low-resolution images. But we can also notice that it has its limit when dealing with sharp edges between large color blobs (for example, the rocks in the first image and the trees in the third image):

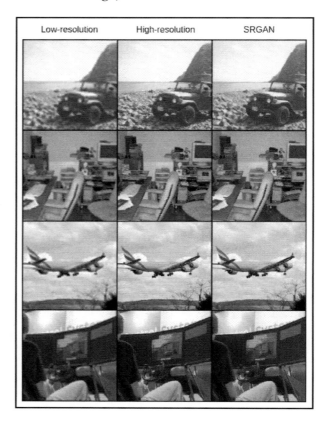

Super-resolution results by SRGAN

Generative image inpainting

We know that GANs, if trained properly, are capable of learning the latent distribution of data and using that information to create new samples. This extraordinary ability of GANs makes them perfect for applications such as image inpainting, which is filling the missing part in images with plausible pixels.

n this section, we will learn how to train a GAN model to perform image inpainting, based n the work of Jiahui Yu, Zhe Lin, Jimei Yang, et. al. in their paper, *Generative Image npainting with Contextual Attention*. Although an updated version of their project has been ublished (`http://jiahuiyu.com/deepfill2`), the source code is not yet open source at the me of writing. Therefore, we should try to implement the model in PyTorch based on the ource code of its previous version for TensorFlow (`https://github.com/JiahuiYu/ enerative_inpainting`).

efore we starting working on addressing image inpainting with GANs, there are a few undamental concepts to understand as they are crucial to comprehend the method.

Efficient convolution – from im2col to nn.Unfold

 you have previously been curious enough to try implementing convolutional neural etworks on your own (either with Python or C/C++), you must know the most painful part f work is the backpropagation of gradients, and the most time-consuming part is the onvolutions (assuming that you are implementing a plain CNN such as LeNet).

here are several ways to perform the convolution in your code (apart from directly using eep learning tools such as PyTorch):

1. Calculate the convolution directly as per definition, which is usually the slowest way.
2. Use **Fast Fourier Transform (FFT)**, which is not ideal for CNNs, since the sizes of kernels are often way too small compared to the images.
3. Treat the convolution as matrix multiplication (in other words, **General Matrix Multiply** or **GeMM**) using **im2col**. This is the most common method used by numerous software and tools and is a lot faster.
4. Use the **Winograd** method, which is faster than GeMM under certain circumstances.

n this section, we will only talk about the first three methods. If you want to learn more bout the Winograd method, feel free to check out this project, `https://github.com/ ndravin/wincnn`, and this paper, *Fast Algorithms for Convolutional Neural Networks*, by ndrew Lavin and Scott Gray. Here, we will give Python code for 2D convolution with ifferent methods.

Before proceeding, make sure you have installed the prerequisites by typing the following command in the Terminal:

```
$ pip install numpy, scipy
```

Now, let's follow these steps:

1. Directly calculate the convolution. Note that all of the following convolution implementations have a stride size of 1 and a padding size of 0, which means that the output size is $image\_size - kernel\_size + 1$.

```python
import numpy as np

def conv2d_direct(x, w):
    w = np.flip(np.flip(w, 0), 1)
    rows = x.shape[0]
    cols = x.shape[1]
    kh = w.shape[0]
    kw = w.shape[1]
    rst = np.zeros((rows-kh+1, cols-kw+1))
    for i in range(rst.shape[0]):
        for j in range(rst.shape[1]):
            tmp = 0.
            for ki in range(kh):
                for kj in range(kw):
                    tmp += x[i+ki][j+kj] * w[ki][kj]
            rst[i][j] = tmp
    return rst
```

As we said before, directly calculating the convolution as per definition is extremely slow. Here is the elapsed time when convolving a 512 x 512 image with a 5 x 5 kernel:

```python
x = np.random.randn(512, 512)
w = np.random.randn(5, 5)

from timeit import default_timer as timer
start = timer()
rst1 = conv2d_direct(x, w)
end = timer()
print('Elapsed time (direct): {}'.format(end - start))
# 3.868343267000455 seconds on an Intel Core i5-4590 CPU
```

We also need to compare its result against a baseline (for example, `scipy.signal.convolve2d`) so that we'll know the computation is correct:

```
from scipy import signal

start = timer()
rst0 = signal.convolve2d(x, w, mode='valid')
end = timer()
print('Elapsed time (reference): {}'.format(end - start))
# 0.017827395000495017

error1 = np.max(np.abs(rst1 - rst0))
print('Error: {}'.format(error1))
# 1.0658141036401503e-14
```

Now we know our calculation is correct, the problem is how to do it faster.

2. Calculate the convolution with FFT:

According to this formula, we can get the result of convolution by performing two Fourier transforms and one inverse Fourier transform:

$$\mathcal{F}\{f * g\} = \mathcal{F}\{f\} \cdot \mathcal{F}\{g\}$$

Since we are dealing with digital images, we need to perform a **Discrete Fourier Transform (DFT)**, which can be calculated extremely fast with a **Fast Fourier Transform (FFT)** method provided by NumPy:

```
def conv2d_fft(x, w):
    # return signal.fftconvolve(x, w, mode='valid')
    size = np.array(x.shape) + np.array(w.shape) - 1
    fsize = 2 ** np.ceil(np.log2(size)).astype(int)
    fslice = tuple([slice(kn-1, int(sz)-kn+1) for sz, kn in
zip(size, w.shape)])
    x_fft = np.fft.fft2(x , fsize)
    w_fft = np.fft.fft2(w , fsize)
    rst = np.fft.ifft2(x_fft * w_fft)
    rst = rst[fslice].real
    return rst
```

Here are the elapsed time and calculation error of an FFT-based convolution:

```
Elapsed time (FFT): 0.17074442000011913
Error: 1.0658141036401503e-14
```

We can see that convolution by FFT is a lot faster than the direct approach and costs almost the same amount of time as `scipy.signal.convolve2d`. Can we do it even faster?

3. Calculate the convolution with im2col.

Let's take a pause and think about the first 2 methods. The direct approach involves 4 `for` loops and a lot of random access to the matrix elements. The FFT approach turns convolution into matrix multiplication but it requires 2 FFTs and 1 inverse FFT. We know low-level computational tools such as BLAS are very good at matrix multiplication. How about we treat the original convolution as matrix multiplication?

Take the convolution between a 3 x 3 image and a 2 x 2 kernel, for example (with a stride size of 1 and padding size of 0):

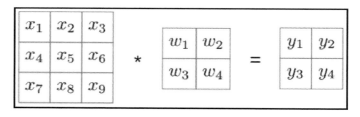

Convolution between image and 2 x 2 kernel

We can stretch the input image into a very long vector (1 x 9), and transform the convolution kernel into a very big matrix (9 x 4) so that our output will have the size of 1 x 4 as expected. Of course, we also need to arrange the elements in the big matrix according to the computational process within the convolution (for example, $y_1 = x_1 w_1 + x_2 w_2 + x_4 w_3 + x_5 w_4$), as shown here:

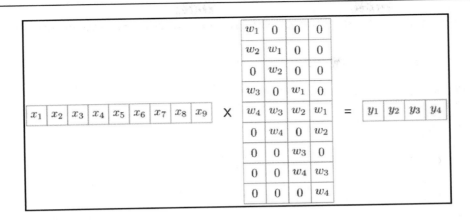

Convolution via sparse matrix multiplication

This way, we need to calculate the matrix multiplication between a very long vector and a large sparse matrix (in which many elements are zeros). Direct multiplication can be very inefficient (both in terms of time and memory). Even though we can speed up sparse matrix multiplication with some numerical algorithms, we won't go into the details of this approach as there is a more efficient way to turn the convolution into matrix multiplication.

Comparing sparse matrix multiplication to a fully-connected layer (nn.Linear) with the same input and output dimensions (also with the same size weight matrix), we can see that the convolution requires much fewer parameters than a fully connected layer (because there are many zeros in the weight matrix and the elements are mostly reusable). This makes CNNs easier to train and more robust to overfitting than MLP, which is also one of the reasons why CNNs have become more popular in recent years.

Considering the size of the kernel is often much smaller than the image, we will try stretching the kernel into a vector and rearranging the elements from the input image to match the kernel vector's dimensions, as shown here:

x_1	x_2	x_4	x_5		w_1		y_1
x_2	x_3	x_5	x_6	$\times$	w_2	$=$	y_2
x_4	x_5	x_7	x_8		w_3		y_3
x_5	x_6	x_8	x_9		w_4		y_4

Convolution via im2col

Now, we can see that we only need to perform dense matrix multiplication with much smaller dimensions. The transformation we perform on the input image is called **im2col**. The result of im2col is easy to comprehend: the elements in one row represent the elements of the input image needed to perform a convolution at a given location (this is known as the **sliding window**) and the ith row corresponds to the ith output element (y_i).

Here is the Python implementation of `im2col`:

```python
def im2col(x, stride=1):
    # https://stackoverflow.com/a/30110497/3829845
    rows = x.shape[0]
    cols = x.shape[1]
    kh = w.shape[0]
    kw = w.shape[1]
    s0, s1 = x.strides
    nrows = rows-kh+1
    ncols = cols-kw+1
    shape = kh, kw, nrows, ncols
    slides = s0, s1, s0, s1
    L = kh*kw

    x_unfold = np.lib.stride_tricks.as_strided(x, shape=shape,
strides=slides)
    return x_unfold.reshape(L, -1)[:,::stride]

def conv2d_gemm(x, w, stride=1):
    w = np.flip(np.flip(w, 0), 1)
    rows = x.shape[0]
    cols = x.shape[1]
    kh = w.shape[0]
    kw = w.shape[1]
    L = kh*kw

    x_unfold = im2col(x)
    y_unfold = np.matmul(x_unfold.transpose(), w.reshape((L, 1)))
    return y_unfold.reshape(rows-kh+1, cols-kw+1)
```

Here are the elapsed time and the calculation error:

```
Elapsed time (im2col): 0.014781345998926554
Error: 1.0658141036401503e-14
```

reating the convolution as matrix multiplication gains the fastest computational speed mong all three methods. It achieves a more than 260x speedup in calculation time ompared to the direct approach. Another advantage of im2col is that it is completely ompatible with CNNs. In CNNs, the convolutions are often performed in channels, which neans that we need to calculate the sum of a group of individual convolutions. For xample, say our input feature map has the size of $[B, C_{in}, H, W]$ and the weight tensor is $[C_{out}, C_{in}, h_k, w_k]$. For each neuron in the C_{out} channels, it is the sum of C_{in} times the onvolution operations between the image $[H, W]$ and kernel $[h_k, w_k]$. With im2col, the onvolution result of a sliding window at a given location is represented by the nultiplication of two vectors (because the convolution itself is the summation of element-ise multiplication). We can apply this pattern by filling all elements inside the same iding window from all C_{in} channels into one long vector so that the output pixel value in ne of the C_{out} channels can be obtained via a single vector multiplication. If you wish to arn more about how channel-wise convolution can be performed in Python, check out nis Stack Overflow post: https://stackoverflow.com/q/30109068/3829845.

urning 4D tensor convolution into 3D tensor multiplication is where nn.Unfold comes in andy. Here is a code snippet showing how to explicitly turning convolution into matrix nultiplication with PyTorch (based on the official document at https://pytorch.org/ ocs/stable/nn.html?highlight=unfold#torch.nn.Unfold):

```
import torch

inp = torch.randn(1, 1, 512, 512)
w = torch.randn(1, 1, 5, 5)
start = timer()
inp_unf = torch.nn.functional.unfold(inp, (5, 5))
out_unf = inp_unf.transpose(1, 2).matmul(w.view(w.size(0),
-1).t()).transpose(1, 2)
out = out_unf.view(1, 1, 508, 508)
# Or using
# out = torch.nn.functional.fold(out_unf, (508, 508), (1, 1))
end = timer()
print('Elapsed time (nn.Unfold): {}'.format(end - start))
error4 = (torch.nn.functional.conv2d(inp, w) - out).abs().max()
print('Error: {}'.format(error4))
```

The output messages are as follows:

```
Elapsed time (nn.Unfold): 0.021252065999760816
Error: 6.67572021484375e-06
```

It is delightful to see that our Python im2col implementation is even faster than PyTorch. We hope this will encourage you to build your own deep learning toolbox!

WGAN – understanding the Wasserstein distance

GANs have been known to be hard to train, especially if you have tried to build one from scratch. (Of course, we hope that, after reading this book, training GANs can be a much easier job for you!) Over the past chapters, we have learned several different model design and training techniques that come from many excellent researchers' experience. In this section, we will talk about how to use a better distance measure to improve the training of GANs, namely, the Wasserstein GAN.

The **Wasserstein GAN (WGAN)** was proposed by Martin Arjovsky, Soumith Chintala, and Léon Bottou in their paper, *Wasserstein GAN*. Martin Arjovsky and Léon Bottou also laid the groundwork in an earlier paper, *Towards Principled Methods for Training Generative Adversarial Networks*. To fully comprehend these papers, you are expected to have fundamental mathematical knowledge in probability theory, measure theory, and functional analysis. We will try our best to keep the mathematical formulae to a minimum and help you to understand the concept of WGAN.

Analyzing the problems with vanilla GAN loss

Let's go over the commonly used loss functions for GANs (which have already appeared in previous chapters):

- $\mathop{\mathbb{E}}\limits_{real}[\log D(x)] + \mathop{\mathbb{E}}\limits_{fake}[\log(1 - D(x))]$, which is the vanilla form of GAN loss

- $\mathop{\mathbb{E}}\limits_{fake}[\log(1 - D(x))]$

- $\mathop{\mathbb{E}}\limits_{fake}[-\log D(x)]$

he experimental results in previous chapters have already shown that these loss functions
ork well in several applications. However, let's dig deep into these functions and see what
ould go wrong when they don't work so well:

tep 1: Problems with the first loss function:

ssume that the generator network is trained and we need to find an optimal discriminator
etwork D. We have the following:

$$P_r(x) \log D(x) + P_f(x) \log(1 - D(x))$$

n this formula, P_r represents the distribution of real data and P_f represents the
listribution of fake (generated) data. x is the real data when calculating $\mathbb{E}_{real}$ and the fake
lata when calculating $\mathbb{E}_{fake}$.

We admit that the notation of x here is a little bit confusing. However, if
we consider that all kinds of data exists in the same data space (for
example, all possible 256 x 256 images with three 8-bit channels), and
some part of the space belongs to the real data while some part belonging
to the generated data. The training of GANs is essentially making the *fake*
part overlap with the *real* part, hopefully, to become the same as the *real*
part.

To find the minimum of the formula, we let its derivatives regarding D to be zero and get
the following:

$$D^*(x) = \frac{P_r(x)}{P_r(x) + P_f(x)}$$

Therefore, the first loss function becomes (when D is optimal) as follows:

$$\mathbb{E}_{real}[\frac{P_r}{\frac{1}{2}(P_r + P_f)}] + \mathbb{E}_{fake}[\frac{P_f}{\frac{1}{2}(P_r + P_f)}] - 2 \log 2$$
$$= 2JS(P_r \| P_f) - 2 \log 2$$

Here, $\text{JS}(P_r \| P_f)$ is the **Jensen–Shannon divergence (JS divergence)**, which is the symmetric version of the **Kullback–Leibler divergence (KL divergence)**:

$$\text{KL}(P_1 \| P_2) = \mathbb{E}_{P_1}[\log \frac{P_1}{P_2}]$$

$$\text{JS}(P_1 \| P_2) = \frac{1}{2}\text{KL}(P_1 \| \frac{P_1 + P_2}{2}) + \frac{1}{2}\text{KL}(P_2 \| \frac{P_1 + P_2}{2})$$

The Kullback–Leibler divergence is usually used to describe the distance between two distributions. It equals the **cross entropy** of P_1 and P_2 minus the **entropy** of P_1, which is why KL divergence is also called **relative entropy**. Keep in mind that KL divergence is not symmetric, because $P_1 = 0$ and $P_2 = 1$ makes $\text{KL}(P_1 \| P_2) = 0$ but $P_1 = 1$ and $P_2 = 0$ makes $\text{KL}(P_1 \| P_2) = \infty$. Therefore, KL divergence is strictly not a distance metric. However, the Jensen–Shannon divergence is symmetric and can be used as a distance metric.

If you have used TensorBoard to visualize the embedding space learned by a neural network, you may have found a useful technique called **t-SNE** that can wonderfully illustrate high-dimensional data in a 2- or 3-dimensional graph (in a much clearer way than PCA). In t-SNE, a revised version of KL divergence is used to map the high-dimension data to low-dimension. You may check out this blog to learn more about t-SNE: https://distill.pub/2016/misread-tsne. Also, this Google Techtalk video can be very helpful to understand KL divergence and t-SNE: https://www.youtube.com/watch?v=RJVL80Gg3lA.

A problem with JS divergence is that when P_r and P_f are apart from each other (with no or little overlapping part), its value remains $\log 2$ no matter how far away P_r and P_f are from each other. It's rather reasonable to assume that P_r and P_f are no way near each other at the beginning of training (since the generator is randomly initialized and P_f could be anywhere in the data space). A nearly constant loss is hardly giving useful information to the derivatives when the discriminator is optimal. Therefore, when using the first form of loss in GANs, a well-trained discriminator will stop the generator from improving itself (**gradient vanishing**).

The gradient vanishing problem in GANs can sometimes be solved by adding annealing noises to the inputs of the discriminator during training. But we will talk about a more principled method later.

Step 2: The problems with the other two loss functions:

Let's take the third loss for example. It can be written as follows:

$$\text{KL}(P_f\|P_r) - \underset{P_f}{\mathbb{E}}[\log(1 - D^*)]$$

$$= \text{KL}(P_f\|P_r) - 2\text{JS}(P_r\|P_f) + 2\log 2 + \underset{P_r}{\mathbb{E}}[\log D^*]$$

In this formula, the last two terms are irrelevant to the generator. The first two terms are, however, aiming for totally opposite objectives (minimizing the KL divergence while maximizing the JS divergence). This causes the training to be very unstable. On the other hand, the employment of KL divergence can lead to **mode collapse**. Failing to generate realistic samples is severely penalized ($\text{KL}(P_f\|P_r) = \infty$ when $P_f > 0$ and $P_r = 0$) but generating only a few kinds of realistic samples is not penalized ($\text{KL}(P_f\|P_r) = 0$ when $P_f = 0$ and $P_r > 0$). This makes the generator more prone to generate samples with less variety.

The advantages of Wasserstein distance

Wasserstein distance (also called **Earth Mover's Distance** or **EMD**) is defined as follows:

$$W(P_r, P_f) = \inf_{\gamma \sim \pi} \underset{(x,y) \sim \gamma}{\mathbb{E}} [\|x - y\|]$$

$$= \frac{1}{K} \sup_{\|f\|_L \leq K} \underset{P_r}{\mathbb{E}}[f] - \underset{P_f}{\mathbb{E}}[f]$$

worry about the preceding equation if you find it hard to understand. It essentially bes the least distance between two variables sampled from all possible joint distributions. In plain words, it is the minimum cost of moving one pile of dirt (in a shape of certain distribution) to form a different pile (another distribution), as shown in the following screenshot:

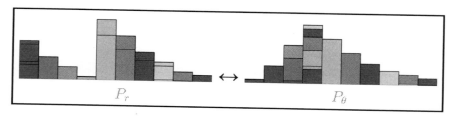

The Wasserstein distance: optimal transportation between two piles (image retrieved from https://vincentherrmann.github.io/blog/wasserstein)

Compared to JS divergence, the Wasserstein distance can properly describe the distance between real data and fake data even when they are far apart from each other. Therefore, the derivatives can be correctly calculated to update the generator network when the discriminator is good.

To find the most suitable function, f, we can simply train a neural network to estimate it (luckily, we are already training a discriminator network). An important condition for the second line of the equation to hold is that all functions, f, are **Lipschitz continuous**:

$$|f(x_1) - f(x_2)| \leq K|x_1 - x_2|, \quad K \geq 0, \quad \text{for any } x_1, x_2$$

Lipschitz continuity is easy to achieve in neural networks by clipping any gradient value that's larger than K to be K (**gradient clipping**), or simply clipping the weight values to a constant value (**weight clipping**).

Remember the simple GAN written in Python in Chapter 1, *Generative Adversarial Networks Fundamentals*? We applied both gradient clipping and weight clipping to ensure stable training. If anyone asks why are you clipping (clamping) the tensors in your GANs, you can give a better answer than *gradient explosion* now.

Finally, the Wasserstein loss is written as follows:

$$\text{G-loss:} \quad - \underset{fake}{\mathbb{E}}\left[D(x)\right]$$

$$\text{D-loss:} \quad \underset{fake}{\mathbb{E}}\left[D(x)\right] - \underset{real}{\mathbb{E}}\left[D(x)\right]$$

However, there are also some issues with gradient clipping when training a very deep neural network. First, if the gradients/weights are clamped to [-c, c] too often, they tend to tick with -c or c by the end of training while only a few parameters have values between the two ends. Second, clamping the gradients to a larger or smaller range could cause "invisible" gradient vanishing or explosion. We call it "invisible" because even though the gradient values are extremely large, they are eventually clamped to [-c, c]. But it will be a complete waste of computational resources. Therefore, Ishaan Gulrajani, Faruk Ahmed, Martin Arjovsky, et. al. proposed to add a penalty term to the discriminator loss, namely, **gradient penalty**, in their paper, *Improved Training of Wasserstein GANs*:

$$\mathop{\mathbb{E}}_{fake}[D(x)] - \mathop{\mathbb{E}}_{real}[D(x)] + \lambda \cdot \mathop{\mathbb{E}}_{\hat{x}}[\|\frac{\partial D(x)}{\partial \hat{x}}\|_2 - 1]^2$$
$$\hat{x} = \alpha \cdot x_{real} + (1 - \alpha) \cdot x_{fake}, \quad \alpha \sim U(0, 1)$$

The penalty gradient is calculated with regards to a random interpolation between a pair of real data and fake data.

In a nutshell, to use Wasserstein loss, you'll need to do the following:

* Get rid of the `Sigmoid` function at the last layer of the discriminator network.
* Don't apply the `log` function to the results when calculating the loss.
* Use the gradient penalty (or simply clip the weights in shallow neural networks).
* Use RMSprop instead of Momentum or Adam to train your networks.

Training GAN for image inpainting

Now, it's finally time to train a new GAN model for image inpainting. You can get the code for the original PyTorch implementation that comes from `https://github.com/DAA233/generative-inpainting-pytorch`. This will be a challenge for you to modify the original code to implement your own. Since you already have the `CelebA` dataset, use it as a training dataset for the experiment in this section.

Model design for image inpainting

The GAN model for image inpainting consists of two generator networks (a coarse generator and a refinement generator) and two discriminator networks (a local discriminator and a global discriminator), as shown here:

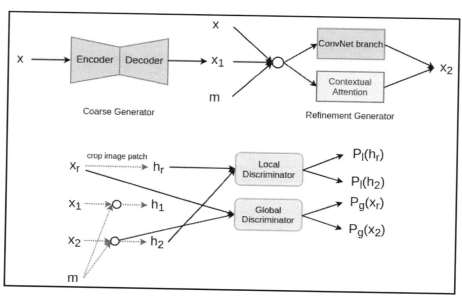

GAN model for image inpainting: Image x represents the input image; x_1 and x_2 represent generated images by coarse and refinement generators, respectively; x, represents the original complete image; and m represents the mask for missing part in the image.

The generator model uses two-stage coarse-to-fine architecture. The coarse generator is a 17-layer encoder-decoder CNN and dilated convolutions are used in the middle to expand the receptive fields. Assume that the size of the input image (x) is 3 x2 56 x 256, then the output (x_1) of the coarse generator is also 3 x 256 x 256.

The refinement generator has two branches. One is a 10-layer CNN and the other is called a **Contextual Attention** branch, which is responsible for finding proper reference location in another part of the image to generate the correct pixels for filling the hole. The initial input image, x; the coarse output, x_1; and the binary mask that marks which pixels are missing in x are fed into the refinement generator together and mapped to a [128, 64, 64] tensor (through 6 convolution layers) before entering the Contextual Attention branch.

the calculation process within the Contextual Attention branch is shown here:

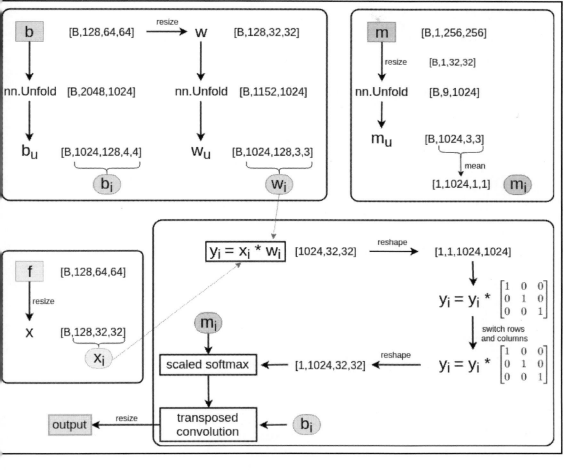

The calculation of Contextual Attention: Image b is the background, f is the foreground, and m is the mask.

We are not going into details about Contextual Attention due to the limited length of content. The important steps are as illustrated in previous diagram. Since we need to find the most relevant parts between the foreground (the pixels to be filled) and the background (the remaining pixels outside the masked hole), a pixel-wise similarity between every pair of image patches from the foreground and background images is calculated. Calculating all possible pairs one-by-one is apparently inefficient. Therefore, nn.Unfold is used to create a sliding-window (with a window size of 3 x 3) versions of the foreground and background images (x_i and w_i). To reduce the GPU memory costs, the images are resized to [128,32,32]. Therefore, there are *32*32=1,024* sliding windows in both images, and the convolution between x_i and w_i will tell us the pixel similarity in each pair of image patches. The location pair with the highest similarity indicates where the attention is focused when reconstructing the foreground patch.

To ensure the robustness against slight shifts of attention, the attention value of each pixel is averaged along horizontal and vertical axes, which is why y_i is convolved with identity matrices twice. The attention scores are calculated via a scaled softmax function:

$$\text{attention score} = \text{softmax}(10 \cdot y_i \cdot m_i) \cdot m_i$$

Finally, a transposed convolution is performed on y_i with the unfold form of the original background as kernel to reconstruct the missing pixels.

Both of the outputs of the CNN branch and CA branch have a size of [128,64,64], which are concatenated into one wide tensor of [256,64,64]. And another 7 convolution layers are used to gradually map the reconstructed feature maps to the [3,256,256] image.

The pixels values in the output images from both coarse and refinement generators are clamped to [-1,1] to suit the discriminator networks.

Two discriminator networks (local discriminator and global discriminator) with similar structures are used to evaluate the quality of generated images. They both have 4 convolution layers and 1 fully-connected layer. The only difference is that the local discriminator is used to evaluate the cropped image patches (in other words, the missing pixels in the original images, with a size of 3 x 128 x 128) and the global discriminator is used to evaluate the whole images (3 x 256 x 256).

Implementation of Wasserstein loss

Here, we let $p_r^{(l)}$ and $p_2^{(l)}$ (outputs of local discriminator) represent the fidelity confidence of the cropped images h_r and h_2, respectively. We let $p_r^{(g)}$ and $p_2^{(g)}$ (outputs of global discriminator) represent the fidelity confidence of whole images x_r and x_2, respectively. Then, the discriminator's Wasserstein loss is defined as follows:

$$\text{w\_loss\_d} = \mathbb{E}[p_r^{(l)} - p_2^{(l)}] + \mathbb{E}[p_r^{(g)} - p_2^{(g)}].$$

The gradient penalty term for the discriminator is given as follows:

$$\text{gp\_d} = \left(\left\| \frac{\partial \text{LD}(\hat{x}^{(l)})}{\partial \hat{x}^{(l)}} \right\|_2 - 1 \right)^2 + \left(\left\| \frac{\partial \text{GD}(\hat{x}^{(g)})}{\partial \hat{x}^{(g)}} \right\|_2 - 1 \right)^2$$

$$\hat{x}^{(l)} = \alpha \cdot h_r + (1 - \alpha) \cdot h_2, \quad \alpha \sim U(0, 1)$$
$$\hat{x}^{(g)} = \beta \cdot x_r + (1 - \beta) \cdot x_2, \quad \beta \sim U(0, 1)$$

The generator's Wasserstein loss is defined as follows:

$$\text{w\_loss\_g} = -\mathbb{E}[p_2^{(l)}] - \mathbb{E}[p_2^{(g)}].$$

The L1 reconstruction loss for the missing pixels is as follows:

$$\text{L1} = 1.2 \cdot \|h_1 - h_r\|_1 + \|h_2 - h_r\|_1.$$

The L1 reconstruction loss for the remaining pixels is as follows (apparently, we don't want to change these pixels):

$$\text{L1\_ae} = 1.2 \cdot \|x_1 \cdot (1 - m) - x_r \cdot (1 - m)\|_1 + \|x_2 \cdot (1 - m) - x_r \cdot (1 - m)\|_1.$$

Finally, the discriminator loss is as follows:

$$\text{w\_loss\_d} + 10 \cdot \text{gp\_d}.$$

The generator loss is as follows:

$$0.001 \cdot \text{w\_loss\_g} + 1.2 \cdot \text{L1} + 1.2 \cdot \text{L1\_ae}$$

With a batch size of 24, the training of the inpainting GAN consumes about 10,097 MB GPU memory and costs about 64 hours of training (180k iterations) before generating some decent results. Here are some of the inpainting results.

Image inpainting results by GAN

Now, we have pretty much learned most of the stuff we need to generate images with GANs.

Summary

We've gotten a tremendous amount of practical and theoretical knowledge in this chapter, from learning about image deblurring and image resolution enhancement, and from FFA algorithms to implementing the Wasserstein loss function.

In the next chapter, we will work on training our GANs to break other models.

Useful reading list and references

- Ledig C, Theis L, Huszar F, et. al. (2017). *Photo-Realistic Single Image Super-Resolution Using a Generative Adversarial Network*. CVPR.
- Shi W, Caballero J, Huszár F, et. al. (2016). *Real-Time Single Image and Video Super-Resolution Using an Efficient Sub-Pixel Convolutional Neural Network*. CVPR.
- Yang E. (May, 2019). *PyTorch internals*. Retrieved from `http://blog.ezyang.com/2019/05/pytorch-internals`.
- Yu J, Lin Z, Yang J, et, al.. (2018). *Generative Image Inpainting with Contextual Attention*. CVPR.
- Lavin A, Gray S. (2016). *Fast Algorithms for Convolutional Neural Networks*. CVPR.
- Warden P. (April 20, 2015). *Why GEMM is at the heart of deep learning*. Retrieved from `https://petewarden.com/2015/04/20/why-gemm-is-at-the-heart-of-deep-learning`.
- Arjovsky M, Bottou L. (2017). *Towards Principled Methods for Training Generative Adversarial Networks*. ICLR.
- Arjovsky M, Chintala S, Bottou L. (2017). *Wasserstein GAN*. ICML.
- Distill. (2016). *How to Use t-SNE Effectively*. Retrieved from `https://distill.pub/2016/misread-tsne`.
- Hui J. (Jun 22, 2018). *GAN—Why it is so hard to train Generative Adversarial Networks!*. Retrieved from `https://medium.com/@jonathan_hui/gan-why-it-is-so-hard-to-train-generative-advisory-networks-819a86b3750b`.
- Weng L. (Aug 20, 2017). *From GAN to WGAN*. Retrieved from `https://lilianweng.github.io/lil-log/2017/08/20/from-GAN-to-WGAN.html`.
- Herrmann V. (Feb 24, 2017). *Wasserstein GAN and the Kantorovich-Rubinstein Duality*. Retrieved from `https://vincentherrmann.github.io/blog/wasserstein`.
- Gulrajani I, Ahmed F, Arjovsky M, et. al. (2017). *Improved Training of Wasserstein GANs*. NIPS.

Training Your GANs to Break Different Models

8

There has been a clear trend that people enjoy using deep learning methods to solve problems in the computer vision field. Has one of your classmates or colleagues ever shown off their latest image classifier to you? Now, with GANs, you may actually get the chance to show them what you can do by generating adversarial examples to break their previous models.

We will be looking into the fundamentals of adversarial examples and how to attack and confuse a CNN model with **FGSM (Fast Gradient Sign Method)**. We will also learn how to train an ensemble classifier with several pre-trained CNN models via transfer learning on Kaggle's Cats vs. Dogs dataset, following which, we will learn how to use an accimage library to speed up your image loading even more and train a GAN model to generate adversarial examples and fool the image classifier.

The following topics will be covered in this chapter:

- Adversarial examples – attacking deep learning models
- Generative adversarial examples

Adversarial examples – attacking deep learning models

It is known that with deep learning methods that have huge numbers of parameters, sometimes more than tens of millions, it becomes more difficult for humans to comprehend what exactly they have learned, except the fact that they perform unexpectedly well in CV and NLP fields. If someone around you feels exceptionally comfortable using deep learning to solve each and every practical problem without a second thought, what we are about to learn in this chapter will help them to realize the potential risks their models are exposed to.

What are adversarial examples and how are they created?

Adversarial examples are a kind of sample (often modified based on real data) that are easily mistakenly classified by a machine learning system (and sometimes look normal to the human eye). Modifications to image data could be a small amount of added noise (https://openai.com/blog/adversarial-example-research) or a small image patch (Tom B. Brown, et al, 2017). Sometimes, printing them on paper and taking pictures of adversarial examples also fools neural networks. It is even possible to 3D-print an object that fools neural networks from almost all perspectives (Anish Athalye, et al, 2018). Although you can create some random samples that look like nothing natural and still cause neural networks to make mistakes, it is far more interesting to study the adversarial examples that look normal to humans but are misclassified by neural networks.

Be assured that we are not going off-topic discussing adversarial examples here. For starters, Ian Goodfellow, known as the father of GANs, has spent a decent amount of time studying adversarial examples. Adversarial examples and GANs might be siblings! Joking aside, GANs are good for generating convincing and realistic samples, as well as generating samples that fool other classifier models. In this chapter, we will first walk through how to construct adversarial examples and attack a small model in PyTorch. Then, we will show you how to use GANs to generate adversarial examples to attack a large model.

Adversarial attacking with PyTorch

There is an excellent toolbox for adversarial attacks, defense, and benchmarks for TensorFlow called CleverHans (https://github.com/tensorflow/cleverhans). Currently, the developers are making plans to support PyTorch (https://github.com/tensorflow/cleverhans/blob/master/tutorials/future/torch/cifar10_tutorial.py). In this section, we will need to implement an adversarial example in PyTorch.

The following code snippet is based on the official tutorial by PyTorch: https://pytorch.org/tutorials/beginner/fgsm_tutorial.html. We will slightly modify the model and the creation of adversarial examples will be performed in batchs. Start with a blank file named AdvAttackGAN.py:

1. Import the modules:

```python
import torch
import torch.nn as nn
import torch.nn.functional as F
import torch.optim as optim
import matplotlib.pyplot as plt

from torchvision import datasets, transforms

print("PyTorch version: {}".format(torch.__version__))
print("CUDA version: {}\n".format(torch.version.cuda))
```

2. Define the device and the perturbation factors:

```python
use_cuda = True
device = torch.device("cuda:0" if use_cuda and
torch.cuda.is_available() else "cpu")

epsilons = [.05, .1, .15, .2, .25, .3]
```

3. Define the CNN model, which is known as the LeNet-5 model:

```python
class Net(nn.Module):
    def __init__(self):
        super(Net, self).__init__()
        self.conv1 = nn.Conv2d(1, 20, kernel_size=5)
        self.conv2 = nn.Conv2d(20, 50, kernel_size=5)
        self.fc1 = nn.Linear(800, 500)
        self.fc2 = nn.Linear(500, 10)

    def forward(self, x):
        x = F.relu(F.max_pool2d(self.conv1(x), 2))
        x = F.relu(F.max_pool2d(self.conv2(x), 2))
```

```
x = F.relu(self.fc1(x.view(-1, 800)))
x = self.fc2(x)
return x
```

4. Define the data loader for both training and testing. Here, we'll use the MNIST dataset:

```
batch_size = 64
train_data = datasets.MNIST('/home/john/Data/mnist', train=True,
download=True,
                            transform=transforms.Compose([
                                transforms.ToTensor(),
                                # transforms.Normalize((0.1307,),
(0.3081,)),
                            ]))
train_loader = torch.utils.data.DataLoader(train_data,
batch_size=batch_size,
                                shuffle=True,
pin_memory=True)

test_data = datasets.MNIST('/home/john/Data/mnist', train=False,
download=True,
                            transform=transforms.Compose([
                                transforms.ToTensor(),
                                # transforms.Normalize((0.1307,),
(0.3081,)),
                            ]))
test_loader = torch.utils.data.DataLoader(test_data,
batch_size=1000,
                                shuffle=False,
pin_memory=True)
```

Note that, to make the defined perturbation factors work for our model, we are not normalizing (whitening) the data by subtracting the mean value and dividing by the standard deviation value.

5. Create the model, optimizer, and loss functions:

```
model = Net().to(device)
optimizer = optim.Adam(model.parameters(), lr=0.001, betas=(0.9,
0.999), weight_decay=3e-5)
criterion = nn.CrossEntropyLoss()
```

6. Define the `train` and `test` functions:

```
def train(model, device, train_loader, optimizer):
    model.train()
    for batch_idx, (data, target) in enumerate(train_loader):
        data, target = data.to(device), target.to(device)
        optimizer.zero_grad()
        output = model(data)
        loss = criterion(output, target)
        loss.backward()
        optimizer.step()
        if batch_idx % 250 == 0:
            print('[{}/{}]\tLoss: {:.6f}'.format(
                batch_idx * batch_size, len(train_data),
loss.item())))

def test(model, device, test_loader):
    model.eval()
    test_loss = 0
    correct = 0
    with torch.no_grad():
        for data, target in test_loader:
            data, target = data.to(device), target.to(device)
            output = model(data)
            test_loss += criterion(output, target).item()
            pred = output.max(1, keepdim=True)[1]
            correct += pred.eq(target.view_as(pred)).sum().item()
    test_loss /= len(test_loader)
    print('\nTest loss: {:.4f}, accuracy: {:.4f}%\n'.format(
        test_loss, 100. * correct / len(test_data)))
```

7. Let's train the model and see what this small model is capable of:

```
model.train()
for epoch in range(5):
 print('Train Epoch: {}'.format(epoch))
 train(model, device, train_loader, optimizer)
 test(model, device, test_loader)
```

The output messages may look like these:

```
PyTorch version: 1.3.1
CUDA version: 10.0.130

Train Epoch: 0
[0/60000] Loss: 2.307504
[16000/60000] Loss: 0.148560
...
Test loss: 0.0229, accuracy: 99.3100%
```

We can see that our small CNN model achieves 99.31% test accuracy after only 5 epochs of training.

8. Now, implement FGSM to create an adversarial example from the read sample and its derivatives:

```
def fgsm_attack(image, epsilon, data_grad):
    sign_data_grad = data_grad.sign()
    perturbed_image = image + epsilon*sign_data_grad
    perturbed_image = torch.clamp(perturbed_image, 0, 1)
    return perturbed_image
```

9. Use `fgsm_attack` to perturbate test images and see what happens:

```
def adv_test(model, device, test_loader, epsilon):
    model.eval()
    correct = 0
    adv_examples = []
    #* grads of params are needed
    for data, target in test_loader:
        data, target = data.to(device), target.to(device)

        # Set requires_grad attribute of tensor. Important for
Attack
        data.requires_grad = True
        output = model(data)
        init_pred = output.max(1, keepdim=True)[1]
        init_pred = init_pred.view_as(target)
        loss = criterion(output, target)
        model.zero_grad()
        loss.backward()

        perturbed_data = fgsm_attack(data, epsilon, data.grad.data)
        output = model(perturbed_data)
        final_pred = output.max(1, keepdim=True)[1]
        # final_pred has shape [1000, 1], target has shape [1000].
Must reshape final_pred
```

```
        final_pred = final_pred.view_as(target)
        correct += final_pred.eq(target).sum().item()
        if len(adv_examples) < 5 and not (final_pred ==
target).all():
            indices = torch.arange(5)
            for i in range(indices.shape[0]):
                adv_ex =
perturbed_data[indices[i]].squeeze().detach().cpu().numpy()
                adv_examples.append((init_pred[indices[i]].item(),
final_pred[indices[i]].item(), adv_ex))
                if (len(adv_examples) >= 5):
                    break
    final_acc = 100. * correct / len(test_data)
    print("Epsilon: {}\tTest Accuracy = {}/{} = {:.4f}".format(
        epsilon, correct, len(test_data), final_acc))
    return final_acc, adv_examples

accuracies = []
examples = []

# Run test for each epsilon
for eps in epsilons:
    acc, ex = adv_test(model, device, test_loader, eps)
    accuracies.append(acc)
    examples.append(ex)
```

Here, we save the first five test images to `adv_examples` to show the predicted labels before and after perturbation. You can always replace the `indices = torch.arange(5)` line with the following line to only show adversarial examples that cause the model to fail:

```
indices = torch.ne(final_pred.ne(target),
init_pred.ne(target)).nonzero()
```

The output messages in the Terminal may look like these:

```
Epsilon: 0.05 Test Accuracy = 9603/10000 = 96.0300
Epsilon: 0.1 Test Accuracy = 8646/10000 = 86.4600
Epsilon: 0.15 Test Accuracy = 6744/10000 = 67.4400
Epsilon: 0.2 Test Accuracy = 4573/10000 = 45.7300
Epsilon: 0.25 Test Accuracy = 2899/10000 = 28.9900
Epsilon: 0.3 Test Accuracy = 1670/10000 = 16.7000
```

We can see that, as `epsilon` increases, more samples are mistakenly classified by the model. The test accuracy of the model drops to 16.7% at worst.

10. Finally, illustrate the perturbed images with `matplotlib`:

```
cnt = 0
plt.figure(figsize=(8,10))
for i in range(len(epsilons)):
    for j in range(len(examples[i])):
        cnt += 1
        plt.subplot(len(epsilons),len(examples[0]),cnt)
        plt.xticks([], [])
        plt.yticks([], [])
        if j == 0:
            plt.ylabel("Eps: {}".format(epsilons[i]), fontsize=14)
        orig,adv,ex = examples[i][j]
        plt.title("{} -> {}".format(orig, adv))
        plt.imshow(ex, cmap="gray")
plt.tight_layout()
plt.show()
```

Here are the first five test images and their predicted labels before and after perturbation with different factor values:

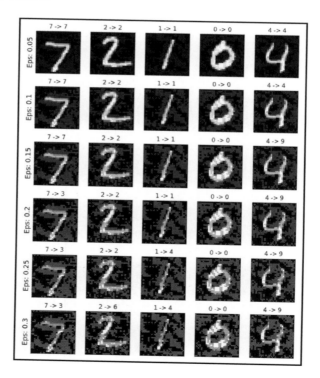

Adversarial examples created from MNIST

Generative adversarial examples

We have been using GANs to generate various types of images in the previous chapters. Now, it's time to try generating adversarial examples with GANs and break some models!

Preparing an ensemble classifier for Kaggle's Cats vs. Dogs

To make our demonstration more similar to practical scenarios, we will train a decent model on Kaggle's Cats vs. Dogs dataset (https://www.kaggle.com/c/dogs-vs-cats), then break the model with adversarial examples generated by GAN. This dataset contains 25,000 training images and 12,500 testing images of either dogs or cats. Here, we will only use the 5,000 training images in our experiment.

For convenience, after downloading the dataset, put images of cats and dogs in separate folders, so that the file structure looks like this:

```
/cats-dogs-kaggle
    /cat
        /cat.0.jpg
        /cat.1.jpg
        ...
    /dog
        /dog.0.jpg
        /dog.1.jpg
        ...
```

The model we are training on this dataset is formed of several pre-trained models provided by PyTorch Hub (https://github.com/pytorch/hub). We will also need to perform transfer training on the pre-trained models to fit our dataset:

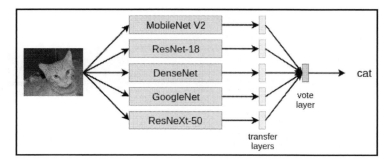

Ensemble model for Kaggle's Cats vs. Dogs

Now, we need to load and preprocess the data, create an ensemble classifier, and train this model. Here are the detailed steps:

1. Create a Python file named `cats_dogs.py` and import the Python modules:

```python
import argparse
import os
import random
import sys

import matplotlib.pyplot as plt
import numpy as np
import torch
import torch.nn as nn
import torch.backends.cudnn as cudnn
import torch.utils.data
import torchvision
import torchvision.datasets as dset
import torchvision.utils as vutils

import utils
from advGAN import AdvGAN_Attack
from data_utils import data_prefetcher, _transforms_catsdogs
from model_ensemble import transfer_init, ModelEnsemble
```

   Here, the custom module files, `advGAN`, `data_utils`, and `model_ensemble`, will be created later.

2. Define the main entry point in `cats_dogs.py`, in which argument values are parsed and the image decoding backend is defined. Here, only some of the lines are shown due to the length. The full source code is available in the `cats_dogs` folder, under the code repository for this chapter:

```python
if __name__ == '__main__':
    from utils import boolean_string
    legal_models = ['resnet18', 'resnet34', 'mobilenet_v2',
'shufflenet_v2_x1_0',
                    'squeezenet1_1', 'densenet121', 'googlenet',
'resnext50_32x4d',
                    'vgg11']
    parser = argparse.ArgumentParser(description='Hands-On GANs -
Chapter 8')
    parser.add_argument('--model', type=str, default='resnet18',
                        help='one of {}'.format(legal_models))
    parser.add_argument('--cuda', type=boolean_string,
                        default=True, help='enable CUDA.')
    parser.add_argument('--train_single', type=boolean_string,
```

```
                                     default=True, help='train single model.')
       parser.add_argument('--train_ensemble', type=boolean_string,
                                     default=True, help='train final model.')
       parser.add_argument('--data_split', type=float, default=0.8,
                                     help='split ratio for train and val data')
       parser.add_argument('--data_dir', type=str,
                                     default='./cats_dogs_kaggle',
   help='Directory for dataset.')
       parser.add_argument('--out_dir', type=str,
                                     default='./output', help='Directory for
   output.')
       parser.add_argument('--epochs', type=int, default=60,
                                     help='number of epochs')
       parser.add_argument('--batch_size', type=int,
                                     default=128, help='size of batches')
       parser.add_argument('--lr', type=float, default=0.01,
   help='learning rate')
       parser.add_argument('--classes', type=int, default=2,
                                     help='number of classes')
       parser.add_argument('--img_size', type=int,
                                     default=224, help='size of images')
       parser.add_argument('--channels', type=int, default=3,
                                     help='number of image channels')
       parser.add_argument('--log_interval', type=int, default=100,
                                     help='interval between logging and image
   sampling')
       parser.add_argument('--seed', type=int, default=1, help='random
   seed')

       FLAGS = parser.parse_args()
       FLAGS.cuda = FLAGS.cuda and torch.cuda.is_available()

       if FLAGS.seed is not None:
           torch.manual_seed(FLAGS.seed)
           if FLAGS.cuda:
               torch.cuda.manual_seed(FLAGS.seed)
           np.random.seed(FLAGS.seed)

       cudnn.benchmark = True

       # if FLAGS.train:
       if FLAGS.train_single or FLAGS.train_ensemble:
           utils.clear_folder(FLAGS.out_dir)

       log_file = os.path.join(FLAGS.out_dir, 'log.txt')
       print("Logging to {}\n".format(log_file))
       sys.stdout = utils.StdOut(log_file)
```

```
print("PyTorch version: {}".format(torch.__version__))
print("CUDA version: {}\n".format(torch.version.cuda))

print(" " * 9 + "Args" + " " * 9 + "| " + "Type" +
      " | " + "Value")
print("-" * 50)
for arg in vars(FLAGS):
    arg_str = str(arg)
    var_str = str(getattr(FLAGS, arg))
    type_str = str(type(getattr(FLAGS, arg)).__name__)
    print(" " + arg_str + " " * (20-len(arg_str)) + "|" +
          " " + type_str + " " * (10-len(type_str)) + "|" +
          " " + var_str)

...

try:
    import accimage
    torchvision.set_image_backend('accimage')
    print('Image loader backend: accimage')
except:
    print('Image loader backend: PIL')

...

main()
```

Here, we use `accimage` as an image decoding backend for `torchvision`. **Accimage** (`https://github.com/pytorch/accimage`) is an image decoding and preprocessing library designed for `torchvision`, which uses Intel IPP (`https://software.intel.com/en-us/intel-ipp`) to improve processing speed.

3. Above the main entry point, define the `main` function, in which we first load and split the training images into a training set and a validation set:

```
FLAGS = None

def main():
    device = torch.device("cuda:0" if FLAGS.cuda else "cpu")

    print('Loading data...\n')
    train_transform, _ = _transforms_catsdogs(FLAGS)
    train_data = dset.ImageFolder(root=FLAGS.data_dir,
transform=train_transform)
    assert train_data

    num_train = len(train_data)
```

```
    indices = list(range(num_train))
    random.shuffle(indices)
    split = int(np.floor(FLAGS.data_split * num_train))

    train_loader = torch.utils.data.DataLoader(
        train_data, batch_size=FLAGS.batch_size,
    sampler=torch.utils.data.sampler.SubsetRandomSampler(indices[:split
    ]),
        num_workers=2)

    valid_loader = torch.utils.data.DataLoader(
        train_data, batch_size=FLAGS.batch_size,
    sampler=torch.utils.data.sampler.SubsetRandomSampler(indices[split:
    num_train]),
        num_workers=2)
```

We split the 25,000 training images into 2 collections, in which 80% of the images are randomly selected to form the training set and the remaining 20% form the validation set. Here, _transforms_catsdogs is defined in data_utils.py:

```
import numpy as np
import torch
import torchvision.transforms as transforms

def _transforms_catsdogs(args):
    train_transform = transforms.Compose([
        transforms.Resize((args.img_size, args.img_size)),
        transforms.RandomHorizontalFlip(),
        transforms.ToTensor(),
    ])

    valid_transform = transforms.Compose([
        transforms.ToTensor()
        ])
    return train_transform, valid_transform
```

Again, we are not whitening the images. However, if you are interested in how to efficiently calculate the mean and standard deviation values of a dataset, the code snippet is provided in the mean_std.py file.

Be comfortable with using multiprocessing.Pool to process your data, which is demonstrated in mean_std.py.

4. Get the pre-trained model files from PyTorch Hub and start transfer learning:

```
if FLAGS.train_single:
    print('Transfer training model
{}...\n'.format(FLAGS.model))
    model = torch.hub.load('pytorch/vision', FLAGS.model,
pretrained=True)
    for param in model.parameters():
        param.requires_grad = False

    model, param_to_train = transfer_init(model, FLAGS.model,
FLAGS.classes)
    model.to(device)

    optimizer = torch.optim.SGD(
        param_to_train, FLAGS.lr,
        momentum=0.9, weight_decay=5e-4)
    scheduler = torch.optim.lr_scheduler.StepLR(optimizer,
step_size=5, gamma=0.1)

    criterion = nn.CrossEntropyLoss()

    # Train
    best_acc = 0.0
    for epoch in range(25):
        model.train()
        scheduler.step()
        print('Epoch {}, lr: {}'.format(epoch,
scheduler.get_lr()[0]))
        prefetcher = data_prefetcher(train_loader)
        data, target = prefetcher.next()
        batch_idx = 0
        while data is not None:
            optimizer.zero_grad()
            output = model(data)
            pred = output.max(1, keepdim=True)[1]
            loss = criterion(output, target)
            loss.backward()
            optimizer.step()
            correct =
pred.eq(target.view_as(pred)).sum().item()
            if batch_idx % FLAGS.log_interval == 0:
                print('[{}/{}]\tloss: {:.4f}\tbatch accuracy:
{:.4f}%'.format(
                    batch_idx * FLAGS.batch_size, num_train,
                    loss.item(), 100 * correct / data.size(0)))
            data, target = prefetcher.next()
```

```
            batch_idx += 1
        # Eval
        . . .
```

The code for evaluation is omitted due to the length. Here, `transfer_init` is defined in `model_ensemble.py` and is responsible for replacing the second to the last layer in each model so that we can train it for any number of classes:

```python
import os

import torch
import torch.nn as nn

def transfer_init(model, model_name, num_class):
    param_to_train = None
    if model_name in ['resnet18', 'resnet34', 'shufflenet_v2_x1_0',
'googlenet', 'resnext50_32x4d']:
        num_features = model.fc.in_features
        model.fc = nn.Linear(num_features, num_class)
        param_to_train = model.fc.parameters()
    elif model_name in ['mobilenet_v2']:
        num_features = model.classifier[1].in_features
        model.classifier[1] = nn.Linear(num_features, num_class)
        param_to_train = model.classifier[1].parameters()
    elif model_name in ['squeezenet1_1']:
        num_features = model.classifier[1].in_channels
        model.classifier[1] = nn.Conv2d(num_features, num_class,
kernel_size=1)
        param_to_train = model.classifier[1].parameters()
    elif model_name in ['densenet121']:
        num_features = model.classifier.in_features
        model.classifier = nn.Linear(num_features, num_class)
        param_to_train = model.classifier.parameters()
    elif model_name in ['vgg11']:
        num_features = model.classifier[6].in_features
        model.classifier[6] = nn.Linear(num_features, num_class)
        param_to_train = model.classifier[6].parameters()
    return model, param_to_train
```

Here's why we can transfer the knowledge learned from one domain (trained on ImageNet) to another domain (Cats vs. Dogs) by simply replacing the last layer (usually a fully connected layer). All of the convolution layers in a CNN are responsible for extracting features from the image and intermediate feature maps. The fully connected layer can be seen as recombining the highest-level features to form the final abstraction of the raw data. It is obvious that good models trained on ImageNet are good at extracting features. Therefore, recombining those features differently is highly likely to be capable for an easier dataset such as Cats vs. Dogs.

Also, `data_prefetcher` is used to speed up the training process. It's defined in `data_utils.py`:

```python
class data_prefetcher():
    def __init__(self, loader):
        self.loader = iter(loader)
        self.stream = torch.cuda.Stream()
        self.preload()

    def preload(self):
        try:
            self.next_input, self.next_target = next(self.loader)
        except StopIteration:
            self.next_input = None
            self.next_target = None
            return
        with torch.cuda.stream(self.stream):
            self.next_input =
self.next_input.cuda(non_blocking=True)
            self.next_target =
self.next_target.cuda(non_blocking=True)
            self.next_input = self.next_input.float()

    def next(self):
        torch.cuda.current_stream().wait_stream(self.stream)
        input = self.next_input
        target = self.next_target
        self.preload()
        return input, target
```

The training of these individual models can be really fast. Here is the GPU memory consumption and validation accuracy after 25 epochs of transfer learning:

Model	Memory	Accuracy
MobileNet V2	1665MB	98.14%
ResNet-18	1185MB	98.24%
DenseNet	1943MB	98.76%
GoogleNet	1447MB	98.06%
ResNeXt-50	1621MB	98.98%

ResNet-34, ShuffleNet V2, SqueezeNet, and VGG-11 are not selected due to either low performance or high memory consumption (over 2 GB).

Saving your model to the hard drive with `torch.save(model.state_dict(), PATH)` will only export the parameter values and you need to explicitly define `model` before loading it in another script. However, `torch.save(model, PATH)` will save everything, including the model definition, to the file.

5. Put together the ensemble classifier in `model_ensemble.py`:

```python
class ModelEnsemble(nn.Module):
    def __init__(self, model_names, num_class, model_path):
        super(ModelEnsemble, self).__init__()
        self.model_names = model_names
        self.num_class = num_class
        models = []
        for m in self.model_names:
            model = torch.load(os.path.join(model_path,
'{}.pth'.format(m)))
            for param in model.parameters():
                param.requires_grad = False
            models.append(model)
        self.models = nn.Sequential(*models)
        self.vote_layer =
nn.Linear(len(self.model_names)*self.num_class, self.num_class)

    def forward(self, input):
        raw_outputs = []
        for m in self.models:
            _out = m(input)
            raw_outputs.append(_out)
        raw_out = torch.cat(raw_outputs, dim=1)
        output = self.vote_layer(raw_out)
        return output
```

Here, the prediction results from all models are combined together to give the final prediction in `vote_layer`.

Alternatively, you can always directly put together the feature maps from the last convolution layers in the pretrained models and train one single fully connected layer to predict the image label.

6. Get back to the `cats_dogs.py` file and start training the ensemble classifier:

```
elif FLAGS.train_ensemble:
print('Loading model...\n')
model_names = ['mobilenet_v2', 'resnet18', 'densenet121',
'googlenet', 'resnext50_32x4d']
model = ModelEnsemble(model_names, FLAGS.classes, FLAGS.model_dir)
model.to(device)

optimizer = torch.optim.SGD(
model.vote_layer.parameters(), FLAGS.lr,
momentum=0.9, weight_decay=5e-4)
 scheduler = torch.optim.lr_scheduler.StepLR(optimizer,
step_size=1, gamma=0.1)

criterion = nn.CrossEntropyLoss()

# Train
print('Training ensemble model...\n')
for epoch in range(2):
model.train()
scheduler.step()
print('Epoch {}, lr: {}'.format(epoch, scheduler.get_lr()[0]))
prefetcher = data_prefetcher(train_loader)
data, target = prefetcher.next()
batch_idx = 0
while data is not None:
optimizer.zero_grad()
output = model(data)
pred = output.max(1, keepdim=True)[1]
loss = criterion(output, target)
loss.backward()
optimizer.step()
correct = pred.eq(target.view_as(pred)).sum().item()
if batch_idx % FLAGS.log_interval == 0:
print('[{}/{}]\tloss: {:.4f}\tbatch accuracy: {:.4f}%'.format(
batch_idx * FLAGS.batch_size, num_train,
loss.item(), 100 * correct / data.size(0)))
```

```
data, target = prefetcher.next()
batch_idx += 1
# Eval
...
```

gain, the code for evaluation is omitted due to the length. Validation accuracy of the
1semble classifier reaches 99.32% after only 2 epochs of training. The training of the
1semble classifier only takes 2775 MB of the GPU memory and the exported model file
ze is no more than 200 MB.

Breaking the classifier with advGAN

he GAN model we'll use for generating adversarial examples is largely borrowed
om https://github.com/mathcbc/advGAN_pytorch. Let's create two files named
dvGAN.py and models.py and put the following code in these files:

1. advGAN.py: Within this file, you will see the following:

```python
import torch.nn as nn
import torch
import numpy as np
import models
import torch.nn.functional as F
import torchvision
import os

def weights_init(m):
    classname = m.__class__.__name__
    if classname.find('Conv') != -1:
        nn.init.normal_(m.weight.data, 0.0, 0.02)
    elif classname.find('BatchNorm') != -1:
        nn.init.normal_(m.weight.data, 1.0, 0.02)
        nn.init.constant_(m.bias.data, 0)

class AdvGAN_Attack:
    def __init__(self,
                 device,
                 model,
                 model_num_labels,
                 image_nc,
                 box_min,
                 box_max,
                 model_path):
        output_nc = image_nc
        self.device = device
```

```
            self.model_num_labels = model_num_labels
            self.model = model
            self.input_nc = image_nc
            self.output_nc = output_nc
            self.box_min = box_min
            self.box_max = box_max
            self.model_path = model_path

            self.gen_input_nc = image_nc
            self.netG = models.Generator(self.gen_input_nc,
        image_nc).to(device)
            self.netDisc = models.Discriminator(image_nc).to(device)

            # initialize all weights
            self.netG.apply(weights_init)
            self.netDisc.apply(weights_init)

            # initialize optimizers
            self.optimizer_G = torch.optim.Adam(self.netG.parameters()
                                                lr=0.001)
            self.optimizer_D =
        torch.optim.Adam(self.netDisc.parameters(),
                                                lr=0.001)

        def train_batch(self, x, labels):
            # optimize D
            for i in range(1):
                perturbation = self.netG(x)

                adv_images = torch.clamp(perturbation, -0.3, 0.3) + x
                adv_images = torch.clamp(adv_images, self.box_min,
                  self.box_max)

                self.optimizer_D.zero_grad()
                pred_real = self.netDisc(x)
                loss_D_real = F.mse_loss(pred_real,
                  torch.ones_like(pred_real, device=self.device))
                loss_D_real.backward()

                pred_fake = self.netDisc(adv_images.detach())
                loss_D_fake = F.mse_loss(pred_fake,
                  torch.zeros_like(pred_fake, device=self.device))
                loss_D_fake.backward()
                loss_D_GAN = loss_D_fake + loss_D_real
                self.optimizer_D.step()

            # optimize G
            for i in range(1):
```

```
        self.optimizer_G.zero_grad()

        pred_fake = self.netDisc(adv_images)
        loss_G_fake = F.mse_loss(pred_fake,
           torch.ones_like(pred_fake, device=self.device))
        loss_G_fake.backward(retain_graph=True)

        C = 0.1
        loss_perturb =
torch.mean(torch.norm(perturbation.view(perturbation.shape[0], -1),
2, dim=1))

        logits_model = self.model(adv_images)
        probs_model = F.softmax(logits_model, dim=1)
        onehot_labels = torch.eye(self.model_num_labels,
device=self.device)[labels]

        real = torch.sum(onehot_labels * probs_model, dim=1)
        other, _ = torch.max((1 - onehot_labels) * probs_model
- onehot_labels * 10000, dim=1)
        zeros = torch.zeros_like(other)
        loss_adv = torch.max(real - other, zeros)
        loss_adv = torch.sum(loss_adv)

        adv_lambda = 10
        pert_lambda = 1
        loss_G = adv_lambda * loss_adv + pert_lambda *
         loss_perturb
        loss_G.backward()
        self.optimizer_G.step()

    return loss_D_GAN.item(), loss_G_fake.item(),
     loss_perturb.item(), loss_adv.item()

def train(self, train_dataloader, epochs):
    ...

def adv_example(self, data):
    perturbation = self.netG(data)
    adv_images = torch.clamp(perturbation, -0.3, 0.3) + data
    adv_images = torch.clamp(adv_images, self.box_min,
       self.box_max)
    return adv_images
```

Part of the code is omitted due to the length. We can see that this GAN model is only responsible for generating the noise part in the adversarial example, which clamped to [-0.3, 0.3] before being added to the original image. During training, MSE loss is used to measure the discriminator loss. L1-loss is used to calculate th adversarial loss for the generator. The L2-norm of the generated perturbation noise is also included in the generator loss. However, the performance of the GAN is highly related to the classifier (`self.model`) we are aiming to break, which means that the GAN model needs to be retrained each time a new classifi is introduced.

The code in `models.py` is omitted here but is available in the code repository for this chapter, since you can basically design the discriminator and generator any way you like. Here, we use a 4-layer CNN as the discriminator network and a 14 layer ResNet-like CNN as the generator network.

Back to `cats_dogs.py`, we need to train the GAN model to learn how to break the ensemble classifier.

2. Redefine the data loader because we need a smaller batch size to fit in the 11 GB GPU memory:

```
print('Training GAN for adversarial attack...\n')
train_loader = torch.utils.data.DataLoader(
    train_data, batch_size=16,

sampler=torch.utils.data.sampler.SubsetRandomSampler
    (indices[:split]),
    num_workers=2)
```

3. Start training the GAN model:

```
model.eval()
advGAN = AdvGAN_Attack(device, model, FLAGS.classes,
                    FLAGS.channels, 0, 1, FLAGS.model_dir)
advGAN.train(train_loader, FLAGS.epochs)
```

4. Attack the ensemble classifier with the GAN:

```
print('Attacking ensemble model...\n')
test_loss = 0
test_correct = 0
adv_examples = []
with torch.no_grad():
    valid_prefetcher = data_prefetcher(valid_loader)
    data, target = valid_prefetcher.next()
    while data is not None:
        output = model(data)
        init_pred = output.max(1, keepdim=True)[1]
        init_pred = init_pred.view_as(target)

        perturbed_data = advGAN.adv_example(data)
        output = model(perturbed_data)
        test_loss += criterion(output, target).item()
        final_pred = output.max(1, keepdim=True)[1]
        final_pred = final_pred.view_as(target)
        test_correct += final_pred.eq(target).sum().item()
        if len(adv_examples) < 64 and not (final_pred ==
target).all():
            indices = torch.ne(final_pred.ne(target),
init_pred.ne(target)).nonzero()
            for i in range(indices.shape[0]):
                adv_ex =
perturbed_data[indices[i]].squeeze().detach().cpu().numpy()
adv_examples.append((init_pred[indices[i]].item(),
final_pred[indices[i]].item(), adv_ex))
                if (len(adv_examples) >= 64):
                    break
        data, target = valid_prefetcher.next()
    test_loss /= len(valid_loader)
    print('Eval loss: {:.4f}, accuracy: {:.4f}'.format(
        test_loss, 100 * test_correct / (1-FLAGS.data_split) /
num_train))
```

It takes about 6 hours to finish 60 epochs of training on the GAN model. The attack result may look like this:

```
Attacking ensemble model...

Eval loss: 2.1465, accuracy: 10.3000
```

We can see that the validation accuracy drops from 99.32% to 10.3% as a result of the adversarial attack by the GAN.

5. Display some of the misclassified images with `matplotlib`:

```
cnt = 0
plt.figure(figsize=(8,10))
for i in range(8):
    for j in range(8):
        cnt += 1
        plt.subplot(8, 8, cnt)
        plt.xticks([], [])
        plt.yticks([], [])
        orig, adv, ex = adv_examples[i*8+j]
        ex = np.transpose(ex, (1, 2, 0))
        plt.title("{} -> {}".format(orig, adv))
        plt.imshow(ex)
plt.tight_layout()
plt.show()
```

Now that everything in the code is finished, it's time to finally actually run our program. We need to do this multiple times, once for each model. Create an empty folder named models in your code folder to hold the saved models.

We'll start the program from the command line:

```
$ python cats_dogs.py --model resnet34 --train_single True
$ python cats_dogs.py --model mobilenet_v2 --train_single True --data_dir
./cats-dogs-kaggle
$ python cats_dogs.py --model shufflenet_v2_x1_0 --train_single True --
data_dir ./cats-dogs-kaggle
$ python cats_dogs.py --model squeezenet1_1 --train_single True --data_dir
./cats-dogs-kaggle
$ python cats_dogs.py --model densenet121 --train_single True --data_dir
./cats-dogs-kaggle
$ python cats_dogs.py --model googlenet --train_single True --data_dir
./cats-dogs-kaggle
$ python cats_dogs.py --model resnext50_32x4d --train_single True --
data_dir ./cats-dogs-kaggle
$ python cats_dogs.py --model vgg11 --train_single True --data_dir ./cats-
dogs-kaggle
```

Once all the models have run, we can finally test our ensemble code:

```
$ python cats_dogs.py --train_single False --train_ensemble True
```

Here are some of the pertubated images generated by the GAN that fooled our ensemble classifier:

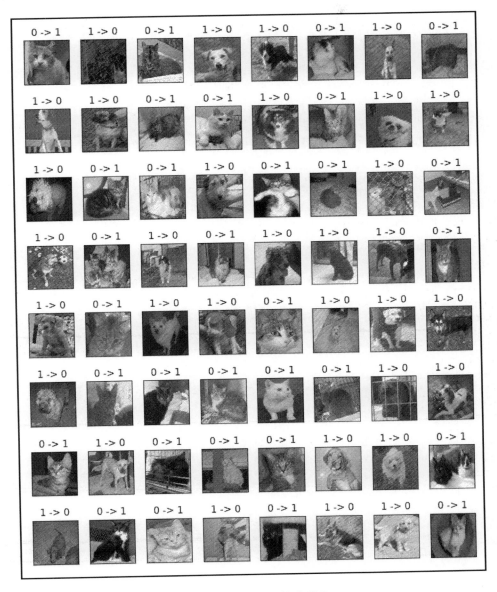

Adversarial examples generated by the GAN

Summary

A lot that has gone on in this chapter. You've learned the basics of Fast Gradient Sign Methods, how to train a classifier with pre-trained models, how to deal with transfer learning, and much more.

In the next chapter, we will show how to combine **NLP** (**Natural Language Processing**) with GANs and generate images from the description text.

References and further reading list

1. Goodfellow I, Papernot N, Huang S, et. al. (Feb 24, 2017). *Attacking machine learning with adversarial examples*. Retrieved from `https://openai.com/blog/adversarial-example-research`.
2. Brown T, Mané D, Roy A, et al (2017). *Adversarial Patch*. NIPS.
3. Athalye A, Engstrom L, Ilyas A. (2018). *Synthesizing Robust Adversarial Examples*. ICML.

9
Image Generation from Description Text

In the previous chapters, we have been mainly dealing with image synthesis and image-to-image translation tasks. Now, it's time for us to move from the CV field to the NLP field and discover the potential of GANs in other applications. Perhaps you have seen some NN models being used for image/video captioning. Wouldn't it be great if we could reverse this process and generate images from description text?

In this chapter, you will learn about the basics of word embeddings and how are they used in the NLP field. You will also learn how to design a text-to-image GAN model so that you can generate images based on one sentence of description text. Finally, you will understand how to stack two or more Conditional GAN models to perform text-to-image synthesis with much higher resolution with StackGAN and StackGAN++.

The following topics will be covered in this chapter:

- Text-to-image synthesis with GANs
- Generating photo-realistic images with StackGAN++

Text-to-image synthesis with GANs

From Chapter 4, *Building Your First GAN with PyTorch,* to Chapter 8, *Training Your GANs to Break Different Models,* we have learned almost every basic application of GANs in computer vision, especially when it comes to image synthesis. You're probably wondering how GANs are used in other fields, such as text or audio generation. In this chapter, we will gradually move from CV to NLP by combining the two fields together and try to generate realistic images from description text. This process is called **text-to-image synthesis** (or text-to-image translation).

We know that almost every GAN model generates synthesized data by establishing a definite mapping from a certain form of input data to the output data. Therefore, in order to generate an image from a corresponding description sentence, we need to understand how to represent sentences with vectors.

Quick introduction to word embedding

It's rather easy to define an approach for transforming the words in a sentence into vectors. We can simply assign different values to all the possible words (for example, let 001 represent *I*, 002 represent *eat*, and 003 represent *apple*) so that the sentence can be uniquely represented by a vector (for example, *I eat apple* would become [001, 002, 003]). This is basically how words are represented in computers. However, languages are much more complicated and flexible than cold digits. Without knowing the meaning of words (for example, a noun or a verb, positive or negative), it is nearly impossible to establish the relationship between the words and understand the meaning of the sentence. Furthermore, it is very hard to find a synonym of a word based on hardcoded values since the distance between the values does not represent the similarity between the corresponding words.

Methods that have been designed to map words, phrases, or sentences to vectors are called **word embeddings**. One of the most successful word embedding techniques is called **word2vec**. If you want to learn more about word2vec, feel free to check out the paper *word2vec Parameter Learning Explained*, `https://arxiv.org/pdf/1411.2738.pdf`, by Xin Rong.

> The term **embedding** means projecting data to a different space so that it's easier to analyze. You may have seen this term being used in some old papers or articles about CNNs, where the output vector of a learned fully connected layer is used to visualize whether the models are trained properly.

Word embeddings are mostly used to solve two types of problems in NLP:

- **CBOW (Continuous Bag-of-Word)** models, which are used to predict a single word based on several other words in the context
- Skip-Gram models, which are the opposite of CBOWs and are used to predict the context words based on the target word

The following diagram provides us with an overview of the **CBOW** and **Skip-Gram** models:

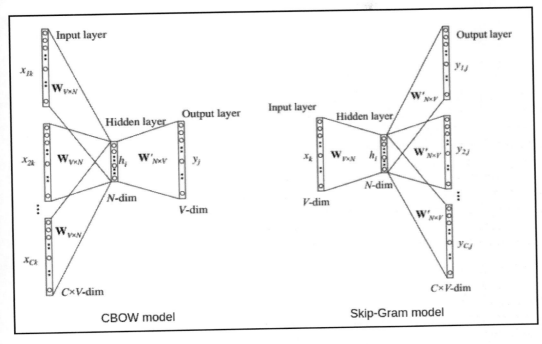

Two types of word embeddings. Image retrieved from Xin Rong, 2014

Another common term in NLP is **language modeling**. Compared to word embeddings, language models predict the possibilities of sentences or, more specifically, the possibilities of words appearing at the next position in a sentence. Since language modeling takes the order of words into consideration, many language models are built upon word embeddings to get good results.

Simply put, a learned word embedding is a vector that represents a sentence that is easier for machine learning algorithms to analyze and understand the meaning of the original sentence. Check out the official tutorial about word embedding to learn how to implement CBOW and Skip-Gram models in PyTorch: https://pytorch.org/tutorials/beginner/nlp/word_embeddings_tutorial.html#sphx-glr-beginner-nlp-word-embeddings-tutorial-py.

Translating text to image with zero-shot transfer learning

In Chapter 8, *Training Your GANs to Break Different Models*, we learned about the basic steps we need to take in order to perform transfer learning in image classification tasks. Under more realistic circumstances, it becomes harder to transfer this learned knowledge to another domain because there can be many new forms of data that the pretrained model hasn't met before, especially when we try to generate images based on description text (or in a reverse process where we generate description text from given images). For example, if the model is only trained on white cats, it won't know what to do when we ask it to generate images of black cats. This is where zero-shot transfer learning comes into play.

Zero-shot learning

Zero-shot learning refers to a machine learning process where we need to predict new samples with labels that haven't been seen before. It is often done by providing additional information to the pretraining process. For example, we can tell the model that the objects known as **white cats** have two properties: a color, that is, white, and the shape of a cat. This makes it easy for the model to know that replacing the white color with black would give us *black cats* when we ask for them.

Similarly, the machine learning process where the new samples are only labeled once per class (or very few samples are labeled per class) is called **one-shot learning**.

In order to establish the zero-shot learning ability between text and image, we will use the word embedding model proposed by Scott Reed, Zeynep Akata, and Bernt Schiele, et al in their paper, *Learning Deep Representations of Fine-Grained Visual Descriptions*. Their model is designed for one purpose: finding the most matching images from a large collection based on a single query sentence.

The following image is an example of image search results from a single query sentence:

Examples of image search results from a single query sentence on the CUB-200-2011 dataset

We won't dive into the implementation details of the word embedding method here and instead use the pretrained `char-CNN-RNN` results provided by the authors.

GAN architecture and training

The design of the GAN model in this section is based on the text-to-image model proposed by Scott Reed, Zeynep Akata, and Xinchen Yan, et al in their paper, *Generative Adversarial Text to Image Synthesis*. Here, we will describe and define the architectures of the generator and discriminator networks and the training process.

The generator network has two inputs, including a latent noise vector, z, and the embedding vector, t, of the description sentence. The embedding vector, t, has a length of 1024, which is mapped by a fully-connected layer to a vector of 128. This vector is concatenated with the noise vector, z, to form a tensor with a size of `[B, 228, 1, 1]` (in which B represents the batch size and is omitted from now on). Five transposed convolution layers (with a kernel size of 4, a stride size of 2, and a padding size of 1) are used to gradually expand the size of feature map (while decreasing the channel width) to `[3, 64, 64]`, which is the generated image after a `Tanh` activation function. Batch normalization layers and `ReLU` activation functions are used in the hidden layers.

Let's create a new file named `gan.py` to define the networks. Here is the code definition of the generator network:

```python
import torch
import torch.nn as nn

class Generator(nn.Module):
    def __init__(self, channels, latent_dim=100, embed_dim=1024,
 embed_out_dim=128):
        super(Generator, self).__init__()
        self.channels = channels
        self.latent_dim = latent_dim
        self.embed_dim = embed_dim
        self.embed_out_dim = embed_out_dim

        self.text_embedding = nn.Sequential(
            nn.Linear(self.embed_dim, self.embed_out_dim),
            nn.BatchNorm1d(self.embed_out_dim),
            nn.LeakyReLU(0.2, inplace=True)
        )

        model = []
        model += self._create_layer(self.latent_dim + self.embed_out_dim,
 512, 4, stride=1, padding=0)
        model += self._create_layer(512, 256, 4, stride=2, padding=1)
        model += self._create_layer(256, 128, 4, stride=2, padding=1)
        model += self._create_layer(128, 64, 4, stride=2, padding=1)
        model += self._create_layer(64, self.channels, 4, stride=2,
 padding=1, output=True)

        self.model = nn.Sequential(*model)

    def _create_layer(self, size_in, size_out, kernel_size=4, stride=2,
 padding=1, output=False):
        layers = [nn.ConvTranspose2d(size_in, size_out, kernel_size,
 stride=stride, padding=padding, bias=False)]
        if output:
            layers.append(nn.Tanh())
        else:
            layers += [nn.BatchNorm2d(size_out),
                nn.ReLU(True)]
        return layers

    def forward(self, noise, text):
        text = self.text_embedding(text)
        text = text.view(text.shape[0], text.shape[1], 1, 1)
        z = torch.cat([text, noise], 1)
        return self.model(z)
```

he discriminator network also has two inputs, which are the generated/real image, x, and
e embedding vector, t. The input image, x, is a tensor with a size of [3, 64, 64] and is
apped to [512, 4, 4] through four convolution layers. The discriminator network has
vo outputs and the [512, 4, 4] feature map is also the second output tensor. The
nbedding vector, t, is mapped to a vector with a length of 128 and expanded to a tensor of
ze [128, 4, 4], which is then concatenated with the image feature map. Finally, the
oncatenated tensor (with a size of [640, 4, 4]) is fed into another convolution layer that
ves us the prediction value.

he code definition of the discriminator network is as follows:

```
class Embedding(nn.Module):
    def __init__(self, size_in, size_out):
        super(Embedding, self).__init__()
        self.text_embedding = nn.Sequential(
            nn.Linear(size_in, size_out),
            nn.BatchNorm1d(size_out),
            nn.LeakyReLU(0.2, inplace=True)
        )

    def forward(self, x, text):
        embed_out = self.text_embedding(text)
        embed_out_resize = embed_out.repeat(4, 4, 1, 1).permute(2, 3, 0, 1)
        out = torch.cat([x, embed_out_resize], 1)
        return out

class Discriminator(nn.Module):
    def __init__(self, channels, embed_dim=1024, embed_out_dim=128):
        super(Discriminator, self).__init__()
        self.channels = channels
        self.embed_dim = embed_dim
        self.embed_out_dim = embed_out_dim

        self.model = nn.Sequential(
            *self._create_layer(self.channels, 64, 4, 2, 1,
              normalize=False),
            *self._create_layer(64, 128, 4, 2, 1),
            *self._create_layer(128, 256, 4, 2, 1),
            *self._create_layer(256, 512, 4, 2, 1)
        )
        self.text_embedding = Embedding(self.embed_dim, self.embed_out_dim)
        self.output = nn.Sequential(
            nn.Conv2d(512 + self.embed_out_dim, 1, 4, 1, 0, bias=False),
            nn.Sigmoid()
        )

    def _create_layer(self, size_in, size_out, kernel_size=4, stride=2,
```

```
    padding=1, normalize=True):
      layers = [nn.Conv2d(size_in, size_out, kernel_size=kernel_size,
        stride=stride, padding=padding)]
      if normalize:
          layers.append(nn.BatchNorm2d(size_out))
      layers.append(nn.LeakyReLU(0.2, inplace=True))
      return layers

  def forward(self, x, text):
      x_out = self.model(x)
      out = self.text_embedding(x_out, text)
      out = self.output(out)
      return out.squeeze(), x_out
```

The training process of both networks can be seen in the following diagram. We can see that training text-to-image GANs is very similar to the vanilla GAN, except that the intermediate outputs (the second output tensors) of the discriminator from the real and generated images are used to calculate the **L1** loss, while the real/generated images are used to calculate the **L2** loss:

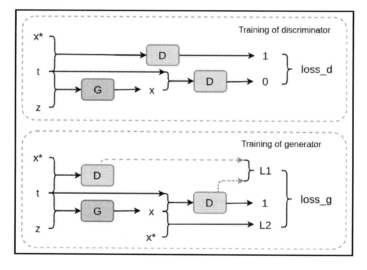

Training process of a text-to-image GAN, in which x^* represents the real image, x represents the generated image, t represents the text embedding vector, and z represents the latent noise vector. The dotted arrows coming out of the discriminator, D, represent the intermediate output tensors

As we introduce the following code, things are going to be presented in a somewhat non-linear fashion. This is to ensure that you understand the processes that are involved at each point.

et's create a new file named `build_gan.py` and create a one-stop train/eval API, just like
e did in some of the previous chapters. We will only show the crucial parts of the training
rocess. You may fill in the blanks yourself as an exercise or refer to the full source code
nder the `text2image` folder in the code repository for this chapter:

```
import os
import time

import torch
import torchvision.utils as vutils

from gan import Generator as netG
from gan import Discriminator as netD

def _weights_init(m):
    # init weights in conv and batchnorm layers
    ...


class Model(object):
    def __init__(self, name, device, data_loader, channels, l1_coef,
l2_coef):
        # parse argument values
        ...
        self.netG = netG(self.channels)
        self.netG.apply(_weights_init)
        self.netG.to(self.device)
        self.netD = netD(self.channels)
        self.netD.apply(_weights_init)
        self.netD.to(self.device)
        self.loss_adv = torch.nn.BCELoss()
        self.loss_l1 = torch.nn.L1Loss()
        self.loss_l2 = torch.nn.MSELoss()
        self.l1_coef = l1_coef
        self.l2_coef = l2_coef
```

Now, let's work on the training process (which is defined in `Model.train()`):

```
    def train(self, epochs, log_interval=100, out_dir='', verbose=True):
        self.netG.train()
        self.netD.train()
        for epoch in range(epochs):
            for batch_idx, data in enumerate(self.data_loader):
                image = data['right_images'].to(self.device)
                embed = data['right_embed'].to(self.device)

                real_label = torch.ones((image.shape[0]),
                 device=self.device)
                fake_label = torch.zeros((image.shape[0]),
```

```
                            device=self.device)

            # Train D
            self.optim_D.zero_grad()

            out_real, _ = self.netD(image, embed)
            loss_d_real = self.loss_adv(out_real, real_label)

            noise = torch.randn((image.shape[0], 100, 1, 1),
             device=self.device)
            image_fake = self.netG(noise, embed)
            out_fake, _ = self.netD(image_fake, embed)
            loss_d_fake = self.loss_adv(out_fake, fake_label)

            d_loss = loss_d_real + loss_d_fake
            d_loss.backward()
            self.optim_D.step()

            # Train G
            self.optim_G.zero_grad()
            noise = torch.randn((image.shape[0], 100, 1, 1),
             device=self.device)
            image_fake = self.netG(noise, embed)
            out_fake, act_fake = self.netD(image_fake, embed)
            _, act_real = self.netD(image, embed)

            l1_loss = self.loss_l1(torch.mean(act_fake, 0),
             torch.mean(act_real, 0).detach())
            g_loss = self.loss_adv(out_fake, real_label) + \
                self.l1_coef * l1_loss + \
                self.l2_coef * self.loss_l2(image_fake, image)
            g_loss.backward()
            self.optim_G.step()
```

Here, we use the Caltech-UCSD Birds-200-2011 (**CUB-200-2011**) dataset, which contains 11,788 annotated bird images. Instead of processing the bird images and training the word embedding vectors by ourselves, we will use the pretrained embeddings by the authors directly (https://github.com/reedscot/icml2016). In the GitHub repository (https://github.com/aelnouby/Text-to-Image-Synthesis), an HDF5 database file containing image files, embedding vectors, and original description text is kindly provided.

't's download the database file (which is around 5.7 GB in size) from the Google Drive
ık that's provided (https://drive.google.com/open?id=1mNhn6MYpBb-
`E86GC1kk0VJsYj-Pn5j`) and put it in a folder (for
ample, /media/john/DataAsgard/text2image/birds). Let's also download the
ıstom dataset class (https://github.com/aelnouby/Text-to-Image-Synthesis/blob/
.ster/txt2image_dataset.py) because it's a little bit tricky to get exported HDF5
ıtabase elements into PyTorch tensors correctly. This also means that we need to install
e h5py library before running the script with `pip install h5py`.

nally, let's create a `main.py` file and fill in the argument parsing code, as we have done
any times already, and call `Model.train()` from it. Again, we omit most of the code in
ıin.py. You can refer to the full source code in this chapter's code repository if you need
ıy help:

```python
import argparse
import os
import sys

import numpy as np
import torch
import torch.backends.cudnn as cudnn
import utils

from torch.utils.data import DataLoader
from build_gan import Model
from txt2image_dataset import Text2ImageDataset

FLAGS = None

def main():
    ...
    device = torch.device("cuda:0" if FLAGS.cuda else "cpu")

    print('Loading data...\n')
    dataloader = DataLoader(Text2ImageDataset(os.path.join(FLAGS.data_dir,
'{}.hdf5'.format(FLAGS.dataset)), split=0),
        batch_size=FLAGS.batch_size, shuffle=True, num_workers=8)

    print('Creating model...\n')
    model = Model(FLAGS.model, device, dataloader, FLAGS.channels,
FLAGS.l1_coef, FLAGS.l2_coef)

    if FLAGS.train:
        model.create_optim(FLAGS.lr)

        print('Training...\n')
```

```
        model.train(FLAGS.epochs, FLAGS.log_interval, FLAGS.out_dir, True)

        model.save_to('')
    else:
        ...
```

It takes about 2 and a half hours to finish 200 epochs of training and costs about 1,753 MB of GPU memory with a batch size of 256. Some of the results by the end of training are as follows:

Images generated by a text-to-image GAN on the CUB-200-2011 dataset

The method that we used in this section was proposed more than 3 years ago, and so the quality of the generated images is not as good as it should be in this day and age. Therefore we will introduce you to StackGAN and StackGAN++ so that you can generate high-resolution results.

Generating photo-realistic images with StackGAN++

The generation of images from description text can be considered as a **Conditional GAN (CGAN)** process in which the embedding vector of the description sentence is used as the additional label information. Luckily for us, we already know how to use CGAN models to generate convincing images. Now, we need to figure out how to generate large images with CGAN.

Do you remember how we used two generators and two discriminators to fill out the missing holes in images (image inpainting) in `Chapter 7`, *Image Restoration with GANs*? It's also possible to stack two CGANs together so that we can get high-quality images. This is exactly what StackGAN does.

High-resolution text-to-image synthesis with StackGAN

StackGAN was proposed by Han Zhang, Tao Xu, and Hongsheng Li, et al in their paper, *StackGAN: Text to Photo-Realistic Image Synthesis with Stacked Generative Adversarial Networks*.

The embedding vector, φ_t, of the description sentence is processed by the Conditioning Augmentation step to create a conditional vector, C. In Conditioning Augmentation, a pair of mean, μ, and standard deviation, σ, vectors are calculated from the embedding vector, to generate the conditional vector, c, based on the Gaussian distribution, $\mathcal{N}(\mu, \sigma^2)$. This process lets us create much more unique conditional vectors from limited text embeddings and ensures that all the conditional variables obey the same Gaussian distribution. At the same time, μ and σ are restrained so that they're not too far away from $\mathcal{N}(0, \mathcal{I})$. This is done by adding a Kullback-Leibler divergence (**KL divergence**) term to the generator's loss functions.

A latent vector, z (which is sampled from $\mathcal{N}(0, \mathcal{I})$), is combined with the conditional vector, , to serve as the input of the **Stage-I Generator**. The first generator network generates a low-resolution image with a size of 64 x 64. The low-resolution image is passed to the **Stage-I Discriminator**, which also takes the embedding vector, φ_t, as input to predict the fidelity of the low-resolution image. The loss functions of the Stage-I Generator and discriminator are as follows:

$$\mathcal{L}_{\mathcal{D}_1} = \underset{real}{\mathbb{E}}[\log D_1(x, \varphi_t)] + \underset{fake}{\mathbb{E}}[\log(1 - D_1(x, \varphi_t))]$$

$$\mathcal{L}_{\mathcal{G}_1} = \underset{fake}{\mathbb{E}}[\log(1 - D_1(x, \varphi_t))] + \lambda \text{KL}[\mathcal{N}(\mu_1, \sigma_1^2) \| \mathcal{N}(0, \mathcal{I})]$$

In the preceding equations, x in $\underset{fake}{\mathbb{E}}$ is the output of the Stage-I Generator $G_1(z, c_1)$, in which is the conditional vector and KL represents the KL divergence.

Then, the low-resolution image is fed into the **Stage-II Generator**. Again, the embedding vector, φ_t, is also passed to the second generator to help create the high-resolution image that's 256 x 256 in size. The quality of the high-resolution image is judged by the **Stage-II Discriminator**, which also takes φ_t as input. The loss functions in the second stage are similar to the first stage, as follows:

$$\mathcal{L}_{\mathcal{D}_2} = \mathop{\mathbb{E}}_{real}[\log D_2(x, \varphi_t)] + \mathop{\mathbb{E}}_{fake}[\log(1 - D_2(x, \varphi_t))]$$

$$\mathcal{L}_{\mathcal{G}_2} = \mathop{\mathbb{E}}_{fake}[\log(1 - D_2(x, \varphi_t))] + \lambda\mathrm{KL}[\mathcal{N}(\mu_2, \sigma_2^2)||\mathcal{N}(0, \mathcal{I})]$$

In the preceding equations , x in $\mathop{\mathbb{E}}_{fake}$ is the output of the Stage-II Generator, $G_2(s_1, c_2)$, in which $s_1 = G_1(z, c_1)$ is the output of the Stage-I Generator and c_2 is the conditional vector.

 Some images that have been generated by StackGAN will be provided in the upcoming sections. If you are interested in trying out StackGAN, the authors of the paper have opensourced a PyTorch version here: `https://github.com/hanzhanggit/StackGAN-Pytorch`.

From StackGAN to StackGAN++

StackGAN++ (also called StackGAN v2) is an improved version of StackGAN and was proposed by Han Zhang, Tao Xu, and Hongsheng Li, et al in their paper, *StackGAN++: Realistic Image Synthesis with Stacked Generative Adversarial Networks*. Compared to StackGAN, there are three main differences in the design of StackGAN++, which are as follows.

- **Multi-scale image synthesis**: It uses a tree-like structure (as shown in the following diagram) in which each branch represents an individual generator network and the size of generated image increases as the tree becomes higher. The quality of the images that are generated by each branch is estimated by a different discriminator network.

- **Employment of unconditional loss**: Besides using label information (calculated from text embedding) to estimate the fidelity of images, additional loss terms, where the images are the only inputs, are added to the loss function of every generator and discriminator (as shown in the following equation).

The loss functions of the discriminator and generator at the i th branch are defined as follows:

$$
\begin{aligned}
\mathcal{L}_{D_i} = {} & - \mathop{\mathbb{E}}_{real}[\log D_i(x, c)] - \mathop{\mathbb{E}}_{fake}[\log(1 - D_i(x, c))] \\
& - \mathop{\mathbb{E}}_{real}[\log D_i(x)] - \mathop{\mathbb{E}}_{fake}[\log(1 - D_i(x))] \\
\mathcal{L}_{G_i} = {} & - \mathop{\mathbb{E}}_{fake}[\log(1 - D_i(x, c))] \\
& - \mathop{\mathbb{E}}_{fake}[\log(1 - D_i(x))]
\end{aligned}
$$

In the preceding equation, the first line in each loss function is called the conditional loss, and the second line is called the unconditional loss. They are calculated by the **JCU Discriminator**, which was illustrated in the previous diagram.

- **Color-consistency restraints**: Since there can be several branches in the tree structure, it is important to ensure that the images that are generated by different branches are similar to each other. Therefore, a color-consistency regularization term is added to the generator's loss function (with a scale factor, of course).

The color-consistency regularization is defined as follows:

$$
\mathcal{L}_{c_i} = \frac{1}{B} \sum_{j=1}^{B} \left(\lambda_1 \| \mu_{s_i^j} - \mu_{s_{i-1}^j} \|_2^2 + \lambda_2 \| \Sigma_{s_i^j} - \Sigma_{s_{i-1}^j} \|_{\mathcal{F}}^2 \right)
$$

In the preceding formula, B represents the batch size, while $\mu_{s_i^j}$ and $\Sigma_{s_i^j}$ represent the mean and covariance of the j th image generated by the i th generator. This makes sure that the images that are generated by neighboring branches have similar color structures.

Training StackGAN++ to generate images with better quality

The authors of StackGAN++ have kindly open sourced the full source code here: `https://github.com/hanzhanggit/StackGAN-v2`. Follow these steps to train StackGAN++ on the CUB-200-2011 dataset. Make sure you have created a **Python 2.7** environment with PyTorch in Anaconda since there will be decoding errors from `pickle` when loading the pretrained text embeddings. You can follow the steps in Chapter 2, *Getting Started with PyTorch 1.3*, to create a new environment:

1. Install the prerequisites by running the following command in your Terminal:

   ```
   $ pip install pyyaml tensorboard-pytorch scipy python-dateutil
   easydict pandas torchfile
   ```

   Make sure you don't have `tensorboard` installed in your Python 2.7 environment since StackGAN++ calls `FileWriter` to write logging information TensorBoard and `FileWriter` has been removed in the latest version of TensorBoard. If you don't want to uninstall TensorBoard, you can downgrade it by running `pip install tensorboard==1.0.0a6`.

2. Download the source code of StackGAN++:

   ```
   $ git clone https://github.com/hanzhanggit/StackGAN-v2 && cd
   StackGAN-v2
   ```

3. Download the CUB-200-2011 dataset from `http://www.vision.caltech.edu/visipedia/CUB-200-2011.html` and put the `CUB_200_2011` folder in the `data/birds` directory, so that the images are located at paths such as `data/birds/CUB_200_2011/images/001.Black_footed_Albatross/Black_Footed_Albatross_0001_796111.jpg`. The compressed file that needs to be downloaded is about 1.1 GB in size.

4. Download the pretrained text embeddings from `https://drive.google.com/open?id=0B3y_msrWZaXLT1BZdVdycDY5TEE` and move the three folders in it to `data/birds`. Make sure that you rename the `text_c10` folder to `text`.

5. Navigate to the code folder and start the training process:

   ```
   $ cd code && python main.py --cfg cfg/birds_3stages.yml --gpu 0
   ```

You only need to make a few changes to the source code of StackGAN++ so that it can run under PyTorch 1.1; for example, you can replace all the `.data[0]` with `.item()` in `trainer.py`. There are also several deprecation warnings that we can fix. You can refer to the source code located under the `stackgan-v2` folder in this book's code repository for this chapter for more information.

6. (Optional) Test your trained model. Specify the model file in the `code/cfg/eval_birds.yml` file like so:

```
NET_G:
'../output/birds_3stages_2019_07_16_23_57_11/Model/netG_220800.pth'
```

Then, run the following script in your Terminal to begin the evaluation process:

```
$ python main.py --cfg cfg/eval_birds.yml --gpu 0
```

The evaluation costs about 7,819 MB of GPU memory and takes 12 minutes to finish. The generated images will be located in the `output/birds_3stages_2019_07_16_23_57_11/Model/iteration220800/singl_samples/valid` folder.

It takes about 48 hours to finish 600 epochs of training on a GTX 1080Ti graphics card and costs about 10,155 MB of GPU memory. Here are some of the images that are generated by the end of the training process:

Image generated by StackGAN++

While this process takes a very long time and a large amount of GPU memory, you can see that the results are very nice.

Summary

In this chapter, we have learned how to generate low-resolution and high-resolution images based on description text.

In the next chapter, we will focus on directly generating sequence data, such as text and audio, with GANs.

Further reading

1. Rong X. (2014). *word2vec Parameter Learning Explained*. arXiv:1411.2738.
2. Reed S, Akata Z, Schiele B, et. al. (2016). *Learning Deep Representations of Fine-Grained Visual Descriptions*. CVPR.
3. Reed S, Akata Z, Yan X, et al (2016). *Generative Adversarial Text to Image Synthesis*. ICML.
4. Zhang H, Xu T, Li H, et al (2017). *StackGAN: Text to Photo-realistic Image Synthesis with Stacked Generative Adversarial Networks*. ICCV.
5. Zhang H, Xu T, Li H, et al (2018). *StackGAN++: Realistic Image Synthesis with Stacked Generative Adversarial Networks*. IEEE Trans. on Pattern Analysis and Machine Intelligence.

Sequence Synthesis with GANs **10**

In this chapter, we will work on GANs that directly generate sequential data, such as text and audio. While doing so, we will go back to the previous image-synthesizing models we've looked at so that you can become familiar with NLP models quickly.

Throughout this chapter, you will get to know the commonly used techniques of the NLP field, such as RNN and LSTM. You will also get to know some of the basic concepts of **reinforcement learning** (**RL**) and how it differs from supervised learning (such as SGD-based CNNs). Later on, we will learn how to build a custom vocabulary from a collection of text so that we can train our own NLP models and learn how to train SeqGAN so that it can generate short English jokes. You will also learn how to use SEGAN to remove background noise and enhance the quality of speech audio.

The following topics will be covered in this chapter:

- Text generation via SeqGAN – teaching GANs how to tell jokes
- Speech quality enhancement with SEGAN

Text generation via SeqGAN – teaching GANs how to tell jokes

In the previous chapter, we learned how to generate high-quality images based on description text with GANs. Now, we will move on and look at sequential data synthesis, such as text and audio, using various GAN models.

When it comes to the generation of text, the biggest difference in terms of image generation is that text data is discrete while image pixel values are more continuous, though digital images and text are both essentially discrete. A pixel typically has 256 values and slight changes in the pixels won't necessarily affect the image's meaning to us. However, a slight change in the sentence – even a single letter (for example, turning *we* into *he*) – may change the whole meaning of the sentence. Also, we tend to have a higher tolerance bar for synthesized images compared to text. For example, if 90% of the pixels in the generated image of a dog are nearly perfect, we may have little trouble recognizing the dog because our brains are smart enough to automatically fill in the missing pixels. However, if you are reading a piece of news in which every one out of 10 words doesn't make any sense, you will definitely find it hard to enjoy reading it. This is why text generation is hard and there's less remarkable progress in text generation than image synthesis.

SeqGAN was one of the first successful attempts of text generation with adversarial learning. It was proposed by Lantao Yu, Weinan Zhang, and Jun Wang, et. al. in their paper, *SeqGAN: Sequence Generative Adversarial Nets with Policy Gradient*. In this section, we will walk you through the design of SeqGAN, how to create your own vocabulary for NLP tasks, and how to train SeqGAN so that it can generate short jokes.

Design of SeqGAN – GAN, LSTM, and RL

Like other GAN models, SeqGAN is built upon the idea of adversarial learning. Some major changes have to be made so that it can accommodate NLP tasks. For example, the generation network is built with LSTM instead of CNNs, similar to some of the other GAN we looked at in the previous chapters. Also, reinforcement learning is used to optimize discrete objectives, unlike the SGD-family methods that were used in previous GAN models.

Here, we will provide a quick introduction to LSTM and RL. However, we won't go too deep into these topics since we want to focus on the adversarial learning part of the model.

A quick introduction to RNN and LSTM

Recurrent neural networks (RNNs) are designed to process sequential data such as text and audio. Their biggest difference to CNNs is that the weights in the hidden layers (that is certain functions) are used repeatedly on multiple inputs and the order of the inputs affect the final results of the functions. The typical design of an RNN can be seen in the following diagram:

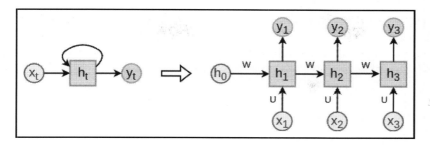

Figure 10.1 Basic computational units of a recurrent neural network

s we can see, the most distinctive characteristic of an RNN unit is that the hidden h_t
ate, , has an outgoing connection pointing to itself. This self-loop is where the name
ecurrent" comes from. Let's say the self-loop is performed three times. The extended
rsion of this computational unit is shown on the right in the preceding diagram. The
mputational process is expressed as follows:

$$h_1 = f(Ux_1 + Wh_0 + b)$$
$$h_2 = f(Ux_2 + Wh_1 + b)$$
$$h_3 = f(Ux_3 + Wh_2 + b)$$

$$y_1 = \text{softmax}(Vh_1 + c)$$
$$y_2 = \text{softmax}(Vh_2 + c)$$
$$y_3 = \text{softmax}(Vh_3 + c)$$

us, after proper training, this RNN unit is capable of handling sequential data with a
aximum length of 3.

NNs are widely used in voice recognition, natural language translation, language
odeling, and image captioning. However, a critical flaw remains in RNN that we need to
ldress with LSTM.

ı RNN model assumes that a strong connection only exists between the neighboring
puts (for example, x_1 and x_2, as shown in the preceding diagram) and that the
nnections between the inputs that are far apart from each other are ignored (for example,
and x_3). This becomes troublesome when we try to translate a long sentence into another
ıguage that has totally different grammatical rules and we need to look through all the
ırts of the sentence to make sense of it.

LSTM (Long Short-Term Memory) was proposed by Sepp Hochreiter and Jürgen Schmidhuber in 1997 to preserve the long-term memory of sequential data and address the gradient explosion and vanishing issues in RNNs. Its computational process is illustrated in the following diagram:

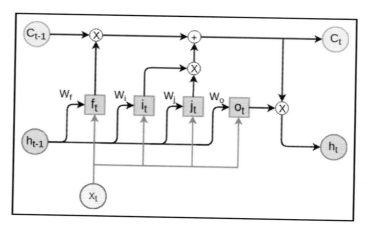

Figure 10.2 Computational process of LSTM

As we can see, an addition term, C_t, is included to help us choose what long-term information should be memorized. The detailed computational process is as follows:

1. h_{t-1} and x_t are passed through the Forget Gate to decide what information should be forgotten:

$$f_t = \text{sigmoid}(W_f \cdot [h_{t-1}, x_t] + b_f)$$

2. The same inputs are also passed through the Input Gate so that we can calculate the updated C_t at the next step:

$$i_t = \text{sigmoid}(W_i \cdot [h_{t-1}, x_t] + b_i)$$
$$j_t = \tanh(W_j \cdot [h_{t-1}, x_t] + b_j)$$

3. The updated C_t and h_t are calculated by the Output Gate:

$$C_t = f_t \cdot C_{t-1} + i_t \cdot j_t$$
$$o_t = \text{sigmoid}(W_o \cdot [h_{t-1}, x_t] + b_o)$$
$$h_t = o_t \cdot \tanh(C_t)$$

hen, the new h_t and C_t are used to calculate the next pair of h_{t+1} and C_{t+1}. Although the tructure of an LSTM cell is much more complicated than the vanilla RNN cell, thanks to he delicate design of the three gates (Forget, Input, and Output), LSTM can be seen in lmost every milestone NLP model in the past few years. If you want to find out more bout LSTM and its variants, check out `https://colah.github.io/posts/2015-08-` `nderstanding-LSTMs` and `https://towardsdatascience.com/illustrated-guide-to-` `stms-and-gru-s-a-step-by-step-explanation-44e9eb85bf21`.

Reinforcement learning versus supervised learning

Reinforcement learning is another optimization method family in machine learning. It is ften used when it's hard to provide standard correct answers for the tasks that the model s trying to solve, especially when the solution involves *free exploration* and the end goal of he task is somewhat *vague* compared to the specific decisions the model needs to make.

for example, if we want to teach a robot to walk, we can use reinforcement learning to let he robot teach itself to walk. We don't need to tell the robot how to move which body part at what time. We only tell it that its final goal is to *take yourself to that location 10 meters in front of you* and let it randomly move its limbs. At some point, a certain combination of movements for the robot's legs will bring the robot a step forward and a certain combination of movements for the robot's arms makes sure it won't fall out of balance. Similarly, reinforcement learning is also used to teach machines to play Go (`https://www.` `alphago-games.com`) and video games (`https://openai.com/blog/openai-five`).

SGD-based optimization methods are often used in supervised learning (they were used in the models in the previous chapters where real data is always used to measure the quality of synthesized data), whereas, in unsupervised learning, the optimization strategies are totally different.

Currently, Policy Gradients and Q-Learning are two of the most commonly used methods in RL. Let's explain them in brief:

1. **Policy Gradient** is a policy-based method. The model directly gives actions (output) based on the current states (input). It alternates between evaluating the policy (takes actions based on states) and updating the policy (updates the mappings between states and actions). It is often used in large and continuous action spaces.

2. **Q-Learning** is a value-based method. It maintains a Q-table that keeps track of the rewards of various actions. It chooses the action that leads to the maximum reward value and then updates the Q-table, based on the new environment as a result of the action. It can be trained faster than the Policy Gradient method and is often used for simple tasks with small action spaces.

So, how can we choose between reinforcement learning and supervised learning (such as SGD methods in CNNs) when both of them are available? A simple rule of thumb is the **continuity** of the search space and the **differentiability** of the objective function. If the objective function is differentiable and the search space is continuous, it's better to use SGD methods. If the search space is discrete or the objective function is nondifferentiable, we need to stick to reinforcement learning. However, if the search space isn't very large and you have extra computing power to spare, **Evolutionary Search (ES)** methods are also a good option. When your variables are assumed to obey Gaussian distribution, you can always give the CMA-ES (`http://cma.gforge.inria.fr`) method a try.

Here are two extra reading materials if you want to learn more about Policy Gradients:

- `https://medium.com/@jonathan_hui/rl-policy-gradients-explained-9b13b688b146`
- `https://lilianweng.github.io/lil-log/2018/04/08/policy-gradient-algorithms.html`

Architecture of SeqGAN

The idea behind SeqGAN is to get it to solve problems that vanilla GANs can't, since they are good at synthesizing discrete data, and discriminator networks can't, since they can't evaluate sequential data with various lengths. To solve the first problem, Policy Gradients are used for updating the generator network. The second problem is addressed by generating the remaining data with the **Monte Carlo Tree Search (MCTS)** method.

The reinforcement learning strategy in SeqGAN is designed as follows. Let's assume that at time t, the generated sequence is denoted as $Y_{1:t-1} = (y_1, \ldots, y_{t-1})$ and that the current action, y_t, needs to be given by the generator network, $G(s_0, Y_{1:t-1})$, in which s_0 is the initial state. The generation of y_t based on $Y_{1:t-1}$ is done by LSTM (or any of its variants). The objective of the generator is to maximize the cumulative rewards:

$$J(\theta) = \mathbb{E}[R_T | s_0, \theta] = \sum_{y \in Y} G_\theta(y | s_0) \cdot Q(s_0, y)$$

Here, R_T is the cumulative rewards, θ is the parameters to be optimized (that is, parameters of G), and Q is called the **action-value function**. The action-value function, $Q(s_0 | y)$, gives us the reward of taking the action, y, by following policy, G_θ, starting from the initial state, .

Normally, we would expect to use the discriminator network to give us reward values. However, the discriminator cannot be used directly to calculate the cumulative rewards because it can only evaluate a full-length sequence, $Y_{1:T}$. At time t, all we have is $Y_{1:t}$. How do we get the rest of the sequence?

In SeqGAN, the remaining sequence, $Y_{t+1:T}$, is generated by the MCTS method. MCTS is a tree-based search method and widely used in chess- and poker-playing programs and video game AI algorithms. All the actions that can be made are represented by nodes in a very large tree. It takes four steps to do a complete search in the Monte Carlo tree, as follows:

1. **Selection**, which is where you select a path from the root node to a leaf node. Normally, the selection of the existing nodes is based on **Upper Confidence Bounds (UCB)**. Nodes with high scores are more likely to be chosen and nodes that haven't been chosen that many times before are more likely to be selected. It is a balance between **exploration and exploitation**.
2. **Expansion**, which is where you add new child nodes to the selected leaf node.
3. **Simulation**, which is where you evaluate the newly added nodes and get the final results (rewards).
4. **Backpropagation**, which is where you update the scores and counts statistics of all the nodes on the selected path.

In fact, only the third step, simulation, is used to generate the remaining sequence, where it performs the simulation (generating the remaining sequence with G) multiple times generate and get the averaged reward.

Therefore, the definition of $Q(s_0|y)$ is as follows:

$$Q(s = Y_{1:t-1}, a = y_t) = \begin{cases} \dfrac{1}{N}\displaystyle\sum_{n=1}^{N} D(\tilde{Y}_{1:T}), & \tilde{Y}_{1:T} \in \mathrm{MC}(Y_{1:t}) & t < T \\ D(Y_{1:t}) & t = T \end{cases}$$

The generator network is an LSTM network with an embedding layer as an input layer and a linear layer as an output layer. The discriminator network consists of an embedding layer, a convolution layer, a max-pooling layer, and a softmax layer. The code that was published by the authors of this paper was written for TensorFlow. Luckily, a PyTorch version can be found on GitHub at `https://github.com/suragnair/seqGAN`. In this version, two differences should be noted: first, the Monte Carlo simulation is only performed once, and second, the discriminator network is also a recurrent network and a variant of LSTM called **Gated Recurrent Unit (GRU)** is used in both networks. Feel free to adjust the network architectures and try out the tricks and techniques we have learned in the previous chapter of this book. Our modified code is also available under the `seqgan` folder in the code repository for this chapter.

Creating your own vocabulary for training

Reading code that's been written by someone else in GitHub is easy. The most important thing we need to do is apply the models we know to new applications and create our own samples. Here, we will walk through the basic steps of creating a vocabulary from a huge collection of text and use it to train our NLP models.

In the NLP model, a vocabulary set is normally a table that maps each word or symbol to a unique token (typically, an `int` value) so that any sentence can be represented by a vector of `int`.

First, let's find some data to play with. To get started, here's a list of NLP datasets available on GitHub: `https://github.com/niderhoff/nlp-datasets`. From this list, you will find an English joke dataset (`https://github.com/taivop/joke-dataset`) that contains more than 200,000 jokes parsed from Reddit (`https://www.reddit.com/r/jokes`), Stupid Stuff (`stupidstuff.org`), and Wocka (`wocka.com`). The joke text will be in three different files (`reddit_jokes.json`, `stupidstuff.json`, and `wocka.json`). Please don't hold us responsible for the content of these jokes!

Now, let's create our vocabulary. First, create a folder named `data` in the project code folder and copy the aforementioned files into it.

ow, let's create a small program so that we can parse the JSON files and put them in CSV
rmat. Let's call it `parse_jokes.py`:

```
import sys
import platform
import os
import json
import csv
import re

datapath = './data'
redditfile = 'reddit_jokes.json'
stupidfile = 'stupidstuff.json'
wockafile = 'wocka.json'
outfile = 'jokes.csv'
headers = ['row', 'Joke', 'Title', 'Body', 'ID',
           'Score', 'Category', 'Other', 'Source']
```

m sure that the import section entries are obvious. The definitions of the constants should
e fairly obvious as well. The headers variable is simply a list of the column names that will
e used when we create the CSV file.

Ve want all of the jokes that will be stored in our files to be in plain text. To do this, get rid
of all the non-letter symbols. This is done by cleaning the text using `clean_str()`, which
ses Python's `str_translate` parameter, as shown here:

```
def clean_str(text):
    fileters = '"#$%&()*+-/;<=>@[\\]^_`{|}~\t\n\r\"'
    trans_map = str.maketrans(fileters, " " * len(fileters))
    text = text.translate(trans_map)
    re.sub(r'[^a-zA-Z,. ]+', '', text)
    return text
```

Feel free to tweak the `filters` string so that you can add or remove any special characters.
The next function will read one of our three JSON files and return it as a JSON object. I've
made it rather generic, so that the only thing it needs to know about is the filename to deal
with:

```
def get_data(fn):
    with open(fn, 'r') as f:
        extracted = json.load(f)
    return extracted
```

Next, we'll create three functions that will handle converting the three JSON objects into CSV files. It is important to remember that none of the three JSON files have the same structure. Due to this, we'll make all three handler functions fairly similar and handle the differences between them at the same time. Each of the functions will take the JSON object that was created by the `get_data` function, as well as an integer value called `startcount`. This will provide a row number for the CSV file. This value will be incremented for each line in the JSON object. Then, we will create a dictionary out of each piece of data and write it to the CSV file. Finally, we will return our counter so that the next function knows what the row value should be. This is the function that will handle the Reddit file:

```python
def handle_reddit(rawdata, startcount):
    global writer
    print(f'Reddit file has {len(rawdata)} items...')
    cntr = startcount
    with open(outfile, mode='a') as csv_file:
        writer = csv.DictWriter(csv_file, fieldnames=headers)
        for d in rawdata:
            title = clean_str(d['title'])
            body = clean_str(d['body'])
            id = d['id']
            score = d['score']
            category = ''
            other = ''
            dict = {}
            dict['row'] = cntr
            dict['Joke'] = title + ' ' + body
            dict['Title'] = title
            dict['Body'] = body
            dict['ID'] = id
            dict['Category'] = category
            dict['Score'] = score
            dict['Other'] = other
            dict['Source'] = 'Reddit'
            writer.writerow(dict)
            cntr += 1
            if cntr % 10000 == 0:
                print(cntr)
    return cntr
```

Next, we have the other two functions: one for the `StupidStuff` file and the other for the `Wocka` file:

```python
def handle_stupidstuff(rawdata, startcount):
    global writer
    print(f'StupidStuff file has {len(rawdata)} items...')
    with open(outfile, mode='a') as csv_file:
        writer = csv.DictWriter(csv_file, fieldnames=headers)
```

```
        cntr = startcount
        for d in rawdata:
            body = clean_str(d['body'])
            id = d['id']
            score = d['rating']
            category = d['category']
            other = ''
            dict = {}
            dict['row'] = cntr
            dict['Joke'] = body
            dict['Title'] = ''
            dict['Body'] = body
            dict['ID'] = id
            dict['Category'] = category
            dict['Score'] = score
            dict['Other'] = other
            dict['Source'] = 'StupidStuff'
            writer.writerow(dict)
            cntr += 1
            if cntr % 1000 == 0:
                print(cntr)
    return cntr


def handle_wocka(rawdata, startcount):
    global writer
    print(f'Wocka file has {len(rawdata)} items...')
    with open(outfile, mode='a') as csv_file:
        writer = csv.DictWriter(csv_file, fieldnames=headers)
        cntr = startcount
        for d in rawdata:
            other = clean_str(d['title'])
            title = ''
            body = clean_str(d['body'])
            id = d['id']
            category = d['category']
            score = ''
            other = ''
            dict = {}
            dict['row'] = cntr
            dict['Joke'] = body
            dict['Title'] = title
            dict['Body'] = body
            dict['ID'] = id
            dict['Category'] = category
            dict['Score'] = score
            dict['Other'] = other
            dict['Source'] = 'Wocka'
```

```
                    writer.writerow(dict)
                    cntr += 1
                    if cntr % 1000 == 0:
                        print(cntr)
        return cntr
```

The second to last function will create the actual CSV file and write the header:

```
def prep_CVS():
    global writer
    with open(outfile, mode='a') as csv_file:
        writer = csv.DictWriter(csv_file, fieldnames=headers)
        writer.writeheader()
```

Finally, we have the main function and the entry point for the program. Here, we will call the preceding functions in any order we like:

```
def main():
    pv = platform.python_version()
    print(f"Running under Python {pv}")
    path1 = os.getcwd()
    print(path1)
    prep_CVS()
    print('Dealing with Reddit file')
    extracted = get_data(datapath + "/" + redditfile)
    count = handle_reddit(extracted, 0)
    print('Dealing with StupidStuff file')
    extracted = get_data(datapath + "/" + stupidfile)
    count = handle_stupidstuff(extracted, count)
    print('Dealing with Wocka file')
    extracted = get_data(datapath + "/" + wockafile)
    count = handle_wocka(extracted, count)
    print(f'Finished processing! Total items processed: {count}')

if __name__ == '__main__':
    main()
```

Now, all we have to do is run the script:

```
$ python parse_jokes.py
```

When we're finished, the joke text will be stored in the `jokes.csv` file. Now, we need to use TorchText to build the vocabulary. TorchText (`https://github.com/pytorch/text`) is data loading tool for NLP that works directly with PyTorch.

Note for Windows 10 users:
At the time of writing this book, there appears to be an issue in
`torchtext\utils.py`. If you install the `torchtext` package directly
from PyPi, you could run into an error while trying to execute some of the
code.

The best way around this is to head over to the GitHub source repository
(`https://github.com/pytorch/text`) and download the source code.
Then, unpack the code into a safe folder. In Command Prompt, navigate
to the folder that contains the source code and enter the following
command to install the library:

```
pip install -e .
```

This will install torchtext directly from the source code.

For other OS, you can install it with the following command:

```
$ pip install torchtext
```

Please make sure that you have installed the latest version of `torchtext` (0.4.0, at the time
of writing this book); otherwise, the code we will use later may not work for you. If `pip`
doesn't install the latest version for you, you can find the `whl` file at `https://pypi.org/
project/torchtext/#files` and install it manually.

We will use the default vocab tool provided by `torchtext` for this. You can also try using
spaCy (`https://spacy.io`) if you want to build vocab for more complex NLP tasks. Create
a new file and call it `mymain.py`. Start by adding the following code to it:

```python
import torchtext as tt
import numpy as np
import torch
from datetime import datetime

VOCAB_SIZE = 5000
MAX_SEQ_LEN = 30
BATCH_SIZE = 32

src = tt.data.Field(tokenize=tt.data.utils.get_tokenizer("basic_english"),
                    fix_length=MAX_SEQ_LEN,
                    lower=True)

datafields = [('row', None),
              ('Joke', src),
              ('Title', None),
```

```
                      ('Body', None),
                      ('ID', None),
                      ('Score', None),
                      ('Category', None),
                      ('Other', None),
                      ('Source', None)]
```

The `datafields` structure describes the CSV file we just created. Each column in the file is described and the only column we want the `torchtext` library to be concerned with is the `'Joke'` column, so we mark that as `'src'` and all the other columns as `'None'`.

Now, we will create the dataset object and start to build a vocabulary object:

```
dataset = tt.data.TabularDataset(path='jokes.csv', format='csv',
                                 fields=[('id', None),
                                         ('text', src)])

src.build_vocab(dataset, max_size=VOCAB_SIZE)
```

We'll use the `torchtext` library's `BucketIterator` to go through the data in the dataset and create sequences of equal length:

```
src_itr = tt.data.BucketIterator(dataset=dataset,
                                 batch_size=BATCH_SIZE,
                                 sort_key=lambda x: len(x.text),
                                 device=torch.device("cuda:0"))
```

Now that we've built our vocabulary, we need to build a small data loader that will feed the batch data into SeqGAN during training:

```
class BatchLoader:
    def __init__(self, dl, x_field):
        self.dl, self.x_field = dl, x_field

    def __len__(self):
        return len(self.dl)

    def __iter__(self):
        for batch in self.dl:
            x = getattr(batch, self.x_field)
            yield x.t()

train_loader = BatchLoader(src_itr, 'text')
```

e also need a mapping from tokens back to words so that we can see the generated text
hen the training process is complete:

```
vocab_max = 0
for i, batch in enumerate(train_loader):
    _max = torch.max(batch)
    if _max > vocab_max:
        vocab_max = _max

VOCAB_SIZE = vocab_max.item() + 1

inv_vocab = {v: k for k, v in src.vocab.stoi.items()}
```

ere, our vocabulary is stored in `src.vocab`. `src.vocab.stoi` is a Python `defaultdict`
at maps words to `int` values. The last line in the preceding code snippet inverses the
ctionary and stores the mappings from the `int` values as words in `inv_vocab`.

ou can test the vocabulary with the following code:

```
sentence = ['a', 'man', 'walks', 'into', 'a', 'bar']
for w in sentence:
    v = src.vocab[w]
    print(v)
    print(inv_vocab[v])
```

you're curious, you can view the contents of `inv_vocab` by adding the following code
ter the preceding code:

```
for i in inv_vocab:
    print(f'Counter: {i} inv_vocab: {inv_vocab[i]}')
```

owever, remember that around 5,000 lines will be printed, so it will be a long list:

```
$ python mymain.py
```

ow, we need to work on the rest of the SeqGAN program. This includes the generator and
e discriminator. As we mentioned in the *Architecture of SeqGAN* section, these modules
n be found at `https://github.com/suragnair/seqGAN`. Download the source code and
npack it into a folder in your working directory.

 train SeqGAN, run the following script under the code folder:

```
$ python main.py
```

The generator network is pretrained with **Maximum Likelihood Estimation** (**MLE**) against the real data for 100 epochs so that it will be trained faster later. Then, the discriminator network is pretrained against real data and some generated data for 150 epochs, in which the generated data is kept the same for every three epochs so that the discriminator becomes familiar with fake data. Finally, both networks are trained together in an adversarial fashion for 50 epochs, in which the discriminator network is trained 15 times more than the generator network. On a single GTX 1080Ti graphics card, the pretraining process takes about **33 hours**, and 17 epochs of the final training can take long as **48 hours** to complete. GPU memory consumption is about 4,143 MB.

The following are some of the jokes that were generated by SeqGAN. Unfortunately, most of the sentences don't make sense due to mode collapse (which means that the same random word will appear anywhere in the sentences in one batch).

Still, let's take a look. Note that sentences shorter than MAX_SEQ_LEN are filled with <pad> at the end and have been omitted here:

- "have you ever make like a tomato of jokes ? . there d call out of vegetables !"
- "the patriots weren't invited camping ! . because i can rather have been born in tents ."
- "trainees. it is a train for christmas pockets"
- "what do you get when you cross a kangaroo and a rhino ? . spanish"

The following sentences were generated by the model:

- "i can't stop a joke . . . . it's all ."
- "i can't see a new joke ."

 Our model also created some jokes that were too inappropriate to print, which is an interesting demonstration of its attempt to emulate human humor!

Speech quality enhancement with SEGAN

In Chapter 7, *Image Restoration with GANs*, we explored how GANs can restore some of the pixels in images. Researchers have found a similar application in NLP where GANs can be trained to get rid of the noises in audio in order to enhance the quality of the recorded speeches. In this section, we will learn how to use SEGAN to reduce background noise in the audio and make the human voice in the noisy audio more audible.

EGAN architecture

peech Enhancement GAN (SEGAN) was proposed by Santiago Pascual, Antonio
nafonte, and Joan Serrà in their paper, *SEGAN: Speech Enhancement Generative Adversarial
twork*. It uses 1D convolutions to successfully remove noise from speech audio. You can
eck out the noise removal results compared to other methods here at `http://veu.talp.`
`t/segan`. There's also an upgraded version, which can be found at `http://veu.talp.cat/`
`ganp`.

ages are two-dimensional, while sounds are one-dimensional. Considering GANs are so
od at synthesizing 2D images, it is rather obvious to consider using 1D convolution
yers instead of 2D convolutions in order to harness the power of GANs when it comes to
nthesizing audio data. This is exactly how SEGAN is built.

e generator network in SEGAN employs an architecture of **Encoder-Decoder** with skip
nnections, which you may be familiar with since we have already met other GANs that
e a similar architecture (such as `pix2pixHD`). The architecture of the generator network is
follows:

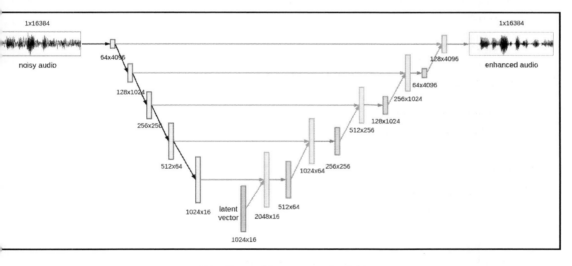

Figure 10.3 Architecture of the generator network in SEGAN

First, the audio samples are cropped to a fixed length of 16,384 and are passed through fiv of the layers of the 1D convolution with a kernel size of 31 and a stride size of 4. The compressed **1,024 x 16** vector (ignoring the batch channel) is concatenated with the latent vector (that's 1,024 x 16 in size) so that it can be fed through another five transposed convolution layers. The feature maps with the same shape in the mirrored convolution an transposed convolution layers are connected with skip connections. This is because the basic structures of noisy and clean audio are pretty much the same and skip connections help the generator reconstruct the structure of enhanced audio a lot faster. Finally, a denoised audio sample with a length of 16,384 is generated.

However, the discriminator network of SEGAN is a single encoder network since all we need from the discriminator is the fidelity score of the input audio. The architecture of the discriminator network is as follows:

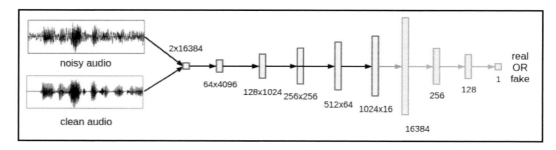

Figure 10.4 Architecture of the discriminator network in SEGAN

The noisy audio and the clean (real data or synthesized data) audio are concatenated together to form a **2 x 16,384** tensor, which is passed through five convolution layers and three fully-connected layers to get the final output, which indicates whether the clean aud is real or synthesized. In both networks, **Parametric ReLU (PReLU)** is used as an activation function in hidden layers.

Training SEGAN to enhance speech quality

Training SEGAN isn't much different from training a normal image-synthesizing GAN. Th training process of SEGAN is as follows:

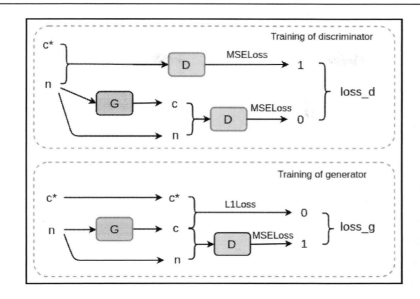

Figure 10.5 The training process of SEGAN. Networks that are updated in each stage are marked with red boundaries. Here, C^* denotes real clean audio, Π denotes noisy audio, and C denotes synthesized clean audio.

rst, the clean audio and the noisy audio from the training data are fed into the scriminator network to calculate MSE loss. The synthesized audio that's generated by the nerator, as well as the noisy audio, are also fed into the discriminator network. In this age, the discriminator network is trained to be better at knowing the difference between al and synthesized clean audio. Then, the generated audio is used to fool the scriminator (by minimizing the MSE loss against 1) so that our generator network will get tter at synthesizing realistic clean audio. Also, the L1 loss between the synthesized audio *) and real audio is calculated (with a scale factor of 100) to force the two to have similar sic structures. RMSprop is used as an optimization method in which the learning rate is t to a very small value (for example, 5×10^{-5}).

ow, let's get some audio data and see what SEGAN can do. A paired clean-noisy audio taset is available here: `https://datashare.is.ed.ac.uk/handle/10283/1942`. We need download both the clean and noisy 48 kHz speech training sets. The `clean` dataset is out 822 MB in size while the `noisy` dataset is about 913 MB in size. There are 11,572 eces of speech inside both sets, most of which are single lines of English spoken by imans. The `noisy` audio is contaminated by several people speaking simultaneously.

The source code of SEGAN for PyTorch has been kindly provided by the authors of the paper: `https://github.com/santi-pdp/segan_pytorch`. Follow these steps to prepare your code and start training SEGAN:

1. Run the following script to get the code and install the prerequisites:

```
$ git clone https://github.com/santi-pdp/segan_pytorch.git
$ pip install soundfile scipy librosa h5py numba matplotlib pyfftw
tensorboardX
```

2. An additional tool called `ahoproc_tools` (`https://github.com/santi-pdp/ahoproc_tools`) is also required. We need to download the source code of `ahoproc_tools` and copy the `ahoproc_tools` inside it into the root folder of `segan_pytorch`. Alternatively, you can access the full source code inside the code repository for this chapter directly. You need to run the following script to make sure that all the submodules have been downloaded:

```
$ git submodule update --init --recursive
```

3. Extract the `.wav` files from the downloaded `.zip` dataset files and move them into the `data/clean_trainset_wav` and `data/noisy_trainset_wav` folders respectively.

4. Finally, run the following script to start the training process:

```
$ python train.py --save_path ckpt_segan+ --batch_size 300 --
clean_trainset data/clean_trainset_wav --noisy_trainset
data/noisy_trainset_wav --cache_dir data/cache
```

First, the training script will create a cache folder (`data/cache`) where it will temporarily store the slicing results of the audio files (because we want the inputs of both networks to be 16,384 in length).

With a batch size of 300, it takes about 10.7 hours to finish 100 epochs of training on a single GTX 1080Ti graphics card and costs about 10,137 MB of GPU memory.

Once the training process has finished, run the following script to test the trained model and remove the background noises from any audio file that's put inside the `data/noisy_testset` folder:

```
$ python clean.py --g_pretrained_ckpt ckpt_segan+/weights_EOE_G-
Generator-16301.ckpt --cfg_file ckpt_segan+/train.opts --synthesis_path
enhanced_results --test_files data/noisy_testset --soundfile
```

Summary

In this chapter, we learned how to generate plain text with SeqGAN and remove background noises in speech audio with SEGAN. We also experimented with how to build a custom vocabulary from a collection of sentences for NLP tasks.

In the next chapter, we will learn how to train GANs so that we can directly generate 3D models.

Further reading

1. Yu L, Zhang W, Wang J. (2017). *SeqGAN: Sequence Generative Adversarial Nets with Policy Gradient*. AAAI.
2. Hochreiter S and Schmidhuber J. (1997). *Long Short-Term Memory. Neural computation*. 9. 1735-80. 10.1162/neco.1997.9.8.1735.
3. Olah C. (Aug 27, 2015). *Understanding LSTM Networks*. **Retrieved from** https://colah.github.io/posts/2015-08-Understanding-LSTMs.
4. Nguyen M. (Sep 25, 2018). *Illustrated Guide to LSTMs and GRUs: A step by step explanation*. **Retrieved from** https://towardsdatascience.com/illustrated-guide-to-lstms-and-gru-s-a-step-by-step-explanation-44e9eb85bf21.
5. Hui J. (Sep 12, 2018). *RL – Policy Gradient Explained*. **Retrieved from** https://medium.com/@jonathan_hui/rl-policy-gradients-explained-9b13b688b146.
6. Weng L. (Apr 8, 2018). *Policy Gradient Algorithms*. **Retrieved from** https://lilianweng.github.io/lil-log/2018/04/08/policy-gradient-algorithms.html.
7. Pascual S, Bonafonte A and Serrà J. (2017). *SEGAN: Speech Enhancement Generative Adversarial Network*. INTERSPEECH.

Reconstructing 3D models with GANs

11

So far, we've learned how to synthesize images, text, and audio with GANs. Now, it's time to explore the 3D world and learn how to use GANs to create convincing 3D models.

In this chapter, you will learn how 3D objects are represented in **computer graphics (CG)**. We will also look into the fundamental concepts of CG, including camera and projection matrices. By the end of this chapter, you will have learned how to create and train 3D_GAN to generate a point cloud of 3D objects, such as chairs.

You will know the fundamental knowledge of the representation of 3D objects and the basic concept of 3D convolution. Then, you will learn to construct a 3D-GAN model by 3D convolutions and train it to generate 3D objects. You will also get familiar with PrGAN, a model that generates 3D objects based on their black-and-white 2D views.

The following topics will be covered in this chapter:

- Fundamental concepts in computer graphics
- Designing GANs for 3D data synthesis

Fundamental concepts in computer graphics

In the previous chapters, we learned about various GAN models for image, text, and audio. Generally, we have been solely dealing with 1D and 2D data. In this chapter, we will expand on our knowledge of the GAN world by looking at the 3D domain. By the end of this chapter, you will have learned how to create your own 3D objects with GANs.

Representation of 3D objects

It is essential to understand how 3D objects are represented in a computer before we dive into the details of the GAN model for 3D data synthesis. The creation and rendering of 3D objects, environments, and animations is called **computer graphics (CG)**, which two of the major entertainment industries, that is video games and movies, heavily rely on. The most important task in CG is figuring out how to efficiently render the most convincing images on the screen. Thanks to the hard work of people in the CG field, we are now getting better visual effects in video games and movies.

Attributes of a 3D object

The most basic attributes a 3D object has are its shape and color. The color of each pixel we can see on a screen is affected by many factors, such as the color of its own texture, the light source, and even the other objects in the scene. This is also affected by the relative directions of the light source and our viewpoint to the pixel's own surface, which are determined by the shape, position, and orientation of the object and the position of the camera. When it comes to shape, a 3D model basically consists of points, lines, and surfaces. An example of the creation of the shape and color of a 3D sports car can be seen in the following image:

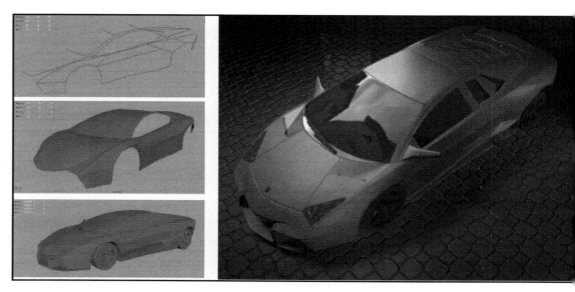

The creation of a sports car in Autodesk Maya shows how lines form surfaces and how textures provide colors in 3D models

surface, either flat or curved, is mostly formed with triangles and quadrangles (which are nerally called **polygons**). A polygon mesh (also called a **wireframe**) is defined by a set of points and a set of segments connecting those points. Normally, having more polygons eans that there will be more details in the 3D models. This can be seen in the following age:

More polygons means more details in 3D models. Images captured in Autodesk Maya.

Sometimes, a set of points (also known as a **point cloud** in some applications) is all we nee
to create 3D objects since there are several widely used methods for automatically creating
segments in order to generate a polygon mesh (for example, the Delaunay triangulation
method). Point clouds are often used to represent the results that are collected by 3D
scanners. A point cloud is a set of three-dimensional vectors representing the spatial
coordinates of each point. In this chapter, we are only interested in the generation of the
point clouds of certain objects with GANs. A few examples of the point clouds of chairs ca
be seen in the following image:

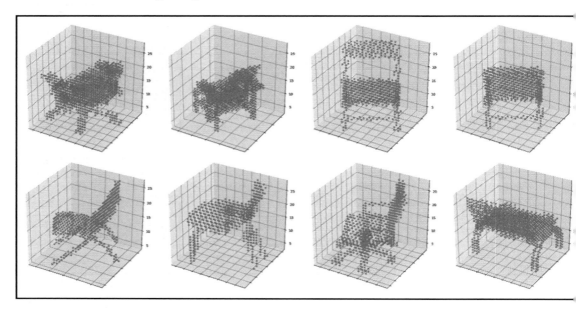

Point clouds of chairs

Camera and projection

Once the shape and color of the 3D objects have been defined, there's still a major factor that will affect the way they look on the screen: the **camera**. The camera is responsible for mapping the 3D points, lines, and surfaces to the 2D image plane, which is usually our screen. If the camera isn't configured correctly, we may not see our objects at all. The process of mapping from the 3D world to the 2D image plane is called **projection**.

There are two different commonly used projection methods in the field of CG: orthographic projection and perspective projection. Let's go over them now:

- **Orthographic projection** is a process that maps everything in a cuboid (that is, a rectangular volume) to a standard cube. For more information about orthographic and perspective projection, please refer to http://www.songho.ca/opengl/gl_projectionmatrix.html.

  In orthographic projection, all the parallel lines in the 3D space are still parallel in the 2D plane, except they have different lengths and orientations. More importantly, the size of the projected image of the same object is always the same, no matter how far away it is from the camera. However, this is not the way our eyes and most cameras capture images of the 3D world. Therefore, orthographic projection is mainly used in **Computer-Aided Design (CAD)** and other engineering applications, where the actual size of the components needs to be rendered correctly.

- **Perspective projection** is a process that maps everything in a frustum (that is, a pyramid without its tip) to a standard cube, as shown in the preceding image. In perspective projection, objects that are closer to the camera look bigger than those far away from the camera. Therefore, parallel lines in the 3D space are not necessarily parallel in the 2D space. This is also how our eyes perceive the surrounding environment. Therefore, this type of projection gives us more realistic images and is often used for rendering visual effects in video games and movies.

Orthographic and perspective projections are used together in some forms of CG software such as Autodesk Maya, as shown in the following screenshots:

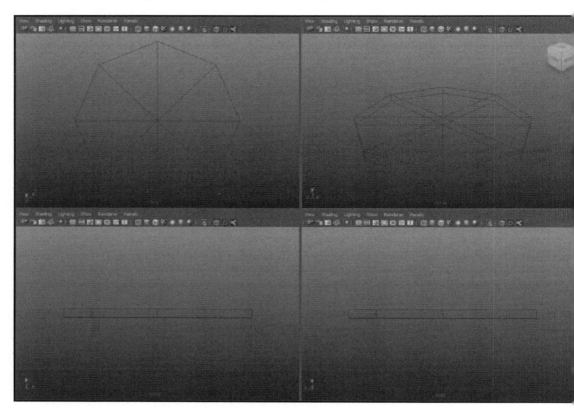

In the user interface of Autodesk Maya, orthographic projection is used to show the top, side, and front views (top left, bottom left, and bottom right), while perspective projection is used to preview the 3D models (top right). Image retrieved from https://knowledge.autodesk.com/support/maya/learn-explore/caas/simplecontent/content/maya-tutorials.html

In this chapter, we will only take a closer look at perspective projection. In computer graphics, **homogeneous coordinates** are often used, which can conveniently represent infinite distance and turn translation, scaling, and rotation using simple matrix multiplication. For a set of homogeneous coordinates (x, y, z, w), the corresponding Cartesian counterpart would be $(x/w, y/w, z/w)$. The mapping from the frustum in the 3D space to the $[-1, 1] \times [-1, 1] \times [-1, 1]$ cube is defined by the **projection matrix**:

$$\begin{bmatrix} \frac{2n}{r-l} & 0 & \frac{r+l}{r-l} & 0 \\ 0 & \frac{2n}{t-b} & \frac{t+b}{t-b} & 0 \\ 0 & 0 & -\frac{f+n}{f-n} & -\frac{2fn}{f-n} \\ 0 & 0 & -1 & 0 \end{bmatrix}$$

the projection matrix, n is the near clipping plane and f is the far clipping plane. Also, t, l, and r denote the top, bottom, left, and right boundaries of the near clipping plane, respectively. The multiplication between the projection matrix and the homogeneous coordinates gives us the corresponding coordinates where the projected points should be. If you are interested in the derivation of the projection matrix, feel free to check out the following article: `http://www.songho.ca/opengl/gl_projectionmatrix.html`.

Designing GANs for 3D data synthesis

3D-GAN, which was proposed by Jiajun Wu, Chengkai Zhang, and Tianfan Xue, et. al. in their paper, *Learning a Probabilistic Latent Space of Object Shapes via 3D Generative-Adversarial Modeling*, was designed to generate a 3D point cloud of certain types of objects. The design and training process of 3D-GAN is very similar to the vanilla GAN, except that the input and output tensors of the 3D-GAN are five-dimensional, rather than four-dimensional.

Generators and discriminators in 3D-GAN

The architecture of the generator network of 3D-GAN is as follows:

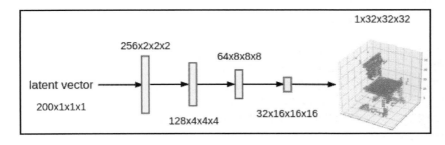

Architecture of the generator network in 3D-GAN

The generator network consists of five transposed convolution layers (nn.ConvTranspose3d), in which the first four layers are followed by the Batch Normalization layer (nn.BatchNorm3d) and ReLU activation function, and the last layer i followed by a Sigmoid activation function. The kernel size, stride size, and padding size a set to 4, 2 and 1 in all the transposed convolution layers, respectively. Here, the input late vector can be gradually expanded to a $1 \times 32 \times 32 \times 32$ cube, which can be considered as a channel 3D "image". In this 3D image, the "pixel" value is actually the possibility of wheth a point exists at these $32 \times 32 \times 32$ grid locations. Normally, we reserve all the points with values higher than 0.5 to form the final point cloud.

In our case, the "pixels" in the 3D image are actually called **voxels** since the points in our point cloud are located at grid points in the $32 \times 32 \times 32$ cube. There are four attributes in a voxel: the x, y, and z coordinates and whether the voxel exists at (x, y, z). Unlike in 2D image synthesizing tasks, such as MNIST, where pixels with values between 0 and 1 (or between 0 and 255, if you prefer) are allowed (for example, at the edge of the digits), the existence of the voxel is a binary decision. Therefore, the tensor of our point cloud is, in fact, a sparse with many zeros and a few ones.

In this section, we will provide the full source code for 3D-GAN. The code files have been organized in the same way as they were in the previous chapters. The networks have been defined in a model_3dgan.py file (be sure to avoid starting your module name with numbers).

The following code is the definition of Generator:

```python
import torch
import torch.nn as nn
import torch.nn.functional as F
import numpy as np

class Generator(nn.Module):
    def __init__(self, latent_dim, cube_len, bias=False):
        super(Generator, self).__init__()
        self.latent_dim = latent_dim
        self.cube_len = cube_len

        self.model = nn.Sequential(
            *self._create_layer(self.latent_dim, self.cube_len*8, 4,
    stride=2, padding=1, bias=bias, transposed=True),
            *self._create_layer(self.cube_len*8, self.cube_len*4, 4,
    stride=2, padding=1, bias=bias, transposed=True),
            *self._create_layer(self.cube_len*4, self.cube_len*2, 4,
    stride=2, padding=1, bias=bias, transposed=True),
```

```
          *self._create_layer(self.cube_len*2, self.cube_len, 4,
stride=2, padding=1, bias=bias, transposed=True),
          *self._create_layer(self.cube_len, 1, 4, stride=2, padding=1,
bias=bias, transposed=True, last_layer=True)
      )

    def _create_layer(self, size_in, size_out, kernel_size=4, stride=2,
padding=1, bias=False, transposed=True, last_layer=False):
        layers = []
        if transposed:
            layers.append(nn.ConvTranspose3d(size_in, size_out,
kernel_size, stride=stride, padding=padding, bias=bias))
        else:
            layers.append(nn.Conv3d(size_in, size_out, kernel_size,
stride=stride, padding=padding, bias=bias))
        if last_layer:
            layers.append(nn.Sigmoid())
        else:
            layers.append(nn.BatchNorm3d(size_out))
            layers.append(nn.ReLU(inplace=True))
        return layers

    def forward(self, x):
        x = x.view(-1, self.latent_dim, 1, 1, 1)
        return self.model(x)
```

The architecture of the discriminator network of 3D-GAN is as follows:

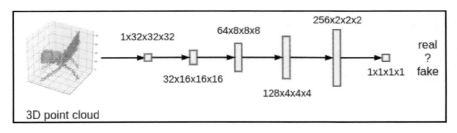

Architecture of the discriminator network in 3D-GAN

The discriminator network consists of five convolution layers (nn.Conv3d), in which the first four layers are followed by a Batch Normalization layer and a Leaky-ReLU (nn.LeakyReLU) activation function, and the last layer is followed by a Sigmoid activation function. The kernel size, stride size, and padding size are set to 4, 2 and 1 in all the convolution layers, respectively. The $1 \times 32 \times 32 \times 32$ cube of the 3D point cloud is mapped by the discriminator network to a single value, which specifies whether the confidence of the input object is authentic.

Imagine what would happen if the dimension of the point cloud was set to $3 \times 32 \times 32 \times 32$. Can you create colorized 3D point clouds, such as fire, smoke, or clouds? Feel free to find or even create your own dataset and try this out!

The following code is the definition of `Discriminator` (this can also be found in the `model_3dgan.py` file):

```python
class Discriminator(nn.Module):
    def __init__(self, cube_len, bias=False):
        super(Discriminator, self).__init__()
        self.cube_len = cube_len

        self.model = nn.Sequential(
            *self._create_layer(1, self.cube_len, 4, stride=2, padding=1,
bias=bias, transposed=False),
            *self._create_layer(self.cube_len, self.cube_len*2, 4,
stride=2, padding=1, bias=bias, transposed=False),
            *self._create_layer(self.cube_len*2, self.cube_len*4, 4,
stride=2, padding=1, bias=bias, transposed=False),
            *self._create_layer(self.cube_len*4, self.cube_len*8, 4,
stride=2, padding=1, bias=bias, transposed=False),
            *self._create_layer(self.cube_len*8, 1, 4, stride=2, padding=1
bias=bias, transposed=False, last_layer=True)
        )

    def _create_layer(self, size_in, size_out, kernel_size=4, stride=2,
padding=1, bias=False, transposed=False, last_layer=False):
        layers = []
        if transposed:
            layers.append(nn.ConvTranspose3d(size_in, size_out,
kernel_size, stride=stride, padding=padding, bias=bias))
        else:
            layers.append(nn.Conv3d(size_in, size_out, kernel_size,
stride=stride, padding=padding, bias=bias))
        if last_layer:
            layers.append(nn.Sigmoid())
        else:
            layers.append(nn.BatchNorm3d(size_out))
            layers.append(nn.LeakyReLU(0.2, inplace=True))
        return layers

    def forward(self, x):
        x = x.view(-1, 1, self.cube_len, self.cube_len, self.cube_len)
        return self.model(x)
```

raining 3D-GAN

ie training process for 3D-GAN is similar to the process for the vanilla GAN. This can be en in the following diagram:

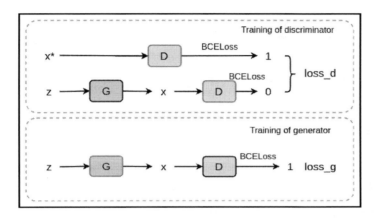

training process of 3D-GAN. Here, x* denotes real data, x denotes fake data, and z denotes the latent vector. The networks whose parameters are updated are marked with red boundaries.

rst, the discriminator network is trained to recognize the real 3D point cloud as true data d the synthesized point cloud that's generated by the generator network as fake data. CE loss (nn.BCELoss) is used as the loss function for the discriminator network. Then, the nerator network is trained by forcing the discriminator to recognize the synthesized 3D oint cloud as true data so that it can learn to get better at fooling the discriminator in the ture. BCE loss is used for training the generator network.

ie following is part of the source code for 3D-GAN training. Create a build_gan.py file d paste the following code into this file. Some of the training tricks have been borrowed om https://github.com/rimchang/3DGAN-Pytorch, which we will discuss later:

```python
import os
import time
from datetime import datetime
import torch
from torch.optim.lr_scheduler import MultiStepLR
import utils
from model_3dgan import Generator as G
from model_3dgan import Discriminator as D
import matplotlib
import matplotlib.pyplot as plt
import numpy as np
import pickle
```

```python
class Model(object):
    def __init__(self, name, device, data_loader, latent_dim, cube_len):
        self.name = name
        self.device = device
        self.data_loader = data_loader
        self.latent_dim = latent_dim
        self.cube_len = cube_len
        assert self.name == '3dgan'
        self.netG = G(self.latent_dim, self.cube_len)
        self.netG.to(self.device)
        self.netD = D(self.cube_len)
        self.netD.to(self.device)
        self.optim_G = None
        self.optim_D = None
        self.scheduler_D = None
        self.criterion = torch.nn.BCELoss()

    def create_optim(self, g_lr, d_lr, alpha=0.5, beta=0.5):
        self.optim_G = torch.optim.Adam(self.netG.parameters(),
                                        lr=g_lr,
                                        betas=(alpha, beta))
        self.optim_D = torch.optim.Adam(self.netD.parameters(),
                                        lr=d_lr,
                                        betas=(alpha, beta))
        self.scheduler_D = MultiStepLR(self.optim_D, milestones=[500,
            1000])

    def train(self, epochs, d_loss_thresh, log_interval=100,
        export_interval=10, out_dir='', verbose=True):
        self.netG.train()
        self.netD.train()
        total_time = time.time()
        for epoch in range(epochs):
            batch_time = time.time()
            for batch_idx, data in enumerate(self.data_loader):
                data = data.to(self.device)

                batch_size = data.shape[0]
                real_label = torch.Tensor(batch_size).uniform_(0.7,
                    1.2).to(self.device)
                fake_label = torch.Tensor(batch_size).uniform_(0,
                    0.3).to(self.device)

                # Train D
                d_real = self.netD(data)
                d_real = d_real.squeeze()
                d_real_loss = self.criterion(d_real, real_label)
```

```
latent = torch.Tensor(batch_size,
  self.latent_dim).normal_(0, 0.33).to(self.device)
fake = self.netG(latent)
d_fake = self.netD(fake.detach())
d_fake = d_fake.squeeze()
d_fake_loss = self.criterion(d_fake, fake_label)

d_loss = d_real_loss + d_fake_loss

d_real_acc = torch.ge(d_real.squeeze(), 0.5).float()
d_fake_acc = torch.le(d_fake.squeeze(), 0.5).float()
d_acc = torch.mean(torch.cat((d_real_acc, d_fake_acc),0))

if d_acc <= d_loss_thresh:
    self.netD.zero_grad()
    d_loss.backward()
    self.optim_D.step()

# Train G
latent = torch.Tensor(batch_size,
  self.latent_dim).normal_(0, 0.33).to(self.device)
fake = self.netG(latent)
d_fake = self.netD(fake)
d_fake = d_fake.squeeze()
g_loss = self.criterion(d_fake, real_label)

self.netD.zero_grad()
self.netG.zero_grad()
g_loss.backward()
self.optim_G.step()

if epoch % export_interval == 0:
    samples = fake.cpu().data[:8].squeeze().numpy()
    utils.save_voxels(samples, out_dir, epoch)
self.scheduler_D.step()
```

You may have noticed that `real_label` and `fake_label` aren't set to 1 and 0 like they usually are. Instead, randomly initialized labels (`uniform_(0.7, 1.2)` and `uniform_(0, 3)`) are used. This technique is very similar to **soft targets**, which use the softmax output of a larger network as labels (instead of "hard" 0 or 1 labels) to train a smaller, yet identical, network in terms of input-output mappings (which is called **Knowledge Distillation**). This trick generates a smoother loss function over time since it introduces an assumption that the labels are random variables. You can always initialize `real_label` randomly and let `fake_label` be equal to `1-real_label`.

We already know that the desired output tensor is sparse and that it should be very easy t fully train the discriminator. Actually, the discriminator will overfit long before the generator is trained properly. Therefore, we only train the discriminator when its training accuracy is not higher than `d_loss_thresh`. Note that learning rate decay is used to optimize the generator.

In the preceding code, we visualized and exported the generated point cloud for every `export_interval` epochs. The code for rendering the point cloud is as follows:

```
def save_voxels(voxels, path, idx):
    from mpl_toolkits.mplot3d import Axes3D
    voxels = voxels[:8].__ge__(0.5)
    fig = plt.figure(figsize=(32, 16))
    gs = gridspec.GridSpec(2, 4)
    gs.update(wspace=0.05, hspace=0.05)

    for i, sample in enumerate(voxels):
        x, y, z = sample.nonzero()
        ax = fig.add_subplot(gs[i], projection='3d')
        ax.scatter(x, y, z, zdir='z', c='red')
        ax.set_xticklabels([])
        ax.set_yticklabels([])
    plt.savefig(path + '/{}.png'.format(str(idx)), bbox_inches='tight')
    plt.close()

    with open(path + '/{}.pkl'.format(str(idx)), "wb") as f:
        pickle.dump(voxels, f, protocol=pickle.HIGHEST_PROTOCOL)
```

The next step is to prepare the training dataset for 3D-GAN. You can download the point clouds of 40 different types of objects from `http://3dshapenets.cs.princeton.edu/3DShapeNetsCode.zip`. After downloading and extracting the `zip` file, move the `volumetric_data` folder to any location you like (for example, `/media/john/DataAsgard/3d_models/volumetric_data`) and choose a category for model training.

The code for loading the training point cloud files is as follows (create a `datasets.py` file and paste the following code into it):

```
import os
import numpy as np
import scipy.ndimage as nd
import scipy.io as io
import torch
from torch.utils.data import Dataset

def getVoxelFromMat(path, cube_len=64):
```

```
        voxels = io.loadmat(path)['instance']
        voxels = np.pad(voxels, (1, 1), 'constant', constant_values=(0, 0))
        if cube_len != 32 and cube_len == 64:
            voxels = nd.zoom(voxels, (2, 2, 2), mode='constant', order=0)
        return voxels


class ShapeNetDataset(Dataset):
    def __init__(self, root, cube_len):
        self.root = root
        self.listdir = os.listdir(self.root)
        self.cube_len = cube_len

    def __getitem__(self, index):
        with open(os.path.join(self.root, self.listdir[index]), "rb") as f:
            volume = np.asarray(getVoxelFromMat(f, self.cube_len),
dtype=np.float32)
            return torch.FloatTensor(volume)

    def __len__(self):
        return len(self.listdir)
```

inally, here is the code for the `main.py` file, which initializes and trains 3D-GAN:

```
import argparse
import os
import sys
import numpy as np
import torch
import torch.backends.cudnn as cudnn
import torch.utils.data as DataLoader
import torchvision.datasets as dset
import torchvision.transforms as transforms
import utils
from build_gan import Model
from datasets import ShapeNetDataset

FLAGS = None

def main():
    device = torch.device("cuda:0" if FLAGS.cuda else "cpu")
    print('Loading data...\n')
    dataset = ShapeNetDataset(FLAGS.data_dir, FLAGS.cube_len)
    dataloader = torch.utils.data.DataLoader(dataset,
                                    FLAGS.batch_size,
                                    shuffle=True,
                                    num_workers=1,
                                    pin_memory=True)
```

```
    print('Creating model...\n')
    model = Model(FLAGS.model, device, dataloader, FLAGS.latent_dim,
FLAGS.cube_len)
    model.create_optim(FLAGS.g_lr, FLAGS.d_lr)

    # Train
    model.train(FLAGS.epochs, FLAGS.d_loss_thresh, FLAGS.log_interval,
                FLAGS.export_interval, FLAGS.out_dir, True)
```

We used code similar to this to create the command-line parser back in Chapter 5, *Generating Images Based on Label Information*. We'll use the same idea here and add a few options into the mix:

```
if __name__ == '__main__':
    from utils import boolean_string
    parser = argparse.ArgumentParser(description='Hands-On GANs - Chapter
11')
    parser.add_argument('--model', type=str, default='3dGan',
                        help='enter `3dGan`.')
    parser.add_argument('--cube_len', type=int, default='32',
                        help='one of `cgan` and `infogan`.')
    parser.add_argument('--cuda', type=boolean_string,
                        default=True, help='enable CUDA.')
    parser.add_argument('--train', type=boolean_string,
                        default=True, help='train mode or eval mode.')
    parser.add_argument('--data_dir', type=str,
                        default='~/data', help='Directory for dataset.')
    parser.add_argument('--out_dir', type=str,
                        default='output', help='Directory for output.')
    parser.add_argument('--epochs', type=int, default=200,
                        help='number of epochs')
    parser.add_argument('--batch_size', type=int,
                        default=128, help='size of batches')
    parser.add_argument('--g_lr', type=float, default=0.0002,
                        help='G learning rate')
    parser.add_argument('--d_lr', type=float, default=0.0002,
                        help='D learning rate')
    parser.add_argument('--d_loss_thresh', type=float, default=0.7,
                        help='D loss threshold')
    parser.add_argument('--latent_dim', type=int,
                        default=100, help='latent space dimension')
    parser.add_argument('--export_interval', type=int,
                        default=10, help='export interval')
    parser.add_argument('--classes', type=int, default=10,
                        help='number of classes')
    parser.add_argument('--img_size', type=int,
                        default=64, help='size of images')
    parser.add_argument('--channels', type=int, default=1,
```

```
                        help='number of image channels')
parser.add_argument('--log_interval', type=int, default=100,
                        help='interval between logging and image sampling')
parser.add_argument('--seed', type=int, default=1, help='random seed')

FLAGS = parser.parse_args()
FLAGS.cuda = FLAGS.cuda and torch.cuda.is_available()

if FLAGS.seed is not None:
    torch.manual_seed(FLAGS.seed)
    if FLAGS.cuda:
        torch.cuda.manual_seed(FLAGS.seed)
    np.random.seed(FLAGS.seed)

cudnn.benchmark = True

if FLAGS.train:
    utils.clear_folder(FLAGS.out_dir)

log_file = os.path.join(FLAGS.out_dir, 'log.txt')
print("Logging to {}\n".format(log_file))
sys.stdout = utils.StdOut(log_file)

print("PyTorch version: {}".format(torch.__version__))
print("CUDA version: {}\n".format(torch.version.cuda))

print(" " * 9 + "Args" + " " * 9 + "| " + "Type" +
        " | " + "Value")
print("-" * 50)
for arg in vars(FLAGS):
    arg_str = str(arg)
    var_str = str(getattr(FLAGS, arg))
    type_str = str(type(getattr(FLAGS, arg)).__name__)
    print(" " + arg_str + " " * (20-len(arg_str)) + "|" +
            " " + type_str + " " * (10-len(type_str)) + "|" +
            " " + var_str)
main()
```

Now, we can run the program by using the following command line. Be sure to provide your proper data directory:

```
python main.py --model 3dgan --train True --epochs 1000 --data_dir
Data_Directory
```

Here, we used the chair category example. It takes about 4 hours to finish 1,000 epochs of training and costs about 1,023 MB GPU memory on a single NVIDIA GTX 1080Ti graphics card. Note that, even though our implementation is heavily based on `https://github.com/rimchang/3DGAN-Pytorch`, the original code costs about 14 hours and 1,499 MB GPU memory to complete the same task.

The following are some of the 3D chair models that were generated by 3D-GAN. As we can see, despite a few outliers and the misplacement of voxels, the models look convincing in general. You can also check out the 3D-GAN website that was created by the authors of the paper, where an interactive showcase of generated chairs has been provided: `https://meetshah1995.github.io/gan/deep-learning/tensorflow/visdom/2017/04/01/3d-generative-adverserial-networks-for-volume-classification-and-generation.html`

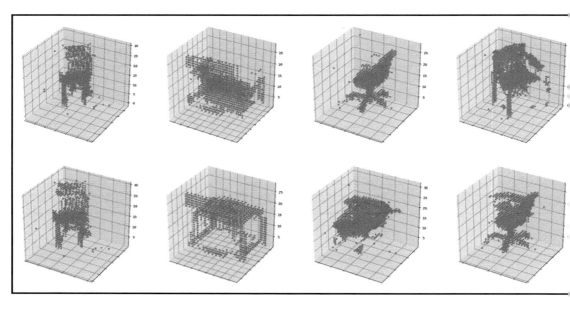

Chair models generated by 3D-GAN

Feel free to select a different object category or even give other datasets a try. Here is a list of point cloud datasets: `http://yulanguo.me/dataset.html`. Here is a list of papers on 3D point cloud from the past years (at the time of writing): `https://github.com/Yochengliu/awesome-point-cloud-analysis`. I hope you can discover new applications with GANs and 3D point clouds!

ummary

this chapter, we learned about the fundamental concepts of computer graphics and how train 3D-GAN to generate 3D objects.

the next chapter, we will take a look back at all the useful tricks we have used in various AN models and introduce more practical techniques that will assist you with model sign and training GANs in the future.

urther reading

1. Ahn S H. (2019). *OpenGL Projection Matrix*. Retrieved from `http://www.songho.ca/opengl/gl_projectionmatrix.html`.
2. Wu J, Zhang C, Xue T. (2016). *Learning a Probabilistic Latent Space of Object Shapes via 3D Generative-Adversarial Modeling*. NIPS.

Other Books You May Enjoy

you enjoyed this book, you may be interested in these other books by Packt:

enerative Adversarial Networks Projects
ilash Ahirwar

BN: 9781789136678

- Train a network on the 3D ShapeNet dataset to generate realistic shapes
- Generate anime characters using the Keras implementation of DCGAN
- Implement an SRGAN network to generate high-resolution images
- Train Age-cGAN on Wiki-Cropped images to improve face verification
- Use Conditional GANs for image-to-image translation
- Understand the generator and discriminator implementations of StackGAN in Keras

Generative Adversarial Networks Cookbook
Josh Kalin

ISBN: 9781789139907

- Structure a GAN architecture in pseudocode
- Understand the common architecture for each of the GAN models you will buil
- Implement different GAN architectures in TensorFlow and Keras
- Use different datasets to enable neural network functionality in GAN models
- Combine different GAN models and learn how to fine-tune them
- Produce a model that can take 2D images and produce 3D models
- Develop a GAN to do style transfer with Pix2Pix

Leave a review - let other readers know what you think

Please share your thoughts on this book with others by leaving a review on the site that you bought it from. If you purchased the book from Amazon, please leave us an honest review on this book's Amazon page. This is vital so that other potential readers can see and use your unbiased opinion to make purchasing decisions, we can understand what our customers think about our products, and our authors can see your feedback on the title that they have worked with Packt to create. It will only take a few minutes of your time, but is valuable to other potential customers, our authors, and Packt. Thank you!

Index

Printed in Great Britain
by Amazon